Constitutional Failure

Constitutional Failure

Carl Schmitt in Weimar

Ellen Kennedy

Duke University Press

Durham and London 2004

Printed in the United States of America on acid-free paper ∞
Typeset in Trump Mediaeval by Keystone Typesetting, Inc.
Library of Congress Cataloging-in-Publication Data appear
on the last printed page of this book.

In Memoriam

TIM MASON

1940–1990

Ich rief den Teufel, und er kam,
Und ich sah ihn mit Verwunderung an.
Er ist nicht häßlich und ist nicht lahm,
Er is ein lieber, scharmanter Mann.
Ein Mann in seinen besten Jahren,
Verbindlich und höflich und welterfahren.
Er is ein gescheuter Diplomat,
Und spricht recht schön über Kirch und Staat.
Blaß ist er etwas, doch ist es kein Wunder,
Sanskrit und Hegel studiert er jetzunder.
Sein Lieblingspoet ist noch immer Fouqué.
Doch will er nicht mehr mit Kritik sich befassen,
Die hat er jetzt gänzlich überlassen
Der teuren Großmutter Hekate.
Er lobte mein juristisches Streben,
Hat früher sich auch damit abgegeben.
Er sagte, meine Freundschaft sei
Ihm nicht zu teurer, und nickte dabei,
Und frug: ob wir uns nicht
Schon einman gesehn beim span'schen Gesandten?
Und als ich recht besah sein Gesicht,
Fand ich in ihm einen alten Bekannten.

—HEINRICH HEINE, "Klagelied eines altdeutschen Jünglings," 1823–24

Contents

Acknowledgments

The subject of this book preoccupied me for many years, and I incurred many debts during that time. The greatest of these is to my institutional supporters in the Federal Republic of Germany and those who were my colleagues and guides when I first began to think and write about German political and constitutional theory. Chief among these were the Alexander-von-Humboldt Stiftung, and my hosts at the University of Freiburg, Professor Wilhelm Hennis and Professor Heinrich August Winkler. No one could ask for a more generous patron, or mentors more knowledgeable than Professors Hennis and Winkler. Additional funding for my work on German political thought was provided by the British Academy, the Nuffield Foundation, the Friedrich Ebert Stiftung, and the Research Foundation of the University of Pennsylvania. The University of York provided exceptionally generous sabbatical leave for my years in Freiburg.

The failure of the Weimar Republic and Carl Schmitt's political theory accompanied me across national boundaries, languages, and cultures during my tenure at the Universities of Manchester, York, and London in England; at Freiburg in Germany; and at the University of Pennsylvania in the United States. Many colleagues listened carefully and critically, and to them I owe much insight: Anja Baumhoff, Joseph Bendersky, Ernst-Wolfgang Böckenförde, Jane Caplan, Michaela Diers, Mary Ann Gallagher, Deborah Harrold, Paul Hirst, Elke Keinath-Vogel, Jack Knight, David Leslie, Hermann Lilienthal, Ingebourg Maus, John McCormick, Anne Norton, Pasquale Pasquino, Pier Paulo Portinaro, Helmut Quaritsch, Keith Tribe, Lawrence Scaff, George Schwab, Kim Lane Scheppele, Ursula Vogel,

Ingebourg Villinger, Albert Weale, and Dörte Winkler. Carl Schmitt generously engaged my interest in Weimar and his work in many conversations at San Casciano and in walks through the hills above the Lenne. The late Professor Dr. Joseph Kaiser and Eberhard Freiherr von Medem allowed me access to the *Nachlaß* soon after Carl Schmitt's death, and Frau Anni Stand, "der gute Geist" of Plettenberg, assisted my research in every possible way. For many of these persons, the subject of this book was written into their lives as tragedy. From them I heard stories of persecution, loss, collaboration, and struggle—the multifarious palette of the historical past when it was still present. Their friendship made the topic less academic than it might have been. At Duke University Press, Valerie Millholland proved a generous and sharp editor whose questions and encouragement were invaluable. To her and to everyone at Duke, my thanks.

Finally: this book is dedicated to the memory of Tim Mason, who told me upon my return to England from Berlin in 1977 that I should read Carl Schmitt.

Constitutional Failure

Introduction

This book began at the Berlin Wall, Easter 1977. From the platform looking eastward, the history of modern Germany, and with it of the modern state system, lay inscribed. The historic old center of palaces, the Opera and Museum island, and the Humboldt University and Neue Wache in neoclassical style were designed in the early nineteenth century by Karl Friedrich Schinkel as a grand parade and public space.[1] Schinkel gave appropriate place to the military in this provincial garrison city on the river Spree. By the end of the century, the fragmented German states would be united through Otto von Bismarck's victory in 1871, and Germany's fantastic development into a major industrial power appeared to erase the failed bourgeois revolution of 1848.[2] Wealth and Great Power ambition shaped "the unpolitical German,"[3] and they destabilized the European balance of powers in 1914. Defeat in the Great War brought, as Johannes Popitz remarked, "a dizzy fall from the heights." When Germany rose again, even more threatening to its neighbors under the Nazi dictatorship, it would fall even further: the achievement of Bismarck's generation was lost in 1945. The Germans were divided and driven from central and eastern Europe, Germany's state sovereignty gone, seemingly forever, and its economy in ruins. What remained was crowded with refugees and under foreign occupation: across the former Reich lay the trip line of the Cold War.

Past and present still traced scars across Berlin. The Wall skirted Hitler's bunker and the remains of the government quarter. Monuments of imperial Germany fell on one or the other side: to the east stood the

Brandenburg Gate; on the west, above a silent Reichstag, flew the gigantic flag of the Federal Republic. On the Linden, once the meeting place of everyone who mattered in Berlin, almost nothing moved below restored facades. On the side streets, Schinkel's magnificent churches still lay in ruins. Streetcars that had once carried Berliners throughout the metropolis, boycotted after 1961 by most in west Berlin, ran beneath the Soviet sector, through dark, sealed station stops, metaphors of the past.

Neither I nor most of my political theory colleagues in England had ever heard of Carl Schmitt. Historians of Germany knew more about Schmitt and Weimar, but few had read him, and there was no significant body of work in English on constitutional debates in the Weimar Republic or their background in broader questions of political theory. An influential collection of essays by Anthony Nicholls and Erich Matthias contained a solitary piece on the most notorious provision of the constitution.[4] In this and other histories of the period, concepts and legal terms such as "liberalism," "parliamentary government," and "democracy" appeared as simple empirical descriptions. Many general histories of Germany tended to see Weimar as a prelude to Hitler.[5] If he figured in them at all, Carl Schmitt, like Martin Heidegger, usually exemplified the moral decay of German academic life. Political science paid little attention to Weimar, none to Schmitt. They appeared, if at all, as examples in empirical political sociology of "breakdown" or "interim regimes."[6]

There was, in short, no context in North America or Great Britain for a discussion of Schmitt's political theory or of the Weimar Republic as a period comparable to those from which the "canon" derives—Greece and Rome, the Middle Ages, England in the Civil War, revolutionary France, or nineteenth-century Europe.

The difference since then is dramatic. In the mid-1970s, only *Der Begriff des Politischen* was available in English, and there was a single monograph.[7] The situation began to change when Princeton published Joseph Bendersky's biography of Schmitt,[8] and three major texts appeared in a list known until then primarily for publishing the Frankfurt school. English versions of *Die geistesgeschichtliche Lage des heutigen Parlamentarismus, Politische Theologie,* and *Politische Romantik* made Schmitt's critique of liberal ideas and institutions available to readers with no German.[9] Translations and new monographs continued to appear in the 1980s and 1990s.[10] Most of the major works, and many important articles, are in English. A new translation of *Legalität und Legitimität* is published simultaneously with this volume, and a translation of Schmitt's constitutional theory, *Verfassungslehre,* is planned.[11]

A critical mass of literature by and about Schmitt is now available in

English that makes it possible to connect Schmitt's work to a more familiar set of texts in political thought. But those would never have been published had there not been a set of questions and problems within liberal constitutions and their state orders that drew their authors to Schmitt in the first place. The ultimate explanation for the burgeoning Schmitt studies lies there.

The Crisis of Liberalism

When Francis Fukuyama proclaimed "the end of history," his survey limited the range of possible political orders to just one—liberal democracy. With the collapse of the Soviet system in eastern Europe, the last alternative to liberalism and a system of government based on it had, Fukuyama argued, disappeared. From now on there would be no more "history" (and no more "politics") because the foundations of political order were no longer in dispute. The prediction proved wrong, and the apolitical era short-lived. The world after the Cold War offers more, not fewer, political choices than the bipolar globe it replaced. In that respect, it resembles more the patterns of European politics between the wars, when liberal ideas and institutions were besieged by various political movements fundamentally hostile to their assumptions about government and society.

Political theory too seems to be moving away from canonical issues of liberalism. The dominance of John Rawls's revival of the social contract model in *A Theory of Justice* (1972)[12] over political philosophy was shaken first by communitarian critiques of its ahistorical individualism,[13] then by postmodern deconstruction of rational self-interest. While such modes of thought still dominate economics and rational choice political science, Rawls himself before his death moved outside the boundaries of *A Theory of Justice.* The argument of that book assumed an innocent "original position" in which individuals would choose rules to govern themselves without knowing their consequences ("the veil of ignorance"). Justice as fairness assumes that there are no first-order differences among the individuals involved in rule making, all of whom would be motivated by rational self-regard, and that the process itself would constitute a just system because it is reasonable—any person so situated would make this same choice. Rawls's perspective thirty years later appeared much more bleak. *Political Liberalism* incorporates an apocalyptic vision of conflict very different from his earlier work:

> What is new about this clash is that it introduces into people's conceptions of the good a transcendent element not admitting of compro-

> mise. This element forces either mortal conflict moderated only by circumstance and exhaustion, or equal liberty of conscience and freedom of thought. Except on the basis of these last, firmly founded and publicly recognized, no reasonable political conception of justice is possible. Political liberalism starts by taking to heart the absolute depth of that irreconcilable latent conflict.[14]

Rawls's new liberalism is political because it detaches decisions about rules from any comprehensive doctrine about the good itself; unlike *A Theory of Justice,* this is a freestanding argument about politics and the basic structure of society, or its constitution. Rawls still assumed that it must be liberal-democratic, but he embedded its institutional design and social structure in "certain fundamental ideas seen as implicit in the public political culture of a democratic society." Conflict arises because that public political culture cannot be assumed to be homogeneous: "A society may also contain unreasonable and irrational, and even mad, comprehensive doctrines. In their case the problem is to contain them so that they do not undermine the unity and justice of society."[15]

With that description of theory and practice, contemporary political theory has come full circle to the central problem of the Weimar Republic and Carl Schmitt's political theory.

The Relevance of Weimar

Rawls introduces his case for political liberalism with a reference to Carl Schmitt, and his argument for it is political in Schmitt's sense—it asserts its truth against all challenges. It would ultimately bring about the situation Schmitt most feared, the end of politics, David Dyzenhaus has argued, because Rawls's homogeneous society "involves, by and large, getting rid of pluralism." It allows only versions of liberalism; the others (by definition unreasonable) are targeted for political action. Reasonable but illiberal beliefs and groups "will find it harder to survive in the social climate liberalism fosters."[16]

The Weimar Republic remains the model of such conflict, and of the failure of political liberalism to master it. While liberal constitutions in North America and western Europe do not appear to be so profoundly challenged today as they were in the Weimar Republic, the situation of such constitutions in the new democracies of eastern Europe is very different. There and here the major fault lines of Weimar liberalism have reappeared: emergency powers, the courts as "defender of the constitution," mobilization of antiliberal politics, ethnic identity politics, illiberal culture, and contested legitimacy. The political changes that ended Soviet rule in central and eastern Europe, and which Fukuyama thought had brought about the complete triumph of liberalism, have, ironically, ushered in a world where politics in Schmitt's sense are *more,* not less, likely.[17] Those changes have also shifted our perspective on Schmitt's work away from an interpretation of it as the prelude to Nazism and toward the immediate problems of the Republic as what Detlev Peukert calls "the crisis of classical modernity."[18] That is ultimately the reason for increased interest in Carl Schmitt's work among English and American political theorists.

Schmitt was primarily a public lawyer—what the Germans call a *Staatsrechtslehrer*—and that discipline conditioned his work as a political theorist. The problems of the Weimar constitution became the focus of Schmitt's political thinking between 1919 and 1933 because the questions of his discipline arose from that text. But unlike most other public lawyers, and in sharp disagreement with the dominant jurisprudential method of the day, Schmitt rejected constitutional formalism in favor of an approach that set questions of public law within politics and history. The law always contains a moment of conflict and decision in which differences are resolved to the advantage of one party and the disadvantage of the other. The attraction of Schmitt for young theorists such as Otto Kirchheimer and Franz Neumann in the 1920s (and for the student generation of 1968) was that Schmitt, too, saw public law as essentially political. Moreover, Schmitt saw those elements in the law as conditioned by "metajurisprudential," or first-order, questions. Both aspects of his work continue to attract commentary today.

Reading Carl Schmitt

Interpreting Schmitt's work requires answering two related questions. The first is not unlike that confronting readers of Rousseau. Like his, Schmitt's work also contains a great variety of substantive political positions, a quality that leads most commentators to describe him with a series of contradictory adjectives. Relativist, nihilist, absolutist, but also rationalist, Catholic, romantic, irrationalist, formalist, normativist, and existentialist have all been used to describe his political theory. Schmitt's personal stance appears sometimes fascist, sometimes liberal, sometimes reactionary, sometimes reformist. During the Third Reich he was described as its "crown jurist" *and* as a Catholic reactionary. Moreover, Schmitt's work frequently contains internal contradictions. His analysis of sovereignty in the Weimar constitution, for example, leads Schmitt to interpret presidential power under Article 48 as "commissarial" but also allows the president "acts of sovereignty."[19] An early review of Schmitt's *Verfassunglehre* focused on the inconsistency in his construction of the central concept of "political unity," describing the state as both the product of political unity *and* the institution that creates such unity in the first place.[20] Waldimar Gurian and Karl Löwith both catalog twists and turns in Schmitt's personal positions and contradictions in his work. Does a single theme or question knit together these disparate pieces of Schmitt's work?

The second question contains an answer to the first. From 1912 onward, Schmitt identified the questions of constitutional law as primarily evaluative. Interpretation, the task of evaluation, cannot be purely conceptual, as Hans Kelsen and the formalists argued. The problem here might be understood as the relationship of norms and rules to some other, justificatory context. Law must work within norms. But what justifies those? Schmitt's conception of that problem led him away from the formal jurisprudence represented by Kelsen and the neo-Kantians before World War I, but it can also be distinguished from the simpler realist position represented by Erich Kaufmann.[21] Between the reality of the state and the norms of law there is another sphere containing the political. For Schmitt, this is both a realm of discourse and of action whose primary focus is the definition of that "comprehensive doctrine" (Rawls) which is "self-evident," needing no further justification. In pluralist societies, however, there cannot be any really self-evident or comprehensive doctrines, only "obvious" procedures for settling disputes about them. Constitutional stability in pluralist societies, then, is the elaboration and acceptance of such obvious procedures. Like the later Rawls, Schmitt too understands the conflict of doctrines as a threat to such obvious constitutional structures that must be mastered politically. Schmitt attacks "Weimar liberalism" because it obscures the reality of doctrinal conflicts within society, treating them as choices without consequences.

Contemporary liberalism still rests on its Enlightenment foundations and on the deontology that is the metaphysical assumption of a secularized and disenchanted world. That the political dilemma of liberal ideas and institutions must be understood as struggle is obvious, even to its most fervent supporters. That struggle alone or that the empirical fact of pluralism cannot justify the principle of a liberalism is not understood. Carl Schmitt's political meets that issue directly in a critique of modern culture and in the assertion of a political theology: in the radical conceptualization of ideas that liberalism since Kant asserted to be immanent.

Modernism in art and literature grew from Nietzsche's deracination of the liberal philosophical order, a development Carl Schorske describes as "the ruthless centrifuge of change," a fragmentation of cultural substance and the values underlying European philosophy in the Enlightenment. The variety of perspectives and their values became "a death-dance of principles," to quote Arnold Schoenberg.[22] Beneath the cultural surface of what was new in art, music, and literature, the rational assumptions of liberalism seemed fractured to many of Schoenberg's contemporaries. Sigmund Freud discovered the irrational as a cause of illness, a diagnosis that he extended from the individual to bourgeois society to the family and back to political society itself. Lesser psychologists such as Gustave Le Bon and Georges Sorel reduced the liberal notion of "society" to a thing more frightening and primal, "the crowd," and the question of where this new world of "mass society" came from and its consequences became the central problem for sociologists such as Emile Durkheim and Max Weber.

Schmitt picks up and elaborates Weber's central question about the ethical-political ramifications of modernity as they manifest themselves in his own time. The origins, political context, and law of the Weimar constitution are central to Schmitt's work, not in its historical singularity but as representative of a particular type of constitution, indeed the dominant type, "the liberal rule of law state" based on political democracy.[23] What makes Schmitt's political theory important derives from Weimar's representative character. A constitution textually like ours in a pluralist society like ours, the central political institutions of the Weimar Republic were under extreme constitutional stress for most of the Republic's brief existence. Its failure is not explained through poor design or the absence of any particular idea. The Weimar document contained a thin constitution in its first half that specified the organization of offices and powers, and in the second part a thick constitution that was a catalog of conflicts. Essentially liberal despite superficial appeals to other doctrines, the whole of nineteenth-century thinking about the state and individual, and the whole of legal positivism and value neutrality, culminate in the document and political culture of the first German republic.

The constitution's crucial provision was not, as has so often been argued, the emergency powers of the president but the provisions of Article 25. In the practical operations of government, this article ensured that all contenders for power had an "equal chance" regardless of their program. Whether loyal or revolutionary, political parties competed for votes on a legally level playing field, and in the history of this constitution, all the assumptions of liberal political theory about the individual were inscribed. As individuals are abstractly equal before the law, so parties were equal in constitutional practice. The sources of fidelity to this regime were the idea of a democratic nation-state declared in the preamble of the Weimar constitution—"the German people have given themselves this constitution"—and the retention of a federal structure, organizationally irrational, but evoking continuity with the past. Machiavelli cautions the prince to woo the goddess of fortune through prudent statecraft. Fortuna appeared to Weimar in the guise of a set of extreme externalities: the Treaty of Versailles, the Great Inflation, the Great Depression—and the susceptibility of elites and the masses to political religions of the Right and Left.

Carl Schmitt's analysis of this constitution began with the historicity of its conceptual architecture in nineteenth-century liberalism. His charge against these elements of the Weimar constitution was consistent: political ideas developed in one social and political context cannot simply be transplanted to another. The concepts of rationality and individual freedom, in particular, appeared to him old-fashioned and outdated in the contemporary context. Individuals, he agreed with Weber, were constrained by the structures of the economy in ways that were more compelling, and restricted the agent more, than liberal theory assumed. Moreover, historical transformations implicated the structure of the state in received conceptions such as the division of public and private that were not adequate to the reality of mass society.

Schmitt shifts our perspective on these questions radically from simple normativism and empiricism to the existential. "The existential is the authentic, the primordial and original, the anti-bourgeois, the uncivilized." If the political is the existential, unsettling and uncomfortable consequences follow—if it cannot be true that one is without enemies, then most certainly there are no political communities that are without enemies and will therefore live in peace because their intentions are good.[24] The diversity of Schmitt's work, its focus on the existential in those terms—as an assumption of the real and present political relations of friend and enemy—precludes a systematic approach, and there is no "grand design" here, even when it addresses first-order theological and metaphysical issues. If revelation and the Christian truth that "Jesus is the Christ" are at the heart of Schmitt's political theory, as Heinrich Meier so forcefully demonstrates,[25] the interpretative task of the political theorist remains, as it always has been, in history, not the afterlife.

The following interpretation of Carl Schmitt's political theory tracks it through the terrain of contemporary issues in the Weimar period as these were thrown out and framed by its constitution. They are addressed in Schmitt's work not as formal logical problems in the positive law but as part of the larger landscape of political ideas in the culture and philosophy of the time. When the following chapters focus on the Republic's institutional problematic, Schmitt's voice lifts us above merely legal interpretation while presenting those issues over which the constitution failed: legitimacy, democracy and representation, the division and balance of powers, and the general crisis of modern values in a disenchanted world.

Although Schmitt's work presents the reader with numerous difficulties, the transformations of our own present have shifted since I stood at the Berlin Wall. Our access to the past that was its context remains obstructed by its history, a field still charged with assumptions that, until quite recently, made reading Schmitt more difficult than other political theorists. A retrospective teleology presents the past to us as if it were never open, but always a foreshadowing of what was, in that present, still future and which is now our past.

It is time to place Schmitt within familiar traditions of political theory and of constitutional theory—to take the risk of assuming that the future was still open as Schmitt wrote and thought about the Weimar constitution.

1 In the Dark Years: 1933–1945

The crisis of European jurisprudence began a century ago
with the triumph of positivism.
—CARL SCHMITT, "Die Lage der europäischen Rechtswissenschaft"

When Carl Schmitt spoke to the faculty of law at Leipzig on December 1, 1944, barely half a year remained for Hitler's "Thousand Year Reich." In twelve years Nazi Germany had laid waste to the European continent and with it the system of nation-states that had been its political structure since 1648. At this point in "the Europe of the dictators," questions of jurisprudence might seem academic indeed.[1] But Schmitt's lecture on "the plight of European jurisprudence" and its text were deeply embedded in Europe's contemporary crisis.[2] Read to law faculties across occupied and fascist Europe between February 1943 and December 1944, the lecture's references to the war are oblique. Schmitt begins with an acknowledgment that the topic itself, *European* jurisprudence, might seem absurd —the second war of the century is evidence enough of Europe's fragmentation. Later he denies that he is addressing "the most obvious subject, the effects of the world war," but also that he will avoid "empty phrases, abstractions and merely formal argument."[3] His topic, the history of Roman law in European jurisprudence since Friedrich Karl von Savigny, had been a controversial subject among legal scholars after 1933 in a debate that set "Romanists" against "Germanists" along the lines of a broadly European versus a narrowly nationalist jurisprudence. The Romanists tended to be "far more international and multilingual and more deeply rooted in the world of liberal-humanist disciplines" than the Germanists. Their respective political and cultural milieus made the one less, the other more, susceptible to "the conglomeration of emotionally charged words that was made up of ethnic-national, corporatist, authoritarian and totalitarian elements and was establishing itself as the ideology of the state."[4] Beyond that, however, basic differences in philosophy divided them. Perhaps because the Roman law was essentially a historic discipline, its practitioners were less politically oriented than the Germanists and less likely to view jurisprudence as the search for "eternal ideas" that could serve as guides to the present than were the Germanists.[5]

Schmitt's starting point is this struggle "for and against the Roman law," but his argument moves beyond its boundaries. The Roman law is not a national question but a European one that raises a general question about the connection between law and justice, and the purpose of political rule.[6] Its concluding pathos hints at the contemporary disjunction between them, suggesting that jurists are called to guard the arcana of law, a vocation that preserves them against "the terror of those weapons of destruction which modern science places in the hands of every ruler."[7] The history of the text suggests more immediate questions about the relationship of law and politics.

Into the Vortex

Schmitt intended "Die Lage der europäischen Rechtswissenschaft" for a Festschrift in honor of his friend Johannes Popitz's sixtieth birthday, a relationship that reveals much about Schmitt's person and place in the political intelligentsia of Weimar and the Third Reich. The two met in 1929 when Schmitt joined the faculty of the Berlin Handelshochschule and published the interpretation of presidential power that took him from largely academic debates into practical politics.[8] Popitz's grasp of economics and his political cunning made him an influential adviser to the government, and the connection gave Schmitt entrée into the circle of conservative politicians and intellectuals around President Paul von Hindenburg.

Although there were differences between them, more united Schmitt and Popitz intellectually than divided them. Their common ground was the diagnosis of Weimar and its remedy, and that led both into active political engagement in Weimar's final crisis. From their different perspectives—Schmitt was a constitutional lawyer, Popitz an economist—they thought that parliamentary governments were unable to manage conflicting economic interests and that partisan politics were destroying confidence in the state and undermining Germany's national independence.[9] Their preferred solution was presidential government because they thought the executive branch was more efficient than the legislative and that its corps of professional civil servants was less corruptible. Both saw the office of president as "the bearer of the principle of the unity of the Reich,"[10] and like Max Weber, they believed that it would counter the dangers of German particularism in the republican constitution. Like him, too, they had misgivings about parliamentary government; their vision of the presidency as the fount of "strong leadership" was not embedded in a balance-of-powers argument but represented an alternative to parliament and its party system.[11]

Both Schmitt and Popitz took part in the public debate on governmental and economic problems caused by the Great Depression and were involved in the political intrigues of the German state crisis from 1930 to 1932. Popitz was a career civil servant who held positions in the Interior Ministry and the Reich Treasury during World War I and high posts in the German state afterward. From 1925 until his resignation on December 21, 1929, Popitz was state secretary in the Finance Ministry under the last parliamentary governments of the Republic. In that position, he advocated a policy of fiscal burden sharing between Reich, *Länder,* and local governments and is regarded as the originator of the German *Finanzausgleich* system of taxation and revenue sharing.[12] An outspoken critic of German federalism, Popitz favored both administrative reforms to create a more unitary state and fiscal policies to stimulate the economy and encourage capital accumulation.[13] When the German Reichsbank undermined a plan for tax cuts in late 1929, Popitz and his finance minister Rudolf Hilferding (Social Democratic Party or SPD) resigned; Popitz did not return to government service until after the Prussian coup of July 20, 1932. The last parliamentary government fell in March 1930. Its successor, headed by Heinrich Brüning (Center Party), governed by emergency decree until Hindenburg dismissed it in late May 1932 and called on Franz von Papen to form a government of "National Consolidation." Popitz and Schmitt were involved in advising the president's counselors behind the scenes and in the decision to remove the government of Prussia that summer. Popitz wrote to his wife regarding the *Preußenschlag* supporting the Reich actions that "at last something has been done that should have been done long ago," but saying, too, that he was "happy not to be directly involved in this."[14]

Schmitt's argument for presidential dictatorship according to Article 48 of the Weimar constitution was widely known and discussed, and he became involved in the presidential cabinets of Franz von Papen (June 1 to

December 3, 1932) and General Kurt von Schleicher (December 3, 1932, to January 30, 1933) through the president's chief of staff, Otto Meißner.[15] When the deposed SPD government of Prussia sued the Reich government, Carl Schmitt defended its actions.[16] The Staatsgerichtshof ruling on October 25 left the commissarial powers of the Reich intact in Prussia but symbolically "restored" the Prussian government. A week later Popitz, with considerable reluctance, accepted appointment as Reich minister without portfolio and commissioner for Prussian finances. He retained that post in the Schleicher cabinet, a failed attempt to form a coalition of military and industrial interests with the Social Democratic working class.[17] As inclusion of the National Socialists began to be discussed in early January 1933, Popitz was skeptical, and he was one of the first dismissed from the cabinet on January 30.[18] In late April, however, Popitz joined the government again as Reich minister and Prussian finance minister, positions he held until his death in 1945.

Both Popitz and Schmitt made careers in government after 1933, and their social and intellectual friendship continued throughout the Third Reich. They were neighbors in Berlin, and the families were often guests in each other's homes. Schmitt's household during the Berlin years was a salon in which everyone in the conservative-national *intelligenz* from Niekisch to Ernst Jünger met, and where artists such as Emile Nolde and David Gillys were also frequent guests. Schmitt and Popitz were influential members of the Deutschen Gesellschaft, a political club of high-ranking civil servants and professors.[19] Although they frequently read and commented on each other's work, Popitz never introduced Schmitt to the Mittwochsgesellschaft, the circle of Berlin civil servants and intellectuals to which Popitz and others in the elite who resisted Hitler belonged.[20] Their shared interests in government and economic issues and Schmitt's broad knowledge of music and literature suggest that he would have been an obvious participant, and his name and work appear several times in the Mittwochsgesellschaft's discussions.[21] Schmitt's absence implies that Popitz believed he would have been an unreliable conspirator against Hitler, and despite their friendship, Popitz never confided in Schmitt. When the coup failed, Schmitt's first reaction was fear that he would be linked to the plot through Popitz.[22]

A diverse group that met fortnightly in the Berlin villas of its members, the society began in 1863 as the Freie Gesellschaft für wissenschaftliche Unterhaltung. All subjects were allowed except "the political events of the day," and the major breaks in German history before the winter of 1932 to 1933 left no traces in the society's records. In the last year of the Republic, that began to change, and the protocols from November 1932 until the group's last meeting on July 26, 1944, contain several presentations on the state, law, and the constitution. Two days after his appointment to the Nazi government, Popitz made a presentation to the society entitled "Recent Developments in Germany," laying out a structural critique of the Republic and arguing that there were only two ways out of the situation, reform or revolution. Reform (by that he meant the presidential cabinets of Papen and Schleicher) had failed; only revolution remained. "The preconditions for revolution were given, because we had tried to prevent the masses gathering behind Hitler's national movement from taking part in government. It [the inclusion of the Nazis] is a revolution because it is a seizure of power in the state, and once in their hands that power has been used against those rights formerly held by individuals and for a fundamental reorganization of the state." This revolution was unique, Popitz continued, because it had been relatively bloodless and, taking an argument from Carl Schmitt, legal.[23] "It began with the capitulation of the government and presidential power—without a 'March on Rome'—through entrusting the leader of this movement with the German Chancellorship and with the exploitation of the defeated constitution which allowed it, with its 2/3rds majority, to accomplish things that are in complete contradiction of the political idea of that [the Weimar] constitution."[24] Popitz concluded with an argument that led many Germans into collaboration. It remains to be seen, he told his listeners that evening, whether this government will succeed in reforming those aspects of political and social life in the Republic that had "cried out for change" through building a new national authority for the state. Would Hitler proceed as the Italian fascists had? Or, Popitz asked in a tone that made his own position clear, would there be room for "personal initiative and the value of the individual which over the long term would allow the emergence of a new leadership class fully aware of its responsibilities and conscious of its ties to the people"?[25]

There is a certain irony in the reaction of Popitz and many other Germans to Hitler's appointment that tends to be obscured by our retrospective vision. Knowing as we do the subsequent development of that regime, it seems obvious in some way that, here at the first moment, persons of goodwill and decency should have reacted to an unfolding tragedy. Instead what we have is the enactment of an old political virtue, temperance, and the counsel to "wait and see" combined with the belief that, despite the governmental instability of the previous year, the institutions of the German state would tame the radical elements in the new government.[26] For many observers, although Hitler's appointment came as a surprise, it seemed to carry no ominous portent, and the mood in Berlin that evening was festive. "That evening I went out to dinner at the 'Kaiserhof' with

[General] Seekt, [foreign minister Walter] Simons, [and state secretary in the Foreign Office Wilhelm] Solf, then to a lecture by Coudenhove on 'Germany's European Task,' " Harry Graf Kessler noted in his diary. "Berlin tonight is in a carnival mood. SA and SS troops, as well as uniformed Stahlhelm members marching through the streets, observers crowding onto the sidewalks. In and around the 'Kaiserhof' there was a real festival; uniformed SS troops standing in lines at the entry and in the hall, SA and SS men patrolling the corridors. . . . I rode over to the Fürstenberg Beer Hall on the Potsdamer Platz. Marching columns of SA men in military formation there too. The highpoint was reached inside the beer hall." Kessler goes on to describe how the men were picked up by "two blonde tarts" at the Fürstenberg: "it was an appropriate conclusion to this 'historic' day that fit in perfectly with the mood."[27] Others, of course, did react powerfully against the appointment. Erich von Ludendorff wrote to Hindenburg, his wartime colleague, "You have delivered up our holy German fatherland to one of the greatest demagogues of all time. I solemnly prophesy that this accursed man will cast our Reich into the abyss and bring our nation to inconceivable misery. Future generations will damn you in your grave for what you have done."[28]

Schmitt's diary for January 31, the day after Hitler's appointment, was terse and pessimistic. "Cancelled my lecture. Couldn't work. Ridiculous circumstances. Read the newspaper. Upset, fits of temper, that's how the day went."[29] On the afternoon of the thirtieth, Schmitt was walking in the Berlin *Tiergarten* as the first demonstrators moved toward the Chancellery in the Wilhelmstraße. His companion was Schleicher's press secretary, Erich Marcks, who remarked to him: "Herr Professor, that was our problem, we could not create enough enthusiasm." Both men regretted Hitler's appointment and would do "all they could to bring the National Socialist adventure to a speedy end."[30] Events in the month between Hitler's appointment as chancellor and the burning of the Reichstag building on February 27 mixed the pattern of revolutionary breaks in political history with the language of government transition, for which Hitler's speech to the nation on January 31 set the tone. The Republic had left "an appalling legacy" of defeat and disunity, a nation undermined by enemies within and without. What was done in fourteen years (1919–1933) must be corrected in four. A pledge of specific programs to help the unemployed and the farming sectors, and "to fulfill the responsibilities of society to those who are old and sick," was combined with a new foreign policy that would restore Germany as a "free and equal nation" among others. Invoking the kaiser's speech to the Reichstag on August 4, 1914, Hitler concluded, "We do not recognize classes, but only the German people."[31]

Speaking to a group of German industrialists a few weeks later, Hitler and Göring made their intentions quite clear; the elections scheduled for March 5 would be used to consolidate the power of the NSDAP and would be, Göring told his audience, "certainly the last for the next ten years, probably the last for the next hundred years."[32] The campaign leading up to the March elections was marked by violence, intimidation, and propaganda branding their opponents as national enemies. The SA and SS, military units of the Nazi Party, were made auxiliaries of the Prussian police, and on Göring's orders, they systematically intimidated other political parties, especially the Social Democrats and Communists. Less than a week before the elections, the Reichstag was set on fire, the pretext for a wholesale roundup of suspects. On the following day, sections of the constitution (personal liberty, free speech, press freedom, assembly and association, privacy of house and communications) were suspended by presidential decree.[33] Local and Länder officials were ordered to carry out measures to "restore public safety and order," and the decree authorized the central Reich government to take over any subordinate governmental unit if this was not done. At the elections the Nazis failed to gain an absolute majority in the Reichstag, despite such intimidation: their vote share rose from 33.1 percent to 43.9 percent, but they still required the nationalists as coalition partners. Nevertheless they held essential institutions of the Reich and had broken the political opposition.

Schmitt held back from the new regime at first. He did not sign a published declaration of university professors and lecturers of support for Hitler after the Reichstag fire and just before the elections.[34] Even after agreeing to work with Popitz on the draft of a law reorganizing federal aspects of the state, Schmitt still found the political circumstances "dreadful."[35] But within weeks he began to accommodate himself to the new men in Berlin.[36] Against the backdrop of continued agitation against "Marxists and Jews," the newly elected Reichstag was opened at the garrison church in Potsdam on March 21 in a ceremony intended to solidify the Nazis' claim to the German, especially the Prussian, national tradition. Three days later, with the necessary two-thirds' majority, the Enabling Law of March 24, 1933, changed the Weimar constitution, effectively consolidating all formal powers in Hitler's hands. Legislative authority was transferred to the chancellor, and while there were formal limitations, the only real remaining limit to Hitler's power was the person of Hindenburg. Within a week, Schmitt had published a commentary.[37] When Schmitt agreed to draft the executive law that would reform relations between the central government and the provincial states, the first step in the Nazis' *Gleichschaltung* of the German state, it was "the turning point in Schmitt's life and work."[38] On May 1 he joined the National Socialist Party. The door to a career under the new regime swung open when the *Westdeutscher Beobachter*, the Cologne party organ, published an article calling Schmitt "the most renowned national constitutionalist in Germany." In early July, on Popitz's recommendation, Herman Göring made Schmitt a Prussian state counselor. He had become "the crown jurist of the Third Reich."

State, Movement, People: Carl Schmitt's Political Theory after 1933

Schmitt's accommodation with the new regime features prominently in much of the literature. Even sympathetic accounts approach his volte-face at least with embarrassment and often with disgust, emotions made so intense by our knowledge after the fact that this trajectory of German politics would end in the most horrific way. The decision for collaboration did not come from enthusiasm, nor was it forced. Carl Schmitt was a constitutional lawyer and a political theorist—our understanding of his choice must start there, with what his professional identity and its intellectual commitments meant in those circumstances, rather than his personal motives. How did the elements of his political theory structure Schmitt's approach to the German circumstances of early 1933? How do those same aspects of Schmitt's political thought shape his argument about the state in this period?

In Schmitt's *Die Diktatur* (1921), Machiavelli's analysis of the dictatorship in a republic provides the basic structure of Schmitt's interpretation of that institution within state theory and the practice of commissarial dictatorships in Europe during the sixteenth and seventeenth centuries. Schmitt's argument that "the dictator is precisely not a tyrant or a form of absolute domination" but "a means peculiar to the republican constitution for the preservation of liberty" is drawn from Machiavelli's *Discourses*.[39] The question implicit in Schmitt's decision for the Nazis in the spring of 1933, however, and to which Machiavelli's work (and life) provides an answer remarkably similar to Schmitt's own, had been stated clearly by him as early as 1913 in a book about the value of the state and individual. "The question is not whether law or power takes precedence, but whether law can be derived from facts," a question that structures Schmitt's normative argument for the state. In that early work, "law" appears as a norm or pure *Sollen* (ought); it is a "pure norm, a value that cannot be justified empirically." On the other side of this "pure value" is the individual, "an empirical existence." In the middle, the fulcrum of the purely normative and the empirical is the state that is the realization of "right" in the world.[40]

In *The Prince,* a text Schmitt knew well and from which the core of his argument in *Der Begriff des Politischen* was drawn, Machiavelli first distinguishes republics from principalities and then categorizes the latter as principalities by inheritance and by acquisition, those that are old and established and new ones acquired by luck or favor or by ability.[41] The Florentine appears first in Schmitt's published work in *Politische Romantik* (1919), the text that marks his transformation from constitutional lawyer into political theorist of law and politics, where the distinction of political realism from romanticism is made by reference to Machiavelli.

Schmitt's concept of the political as a "sphere without substance," purely an intensity of association or dissociation, and his theory of the presidency under Article 48 were the theoretical and practical end points of his movement away from normative theories of politics toward a "Machiavellian" realism about them, which, in 1933, included the complex of problems contained in the category of principalities by acquisition. The political can be "about" anything—but its criterion, the intensity of association or dissociation into friend or foe, liberates political decisions from moral criteria and states theoretically the maxims of political realism that Machiavelli derives from historical study.[42]

The passages of *The Prince* in which Machiavelli offers advice to new princes on the dangers of their situation and how they should act to secure themselves are what make Machiavelli, like some other political theorists, "a sign," something that exists independently of his work or person.[43] Writing for a popular audience on the four hundredth anniversary of Machiavelli's death, Schmitt dismisses Machiavelli as a statesman and political theorist but proceeds to use him as *the* sign in postwar Europe of political realism. The most shocking passages are "simple political truths" that should not outrage the political observer, and more: for Schmitt, they reveal the essence of the political as "an eternal part of human nature." In Machiavelli's voice and quoting from *The Prince,* Schmitt writes, "My views would be immoral if men were good; but they are not."

The article on Machiavelli condenses Schmitt's argument about the political, making it available for ready use. Politics is about the use of force; its art is to seem, not to be; piety and good intentions are more often signs of deceit than of virtue; what is wrong for the private man is right for the prince. Six years later, after Hitler had been chancellor of Germany for half a year, Machiavelli's categories, blended with Schmitt's own analysis of the circumstances, render a specific understanding of Germany's constitutional reality. Hitler came to power through luck, the patronage of others, and the ability to manipulate central institutions of the Reich. Once in office, the National Socialists moved quickly, as Machiavelli had advised new princes, to suppress their enemies and consolidate power.[44] The decay of republican government was the subject of the *Discourses,* as it was Schmitt's subject throughout most of the Weimar Republic. Like Machiavelli, Schmitt too came to terms with the new state, and for a time quite successfully.

By May 1933, Schmitt thought of the Third Reich as a new state, and his work in the first year of Hitler's regime locates it as a revolutionary break with its predecessor. The end of the Republic came much as Schmitt had predicted the previous summer in *Legalität und Legitimität* (1932). The formal guarantees of the constitution are not independent of the political circumstances, Schmitt argued, and "the law cannot protect itself."[45] It was the dead end of a long debate between legal positivists such as Gerhard Anschütz and Richard Thoma and antipositivists such as Schmitt, Erich Kaufmann, and Rudolf Smend about constitutional protection. Schmitt and the others maintained that amendment (Article 76) should be limited by the constitution's "fundamental political decision" contained in its core institutions—a constitution is more, that is, than the sum of its laws.[46] For Anschütz and Thoma, those did not limit constitutional change; all could be (and ultimately were) abolished by a Reichstag vote.[47] As late as January 1933, with the publication of the fourteenth edition of his definitive commentary, Anschütz regarded Schmitt's argument about the limitations of constitutional amendment as "a political demand."[48] Their resulting positions in 1933 were bizarre: Anschütz, who on the grounds of his own argument must accept the Enabling Law as constitutional, rejected its political consequences; Schmitt, who must reject it as unconstitutional, accepted it politically. That he *also* accepted it constitutionally can be understood in terms of the same political theory of the Republic's constitution that he had offered in the *Verfassungslehre* (1928): it was a fundamental political decision, or as an earlier generation of positivists had themselves declared in other constitutional circumstances, it had "the normative power of the factual."[49]

Excursus: The Languages of National Socialism

As his decision for Hitler drew Schmitt's political theory into a revolution, so its reading throws us into a maelstrom: the past is not history, the language of political theory is polemic, assured positions have disappeared. "I am the last conscious representative of the *jus publicum Eu-*

ropaeum, its last teacher and student in an existential sense and I have experienced it as Benito Cereno did the voyage of the pirate ship."[50] So Carl Schmitt wrote in the summer of 1946.

The comparison suggests that Schmitt's role in the Third Reich was like that of Melville's sailor, forced to cooperate with the pirates in an ultimately vain hope of saving himself. The metaphor of ships and sailing is an old one in political philosophy. It suggests a risky enterprise, one that requires practical knowledge (what Gilbert Ryle called "knowing how"), and one in which the helmsman's authority derives from the common good of the crew and the ship itself. Schmitt's reflection reverses this classical image, presenting the ship of state as a pirate ship, himself as the hostage whose knowledge must be turned to buccaneer's work. To the extent that Schmitt wanted to conserve "the state," it had to be reconstructed in terms acceptable to the new powers in Germany, but that project, like steering a pirate ship, could easily turn into its self-destruction. Among German lawyers, those working in constitutional and public law were most endangered by the regime change, for theirs was the most intrinsically political branch of law.[51] What was true of the law in general between 1933 and 1945 was especially true of constitutional law: "a quick penetration of new National Socialist terms into the old conceptual world and a remarkable resistance to all attempts at innovation."[52] Schmitt's work demonstrates both aspects of the accommodation to Nazism.

Even after liberalism had been destroyed as the principle of the Weimar constitution, the political ideas and institutions of liberalism remained the focus of Schmitt's political theory, a thesis to which National Socialism was both antithesis and synthesis. The radical turn in his thought was apparent by the end of 1933. His analysis of the new constitutional circumstances, *Staat, Bewegung, Volk,* appeared in a prominent series ("The German State of the Present") that he edited for a leading National Socialist press, the Hamburg firm of Hanseatischer Verlag. It was based on his presentation at the Conference of German Lawyers at Leipzig that September, expanding the argument about the dualism of nineteenth-century liberal thought, with its central images of representation (king/people), public/private, and state/society. Against those, Schmitt sets the National Socialist "tripartite division of political unity"—the elements of state, movement, and people that a contemporary reviewer compared to Hegel's tripartite division in *The Philosophy of Right* of family, civil society, and the state.[53] The superficial resemblance reflects the deeper structure of Schmitt's work—he can approach the new system only through a dialectic of the old, liberal world it has replaced. Hegel's *Beamtenstaat* survives here as a governing idea of "German state theory" as opposed to the dualism of nineteenth-century liberal thought. The "twentieth-century state" of Adolf Hitler reclaims that work in new circumstances.[54]

Although the circumstances were new, Schmitt's argument applied categories and concepts from earlier works. The *Verfassungslehre* (1928) distinguished among various types of constitutions. There was not only one constitution, as liberal constitutionalism asserted, but many different meanings of a constitution: the "positive" constitution is "an all-inclusive decision about the kind and form of political unity" in contrast to the constitution as "a multitude of particular laws."[55] In *Staatsgefüge und Zusammenbruch des zweiten Reiches* (1934), Schmitt demonstrates how dualistic forces within the "absolute" constitution of the Republic,[56] the pluralism and polyarchy described in *Der Hüter der Verfassung* (1931), destroyed the Weimar state. Those have been overcome in the unitary constitution of the Third Reich, for which the Enabling Law of March 24, 1933, is "the provisional constitution." Although specific parts of the Weimar constitution remain "valid by default" (the constitution was never formally repealed or abrogated), it is "no longer in effect," and with that, "the world of liberal ideas and institutions" has been set aside.[57] The Weimar constitution is "mere text" that can no longer be used to criticize National Socialism—that is either a "mere game" or "subversion." The absolute constitution of the Third Reich elevates and transforms Weimar's dualism into a harmonious tripartite unity where the state is its static part, the movement its dynamic or political part, and the people its passive or apolitical part.

Leadership *(Führung)* is the element that transforms those parts into a whole, but Schmitt's attempt at a political theory of this central element in Nazi thought fails miserably, and perhaps not surprisingly. The notion of leadership remains amorphous, no matter how many adjectives are appended to it, and the text retreats constantly into a description of liberal organization and its opposite in "leadership" or simply an assertion of what it is not—"Leading is not commanding, dictating, central-bureaucratic governing, or any of the usual kinds of ruling"—so that Schmitt finally calls on a political theology to explain its meaning. Leading is to governing what grace is to the soul, and Carl Schmitt in 1933 can think of no better metaphors for it than those of traditional political theory or the Bible: the shepherd and his sheep (Catholicism); the physician, the shepherd, the helmsman (Plato); the horseman (Taine).[58]

Schmitt's political theory during the Republic developed as a critique of legal formalism and constitutional positivism in the work of the leading school of jurisprudence. *Staat, Bewegung, Volk,* and much else after 1933, builds on that argument: the *Verfassungslehre* identified core constitutional values or principles that must be defended politically; in *Legalität und Legitimität* the formal legal aspects of the constitution are subordinated to a principle of legitimacy that cannot be legality itself. Throughout the 1920s, Schmitt constantly emphasized the primacy of the political over the legal. Leo Strauss read Schmitt's political theory as a treatise about "the order of human things" in an age when "liberalism has failed" but could still produce a "smoke screen" to cover the truth of man's nature as a political animal: "When it is said that the political is a basic characteristic of human life, in other words that man ceases to be man if he ceases to be political, this statement also, and precisely, means that man ceases to be human when he ceases to be political." For Strauss, the political is both real and necessary, and Schmitt's "affirmation of the political is ultimately nothing other than the affirmation of the moral."[59] The affirmations of the political in Schmitt's work after 1933 are something less than moral—unless one collapses that concept, as Schmitt's own theory of "concrete orders" tended to do, back into the political distinctions of race and nation.[60]

That implication is obvious in *Staat, Bewegung, Volk.* The political as a pure intensity must be constituted as substance, as a way of life, as more than "mere text," and it appears here as a national and racial project. The Enabling Law, a "provisional constitution" of the Third Reich, returns Germany to "its own foundation" *(eigenen Boden)* from the foreign territory of Weimar and Versailles, and we can read *Staat, Bewegung, Volk* as the provisional political theory of German fascism. Leo Strauss had seen the friend/enemy relationship that is the heart of Schmitt's concept of the political as a necessary condition of morality; but Schmitt's political theory after 1933 certainly demonstrates that it is not a *sufficient* condition of morality as Strauss understood it, even though it may be both the necessary and sufficient conditions of political life as Schmitt understood it. No single text makes that so clear as "The Führer Protects the Law," Schmitt's notorious defense of the 1934 purge of Röhm's SA on June 30, 1934. In the putsch, carried out by Himmler's SS with the help of the German army, Röhm and 150 to 200 SA men were murdered. So too were some of Hitler's former rivals and opponents, including General Kurt von Schleicher and his wife, and others from the national and Catholic Right including vice-chancellor Franz von Papen's adviser Ernst Jung. Papen himself was put under house arrest. The Röhm purge might just be a case of "the revolution eating its children," but it also established "the arbitrary power of the Führer as a principle." With the death of Hindenburg on August 2, the army swore an oath of loyalty to Hitler, and the cabinet passed a law combining both offices, the chancellorship and the presidency, into one person, the "Führer and Chancellor."[61]

This "second revolution" was legitimized by Schmitt's article in the August 1 issue of the *Deutsche Juristen Zeitung,* a text that remains unmatched for its political calculation and what many have seen as the cynical destruction of law in Germany. Helmut Quaritsch's discussion of Schmitt's Röhm purge article moves away from simple damnation ("opportunistic capitulation" is Bracher's description) by asking why Schmitt wrote the piece in the first place, and why it was reproduced in his essay collection *Positionen und Begriffe im Kampf mit Weimar-Genf-Versailles, 1923–1939.*[62] "With this article," Quaritsch writes, "as the only jurist of importance, Schmitt justified an act that could not be defended juridically." All the other professors were silent—only Schmitt spoke out for Hitler. In Hitler, Schmitt wrote, all the lessons of German history are alive, and all justice originates in him. He decides what is right and lawful, and he is also the last judge in every case. Hitler is also sovereign; he decides what is an emergency and, in accordance with his position as the source and judge of law, what shall be done. There is "only one representative of the political will in our state, the National Socialist Party," whose task it is to preserve national unity. The article closes with a violent rejection of due process as "the national poison [*Volksvergiftung*] of the last decades . . . an artifice of anti-German propaganda."[63]

After the war, Schmitt often claimed that he had been compelled to write this piece and that besides its forced justification of the SA purge, he had called for the murders of Schleicher and the others to be prosecuted. Whatever the truth of that might be, the answer to Quaritsch's second question—why include it in the 1939 collection?—illuminates Schmitt's own position within the corps of Nazi jurists. As a relative latecomer to the party, he was regarded with suspicion by others, such as Otto Koellreutter, professor of public law at Munich.[64] Schmitt's appointment to the plum posts of his profession and to the chair of public and constitutional law at Berlin, the country's leading university, engendered the envy and hostility of many others.[65] And even academic debates had a deadly undercurrent.

The *Rechtsstaat* controversy of 1933 to 1935 among German lawyers turned on whether the language of Rechtsstaat theories should be adopted by the new regime.[66] An important faction of National Socialist jurists favored retaining the term and argued that the Third Reich was a "true" Rechtsstaat, unlike the Republic, which was neither "Recht" nor "Staat." Schmitt sometimes seemed to agree with that position. Three months before the Röhm purge, he wrote that the term could be used when prefaced by the word "National Socialist" to distinguish it from a state in which "laws, not a leader personally," rule.[67] But in a 1935 article summarizing the debate, he moved away from it. Rechtsstaat theory subordinated state to society, which is to say, to the economy and the individual, removing the content of law and the state and replacing it with "procedure." It originated as a concept between two others: against the Christian idea of the state, or the religious state, and the moral idea of the state, "namely the Prussian civil service state of Hegel's philosophy."[68] That is the origin and heritage of the Rechtsstaat, and "everything else follows from that beginning: the division of law from religion and morality; the 'purely juridical' concept of law . . . the transformation of law and justice into a positivistic 'civilly imperative standard' whose entire justice consists in legal security, i.e., in predictability."[69] Thinking of the state primarily in legal terms, however, ignores substantial factors in which the political originates, and which are revealed by polemics, conflicts, and disagreement over the ends of life. The vision of National Socialism developed here is transcendent and positions the state above society, not as a neutral process for individual goals but as the "powerful realization of a concrete order."[70]

Schmitt's rhetoric deconstructs the concept, then allows for its National Socialist interpretation for the sake of "coordinating" (*Gleichschaltung*) the state apparatus,[71] but finally rejects it as un-German, bound to its time and place in the dualism of nineteenth-century liberal thought: "In a tripartite construction, in a living political unity of the state, movement and people, the word *'Rechtsstaat'* will become superfluous to the extent that the edifice of a fundamentally new order is realized."[72]

The immediate effect of Schmitt's texts from 1933 to 1935 is revolutionary, the announcement of a new order in place of the old, and suggests more than the obvious replacement of one set of institutions and arrangements by another. What is left of the old order is transformed, filled with a new substance that makes what is apparent (the formal continuation of the Weimar constitution until May 1945) false. In these works, Schmitt reviews and summarizes the political theory and constitutional arguments he had developed in Weimar, tracing the origins of Hitler's success back along those critical elements of Schmitt's own analysis of the republican constitution. *That* the republican constitution failed, and *how* it failed, proved the truth of his case against liberal formalism and neutrality. The Enabling Law "pronounces the death of the old system" that Schmitt had predicted in *Legalität und Legitimität* (1932), and even old opponents, such as Gerhard Anschütz, must be conquered again after 1933.[73] The atmosphere of these texts brings to mind Milton at the height of the English Civil War, whose history was a key to Carl Schmitt's own thinking. As he justified the regicide, so Schmitt justified Hitler's seizure of power: "Let men cease therefore out of faction and hypocrisy to make out-cries and horrid things of things so just and honorable."[74]

A Higher Third: The State Philosophy of Johannes Popitz

In this revolutionary phase of Carl Schmitt's work, the question of his character meets the content of his political theory. He accommodated himself to the Nazi regime, and more, when others such as Rudolf Smend or Erich Kaufmann and Herman Heller who shared Schmitt's positions in the Weimar controversy over legal positivism chose passivity or exile.[75] Schmitt himself, and his defenders too, have argued that his decision for Hitler was like that of many other German conservatives, including Johannes Popitz, who believed that a political and cultural elite would emerge on the basis of this mass democratic movement, which could reform and stabilize the German political system and the economy in the Great Depression. Their expectations failed utterly to appreciate the radical nature of German fascism, and the limits of their own power in the state under Hitler. Far from conserving it, the Nazis led the German state and nation to destruction, and much of the world with them.

Schmitt understood, at the latest by the outbreak of the war, that "the state" was no longer the ordering institution of the political.[76] Beginning with his book on Hobbes's *Leviathan* and throughout numerous articles on international law and the history of political thought, Schmitt tried to identify the real powers that had replaced the state. His project in these years (1938–1945) and after the war tried to do for this new era of world history what the critique of liberalism in Weimar had done: the analysis of a failed institution, the state, and its underlying ideas. Its provisional successor was a new form of regional power, which he called (in conscious reference to Germany's place on the continent since Charlemagne) a *Reich*, and its locus was a hegemonic territory like that declared over the Americas by President Monroe.[77] Significant as these ideas were for the empirical theory of the state, they were more important for the political philosophy underlying modern institutions of governance, especially the ideas of political obligation, consent, and the varieties of liberty that had been derived from general theories of politics since Plato and Aristotle.

By contrast, Johannes Popitz consistently advanced an idea of the state influenced by Hegel's nineteenth-century conservative students, particularly Lorenz von Stein.[78] It was for Popitz the task and duty of civil servants to realize certain specific values inherent in Hegel's concept of the state as the higher third above family and civil society in which the ethical content of a particular people and their place in world history come to life. He often sought to draw a parallel between Weimar and the German states of the mid–nineteenth century, from which he drew practical political and ethical conclusions. Speaking to a group of professional civil servants in 1931, Popitz compared their circumstances with that of von Stein and his time. Our situation is like theirs in three respects, Popitz said, "a crushing burden of reparations after a terrible fall from a glorious height, the complete failure of the state organization, whose growth and strength had been the wonder and envy of the world, and a new *Zeitgeist* whose constitutive values are not understood and not least because of that, storms destructively into an inherited world of ideas."[79]

For Popitz, the state was an instrument of well-conceived law, but also more than the law. Like Hegel, he understood it as something above and beyond particular individuals, a value greater than one person's fate or that of a generation.[80] The substance of its ethic was not simply, for Popitz, a prevailing "opinion" but truth as the self-revelation of world spirit in time whose meaning in specific circumstances would be understood only at the end of time. Popitz was not a political philosopher—he did not pursue the problematic quality of such claims in a strictly philosophical sense. They were, rather, practical assumptions about what he, as a professional civil servant and member of government, was morally charged to do. This is the ultimate source of Popitz's revulsion at the interest group politics of the Republic, in which German particularism, always the greatest threat to the state as an idea and as a political unity, seemed to have gained the upper hand. If there is only "interest," whether of the group or the individual, then nothing justifies the tragic character of political authority. He never wavered from that conception. Indeed it remained, embedded in the great figures of German culture, his point of orientation to the last.[81] It was also the issue over which he differed fundamentally with Carl Schmitt.

The maintenance of the Reich—a unified German state in the face of particularist political movements in important Länder such as Bavaria—was Popitz's central concern during the Republic, and his policy studies and advice to governments on matters of fiscal administration and taxation reflect that general theme. While there were ideological, even mystical, notions of the Reich in German political culture of the period, which extremists such as Hitler exploited, Popitz treated the question as a practical political issue: the preservation of German unity after the nation's defeat in World War I. After 1933 the term took on a different tenor; it was already permeated by Nazi ideology before 1939, but as the German armies moved east, they tried to legitimate their conquests through a new, even more radical Reich ideology that was explicitly racial. The extermination of Jews, Poles, Gypsies, and other "subhumans" was carried out in the name of this "manifest destiny."

In his presentations to the Mittwochsgesellschaft from 1933 to 1944 there is no trace of such ideological uses, although questions of the German state's survival, and thus of the Reich, figured more or less prominently in all of them. Popitz's talk "The Two Meanings of the Concept Reich," on December 11, 1940, can be read as both an explicit rejection of Carl Schmitt's emergent theory of *Großraum* and a subtle rejection of Nazi race theory.[82] It began with the question of whether the concept of Reich can be distinguished from that of the state and still be a legally and administratively useful concept. A review of the word's etymology identifies "Reich" with a medieval appeal to the city of God *(civitas dei)* and the Roman Empire. Both suggest a religious and theological concept, which the Germans adopted in various titles that "not only contradicted reality but aroused the resentment of other states."[83] Constitutional and state law suggests two other meanings. One is the federalist idea advanced before 1933 by the Bavarians and by Austria before the Anschluß (1938). The Reich in this sense refers to a "higher state" than those of its members, but its reality, while appearing, especially from outside Germany, to unify "Reich-and-Kaiser," was actually an umbrella for the polycratic and centrifugal interests of the member states. Thus "Reich" has been "either a romantic dream or the reality of a weak Germany."[84]

The second idea is, Popitz asserts, completely new. It advances the notion of a politically unified people influencing nations beyond its own state borders and even exercising special rights over them.[85] In the theory of Carl Schmitt, these "special territories" are a Großraum for which "Reich" is the legal designation. It has been argued by proponents of this new concept, Popitz remarks, that "it will be politically useful after a victorious war." This theory, however, is nothing but the assertion of the power principle. Is there any sense in which a new conception of Reich should be used? Only if it reminds Germans of "their mission in central Europe": to protect German nationals and to develop a regional economic and political structure. Despite the language of a national calling Popitz uses here, he offers a subtly different view of German policy than the official one—or that proposed by Carl Schmitt in his writings on the subject. It is significant for what it does *not* say and how it does *not* say it. Germany at the end of 1940 occupied most of western Europe and much of central Europe; plans to invade Russia were already being made. Popitz's failure to use the ideological language underlying German expansion and his rejection of the power principle attributed to Carl Schmitt suggest the dialogue of Socrates and Thrasymachus in *The Republic* and the administrative concerns of a civil servant.[86]

The more general of those concerns is the most important for placing his and Carl Schmitt's work in the context of their times. Schmitt's Großraum theory turned on his assertion of "the end of the state," which depended in turn on a reading of Jean Bodin's political theory. Schmitt discussed with Popitz a paper entitled "The State as the Concrete Concept of a Historical Epoch," who rejected its premise: unless the state remained a general idea, Popitz argued against Schmitt, its substance (its ethical rational content) would be surrendered to factions and parties.[87] The historical elements of Schmitt's argument were taken from Otto Brunner's *Land und Herrschaft* (1939),[88] which had, in turn, been influenced by Schmitt's *Der Begriff des Politischen* (1927). Brunner challenged the prevailing approach to medieval history that employed the modern concept of the state to understand the premodern period. Scholarship based on the assumption that the state is a universal idea was erroneous, Brunner argued, because it concealed the systemic relations of territory to households, clans, and lords in the high and late Middle Ages. At stake, according to Brunner, was more than the accurate description of a time and place in European history or a narrative based on the close reading of sources. Brunner's book was actually a new kind of constitutional history that confronted the difficulties of writing about constitutions through the hegemonic lens of nineteenth-century political thought, with its emphasis on the liberal-bourgeois Rechtsstaat. It presented, instead, a model of land and lordship that revealed both the "lawfulness" of the medieval institution of feud and the original violence of the law. "The feud," Brunner writes, "is an expression of Right," which the categories of positive legal theory exclude.[89] In so doing, the origins of the modern state are obscured, and the worlds of law *outside* its conceptual framework and political theory ignored. The feud, while characteristic of an area of premodern Europe,[90] was not its central constitutional idea—that was peace: "a special kind of peace that included 'legitimate force' within it."[91] The "special kind of peace" Brunner refers to was the elaborate structure of friend/enemy relations, around which were based the declaration of a feud, its procedure, the prohibition of certain kinds of violence, and ultimately the achievement of justice that resulted in reconciliation of the parties concerned. In this account, "law" emerged as the nexus of feud *and* peace, both of which are limited and distinguished from mere criminality (brigandage) by Brunner.

What do "state" and "right" mean under these circumstances? Brunner's answer, like his conception of the feud/peace problematic in the Middle Ages, drew on Carl Schmitt's political theory. The analysis of enmity relies on Schmitt's conception of the political as a criterion of identity, "friend" or "enemy"; and Brunner's construction of the medieval and early modern constitution assumes that a constitution is "the total condition of political unity and order."[92] Hobbes defined the modern state abstractly as a condition of commonwealth achieved through sovereignty that put an end to "nature," or civil war. Working historically, Brunner too describes the emergence of the modern state as a condition of peace that gradually eliminated recourse to the feud as the primary means of seeing justice done.[93]

Although Schmitt was drawn to Hobbes's theory for its account of the origin of political obligation, Bodin was the more important theorist of the state for his work, and the articles on Reich and Großraum during the war return to arguments in *Politische Theologie* (1921). The strength of Bodin's "legal-decisionist" theory lay in the construction of a legal logic of the state and his acute grasp of Europe's sectarian fragmentation. After the concept of Christendom as a supernational order with its central religious authority in Rome had been exhausted in religious war, Bodin's sociological theory of sovereignty as an empirically recognizable institution severed the knot of theological dispute over secular authority. With Bodin the word "state" begins to define an epoch, the age of the modern state, with its marks of sovereignty. "No matter how much power [other institutions] have," Bodin writes, "if they are bound to the laws, jurisdiction and command of someone else, they are not sovereign."[94] With that, Bodin detached the question of political domination not only from theology but from justice as well. Indeed, the sovereign is *less* bound to "do justice" than are magistrates and subjects; because only the sovereign can make law "affecting all subjects in general, or dealing with general interests; law is the command of the sovereign."[95]

Schmitt's theory emphasizes that the sovereign's decisions are political, not moral, as sovereign authority is political, not theological. It is, rather, the nullification of all theological causes in what political order is or how it is constituted. Political conflict, which makes sovereignty necessary, can arise from any or all of the other spheres (ethical, aesthetic, or economic), but none of them constrain or limit sovereignty.[96]

Popitz gave his last presentation to the Mittwochsgesellschaft, "Is There a General Theory of the State?", less than a month before the July 20 coup against Hitler.[97] The talk began by acknowledging that Brunner's and Carl Schmitt's work made it difficult to think of the state as anything but the political organization of nineteenth-century Europe, but Popitz rejected his friend's argument as opaque and dangerous. Popitz undermined Bodin's (and Schmitt's) empiricism in the "marks" of statehood and excluded from the start its simple identification with a particular juridical construction or with its functions.[98] Granted, there are four empirical marks of the state: (1) an identity that distinguishes this group from that, (2) a territory, (3) a governing force or power, and (4) a lasting sense of purpose that gives meaning to their submission to government. What might the most general concept be on which those are based? Popitz asked, and quickly excluded the most obvious in the history of political thought. Neither Kantian reason nor Aristotelian order will do. He also rejected—a startling argument in Nazi Germany—a natural "organism" (such as that found in Othmar Spann's work), the association *(Verband)* with its rituals of obedience and loyalty, and the *Volk* "with everything one thinks constitutes it, common language, race, religion, culture, etc."[99]

Of the four marks of the state, Popitz discards the first as contributing nothing.[100] He retains "territory" while relaxing Weber's strict definition of its boundaries. Brunner had shown the third mark, government, not to have been an exclusive property of the state, whose powers and structures grew up from families, clans, and the Länder of the nobility, rather than the reverse, as nineteenth-century political theory and jurisprudence assumed. The state, Popitz argues, must at some point have achieved an overwhelming power vis-à-vis other political organizations, however, and that marked the beginning of modern political organization. Only the condition of being governed and of governing holds for all people at all times.[101] "The state is a group of men constantly renewing itself and living within a territory that is held together by governing force and superior to all other governing powers in this territory."[102] Popitz says nothing—or the reporter for this session omits its record—about the factor of meaning or a shared sense of purpose that justifies governing force, which his fourth criterion recognizes.

We know from Popitz's involvement with the oppositional elite that he had long since ceased to credit the Nazi state with such meaning or purpose. In a constitutional draft of 1943, he emphasized the "inviolability of law, an independent judiciary, security of the person, family and property and personal liberties."[103] Ulrich von Hassel, who lost faith in the Nazi regime as early as December 1939, noted in his diary that "the atmosphere [at Popitz's talk in June 1944] was depressed, Beck [is] hopeless about the coup."[104] Popitz, like Schmitt, believed that internal pluralism and external integration into the international system of states had destroyed the nineteenth-century state.[105] The similarity of their views on this subject is remarkable. Yet Popitz clung to an idea of the "true" state, and to his own (generalized) identity as a civil servant who was a member, in Hegel's terms, of the "universal class."[106] Beliefs such as those fell into the silence of summer 1944.[107] In the protocol for July 26, 1944, Paul Fechter notes: "This was the last meeting of the Mittwochsgesellschaft. Beck and Jessen were already dead, Popitz under arrest; Hassell was arrested the next day. The lecturer dramatically shortened his presentation on a literary topic—the meeting also ended much sooner than usual. A report on the substance of the presentation is unnecessary." Four other members were present: Eduard Spranger, Ulrich von Hassell, Johannes Stroux, and Ludwig Diels. Von Hassell was also brought before the Volksgerichtshof and executed at Plötzensee. The Gestapo held Spranger for seven weeks before appeals from the Japanese embassy secured his release.[108] A sign of the reigning confusion is that Jens Jessen would not be executed until November 30, 1944. Diels's unpublished diary notes that Fechter spoke unconvincingly about the power of speech over novelists and poets. It was "a lovely summer evening," but all were depressed by the circumstances. Diels lay awake from quarter to one until nearly three in the morning.[109] Later Fechtner remembered the evening thus: "I spoke about some sort of literary topic, but neither I nor the others could concentrate on a subject so removed, so I just left out a good bit of the talk. On the empty chairs around me sat the shadows of the others, the dead, the arrested; when someone asked von Hassell how he was, he laughed and replied with a sigh, 'Well, it's not in the newspapers yet . . .' It was a macabre end to eighty years of intellectual life."[110]

The State after Its End: Carl Schmitt's Political Theory

In the text Schmitt wrote for Popitz's Festschrift, the conflict between legality and legitimacy is the final consequence of European legal positivism that reduced the state to merely mechanical functions, a technique of planning driven ever more intensely by the demands of the market and the economy until its political institutions were hollowed out. The circumstances of its composition and the larger context of the war lend his argument an oblique quality that may account, in part, for the author's insistence on his "purely academic" intention. There is no direct criticism of the regime, and nothing in Schmitt's thought would have led him to the risky enterprise of resistance. But his use of the present tense in describing the effects of positivism on "law that is more than mere statute,"[111] and his inclusion of contemporary state practices with those of the liberal nineteenth century, give this text an artful quality of representation that proceeds through a sequence of comparisons and references to figures in the history of political and jurisprudential thought which suggest his own and Popitz's positions on the question of the state.[112]

Popitz had read the lecture and disagreed with its approach, Schmitt remarks, primarily because of the connection it made between jurisprudence and philosophy:

> Popitz thought that concepts such as person, reciprocity and many others were purely philosophical in origin, and that jurisprudence could not avoid reliance on philosophy. The influence of Greek philosophy and the Roman law were the great examples of this for him. I thought, to the contrary, that a jurisprudence freed from the dead end of general concepts was superior to all philosophy. To me, Socrates, Plato and Aristotle were primarily teachers of law, and not what one today calls philosophers. Of course I did not mean by "teachers of law" or "jurisprudence" someone who can lecture on his subject in the teaching and examining business today. The philosophy of law, for me, does not mean applying a vocabulary developed from a given philosophical system to legal questions, but the development of concrete concepts out of the immanence of a concrete legal and social order.[113]

The key figures are Savigny and Hegel, but Schmitt takes care not to identify himself with the author of *The Philosophy of Right* while making use of Hegel's concepts and categories to explain the crucial moments of the state's transformation that have rendered the substance of legal knowledge irrelevant to their practical goals.[114] Instead he draws subtle parallels between his own position in the Third Reich and that of Savigny under Friedrich Wilhelm IV on the eve of 1848 by advancing Savigny's "Vom Beruf unserer Zeit für Gesetzgebung und Rechtswissenschaft" (1814) and "Stimmen für und wider neue Gesetzbücher" (1816) as texts "exactly concerned with my topic."[115] These citations lead the reader to connect Schmitt with Savigny's perspective on the "vocation of jurisprudence" and his critique of codification with Schmitt's own critique of positivism in the opening chapters of *Politische Theologie* (1922).

The conversations with Popitz trace a pattern of state decline along the moments of Germany's modern development,[116] until on the eve of Hitler's appointment to the chancellorship and the rapid consolidation of National Socialist power over the liberal constitution in the spring of 1933, the state as the source of order and the locus of authoritative decisions had been replaced by the notion of "free competition" and "the self-organization of society."[117] The basis for that turn in Schmitt's thought was laid by his argument (against Popitz) that the state is temporally and geographically limited, and neither a philosophical nor a general or universal concept, but a "concrete idea bound to an historical epoch,"[118] which could keep the peace internally and externally:

> There really was a time in which it was meaningful to identify the concepts "state" and "political." For the classical European state had achieved something fantastic: it established an internal peace that excluded "enmity" as a legal concept. It succeeded in eliminating the feud, an institution of medieval law, and ending the religious wars of the 16th and 17th centuries which had been fought by both sides as especially just wars, and in creating within its boundaries peace, security and order. The formula, "peace, security and order" served famously as the definition of the police. Internally in such states, there really was only police and no more politics, unless one calls ambitions, rivalries, alliances and attempted rebellion by malcontents, in short, "disturbances," politics.[119]

The political as friend/enemy relations clarifies the achievement of the modern state: its "constitution" defines an area from which the political in precisely those terms (the medieval feud, the religious or civil war) is excluded. In the course of its historical development, the state turned "law" *(Recht)* into the laws that come from the state—its monopoly on making law excludes any other source of law—laws that it can use, and the typical form of this is codification. Old social forms lose their meaning and purpose.

That context explains, Schmitt argues, jurisprudence as a *political,* not a legal, science whose predicament derives from "concrete concepts developed within an immanent legal and social order."[120] Schmitt's history of jurisprudence in the nineteenth and twentieth centuries contains another hidden narrative that could not have been lost to his audiences: the emergence of the totalitarian state from within the decay of the European nation-state. His argument connects the claims of jurisprudence about what law is to the stages of the state's crisis, manifest here as one of lawmaking, or the functions of the legislative state, and Schmitt's diagnosis of that change is surprisingly consistent from 1914 until this lecture. Its formulation is the core of Carl Schmitt's political theory of constitutional failure: the circumstances of industrial society erode the foundations of the modern state. The specific causes of this are various in Schmitt's accounts, but they always include an ideological transformation in which apparently identical concepts have radically different meanings. Thus the normative structure of the state remains only as a "technique" for government.[121]

Obligation and Resistance: Schmitt and Popitz at the End of the Third Reich

By summer 1944 the horizon beyond the immediate seemed to have disappeared for Schmitt and Popitz. Was there anything beyond the power principle that Popitz had so firmly rejected in his friend's work? His last presentation to the Mittwochsgesellschaft held out no promise of that, and all the society's members were conscious of the coming catastrophe.[122] The conclusion of Schmitt's paper on jurisprudence rings hollow. In a world from which justice (Popitz) and security (Schmitt) are both absent, their refuge is the science of law. Even under terror, Schmitt wrote, "a jurisprudence thrown back on its own resources will know how to find the secret crypt in which the seed of the spirit will be protected against every prosecutor."[123] Circumstances in autumn 1944 made publication of a Festschrift for Popitz impossible, but Schmitt continued to work on the collection.[124] On December 2, Popitz's sixtieth birthday, the day after Schmitt lectured at Leipzig, Popitz had been in prison for five months. Arrested in the early morning of July 21, he was still Reich minister of state and Prussian finance minister, the only member of the Nazi government charged with conspiracy against the regime.[125] Sentenced by the "People's Court" (Volksgerichtshof) to death in October 1944, Popitz was led once to the execution room, only to be brought back and ordered to work on administrative and financial reform documents. He was finally executed on February 2, 1945.

Schmitt was arrested in Berlin by the Russians in April 1945 but was released after interrogation. In June 1945 the Americans arrested him and had him fill out a questionnaire, released him, then arrested him again. Interrogated throughout that fall, Schmitt was held in Berlin and Nuremberg as a possible defendant in one of the war crimes trials until April 1947. He was never charged with war crimes, but like Martin Heidegger, Schmitt's support for the regime cost him his university post.[126] Upon his release, the chief American prosecutor, Robert Kempner, advised Schmitt to leave Berlin—by then an outpost in the Cold War surrounded by Russian troops—and he returned to his family home in Plettenberg (Sauerland), where his sister still lived. He never again held a formal appointment in any academic institution, but the house that Schmitt, in conscious reference to Machiavelli, called San Casciano remained a destination for intellectuals until his death in 1985.[127] He later compared the incarceration at Nuremberg with other times in his life when he felt threatened—the communist revolution in Munich, the murder of conservatives during the Rhöm purge, the SD attack on him in 1936, the arrest and execution of Popitz. It became, his biographer writes, "a litany he included in every discussion about his life."[128]

Conclusion: *Recht im Unrecht*—Law and Political Obligation under Tyranny

Both men opposed the National Socialists before 1933, but neither was sympathetic to the Weimar system. As conservative nationalists, they would have preferred a different solution to the Republic's dilemmas, not Hitler's radical alternative. An account of how and why they became involved in this regime is not my main concern, nor is the interrogation of individual guilt or innocence. The history of their political ideas does not rule out moral questions, as Michael Stolleis has argued, and can in fact sharpen them.[129] Hans Mommsen argued in a study of the German resistance to Hitler that "it consisted of groups of individuals loosely connected to one another and arose on the basis of personal acquaintance in those remaining social niches that had not been fully destroyed by the National Socialists."[130] The same cannot be said of how men such as Schmitt and Popitz came to support the Third Reich, although personal factors—their friendship with each other and their ties to the main actors in the crisis of 1932—certainly played a role. More systematic commitments led both men to collaboration. A considerable body of work on Schmitt and on the political elites of the Republic explains their opposition to democracy and collaboration, first with authoritarianism, then with fascism, in terms of the "social function" of ideas.[131] It has also been suggested that a state philosophy such as that represented by Popitz was "a particular optic of enquiry . . . that allows *Staat* to fix the terms in which *Gesellschaft* may be studied."[132] Those studies allow us to see that of all the two men's intellectual commitments, their respective theories of the state led Schmitt and Popitz into political alliance before and after 1933, but those studies do not explain their ultimately very different courses under the regime. The political philosophy of the state does, however, ground *any* critique of German fascism, as it grounds justification beyond the terms of prudential obligation as defined by Schmitt and (on a certain reading) by Hobbes.[133]

The texts and their context are important nonetheless because of what they tell us about the circumstances of life under such regimes, including the persistence of an intellectual culture of law and the state. That Germans continued to discuss the grounds of law and debate the character of the state under the circumstances of Nazism may seem absurd, and many find analysis of their arguments, particularly those of immediate participants in the regime, such as Schmitt and Popitz, morally revolting. Yet these debates provide concrete instances of all three possible conceptions of law and the state under National Socialism: (1) that no tyranny is ever total, (2) that there was no higher law than the positive law, and (3) that there was no positive law because it conflicted with the natural law. In the arguments of those involved, we can see something of the terrifying reality in Nazi Germany inherent in questions central to modern political theory. They echo the conflict of natural and positive law, leave the grounds of political obligation unclear, and raise the question of what political philosophy is for.

2 The Sovereign Moment: Sources of Schmitt's Theory of the State

Mensch begreif der Weltennoth!
Sieh was allen Wesen droth!
Denn der Tod ist Urgebot!
—THEODOR DÄUBLER, *Nordlicht*

Was durch mein *Entweder/Oder* in Erscheinung tritt,
ist das Ethische.
—KIERKEGAARD, *Entweder/Oder*

Carl Schmitt belonged to a generation of German intellectuals who grew up in prosperity and security before World War I, a generation who in the years after the war rebelled not just against the new Republic but also against its cultural and metaphysical assumptions. These were the inheritance of the previous century: belief in progress and technology, and instrumental rationality. At the very moment when liberalism—their political doctrine—triumphed in Germany, it seemed to many intellectuals, Schmitt among them, that its foundations were a sham and shallow pretense.

Like their contemporaries elsewhere in Europe, the German "generation of 1914" viewed their postwar lives across the confusion and destruction of the Great War. For Germans, however, the gulf between life before and after 1914 was even deeper. Defeat and the Versailles treaty brought a complex set of national and international issues that plagued the new Republic and proved explosive tinder for its fledgling constitution. After

Germany's unification less than a half century before, after divisive struggles over the constitutional order and boundaries of a German state, the Great War stripped Germany of sensitive territory on the eastern and western frontiers with Poland and France. Reparations to the Allies made the Weimar Republic the first "debtor nation." As elsewhere in central and eastern Europe, monarchy gave way to a liberal-democratic republic, and in Germany, revolution and civil war came with defeat. Schmitt's generation came to democratic politics shaped by four years of mechanized destruction and the memory of male community in the trenches. Amid the Republic's recurrent crises, Weimar seemed an unacceptable alternative both to prewar *Bürgerlichkeit* and to the heroic *Fronterlebnis* of 1914 to 1918. This was the immediate context of Carl Schmitt's political thought. It constituted "a rebellion against the age" that paradoxically "did not exclude collaboration with it."[1]

The distinctively German modernism of Weimar owed its form and intellectual content to the literary and artistic style of gallery and café life in imperial Germany. Its atmosphere fostered an extraordinarily creative impulse during the first third of the twentieth century in art and architecture and in the modernist spirit. Walter Gropius and the Bauhaus, Freud's psychology and *Existenz* philosophy, modern sociology, and the discoveries of Ernst Mach and Einstein in physics were all products of German-speaking Europe. Peter Gay has described this as "the Weimar ideal," and it was far more than a new style.[2] The revolution of 1918, the republican constitution—these were signs of a new consciousness, part political, part social, that produced Weimar's recurrent crisis of fidelity.[3] The war and the suffering of civilians on the home front, the sudden collapse of monarchy and of the western front—this trauma found expression in a mass culture not clearly theistic but with a powerful current of irrational sentiment. Theological assumptions that had once legitimated the state gave way to a more pluralistic, and thus potentially more conflicted, moral sphere:

> Bourgeois egoism, which had become common in the form of secular utilitarianism, freed itself from rational natural law foundations, and become unproblematic as "common sense." Since the middle of the 19th century this process of the *Aufhebung* of religion and philosophy has become obvious—a highly ambivalent set of events. Religion is not even a private affair anymore; but the atheism of the masses threatens the utopian content of tradition. Philosophy has been stripped of her metaphysical claims, but the reigning scientism has also collapsed those constructs in terms of which a miserable reality must justify itself.[4]

Well before Habermas, Schmitt's early work traced this process and its consequences for the European state. His skepticism about liberal democracy did not, however, prevent him from seeking a resolution of Weimar's political problems in the political and its constitution.

"A Carousel of Bourgeois Feelings": The Generation of 1910

Gottfried Benn characterized expressionism as part of the futurist style "also called cubism" whose varieties were unified in "a ruthless going-to-the-root-of-things, beyond where they are individually and sensually tinted, falsified, confused, used in a psychological process."[5] This reckless drive for the absolute took the shape, in Carl Schmitt's political theory, of his oft-repeated declaration that his was a "purely scientific" *(wissenschaftlich)* interest and his insistence on radical thinking about concepts.[6] From an early discovery of modernism and expressionism, Schmitt created the figure of liberalism that guided his analysis of Weimar's institutions, a gestalt and doctrine that was part romantic and part positivistic and that was the spirit of his age.

Schmitt was not alone in his reaction to liberalism and bourgeois society, but the cultural critique of them offered by Georges Sorel and Jacob Burckhardt appears not to have influenced his own view, nor did contemporary sociological studies such as those of Ostrogorski and Michels.[7] Rather, Schmitt's antiliberalism was literary and theological at its core. In "The Problem of Form" Kandinsky warned that form is "always transient, relative . . . nothing more than the necessary medium through which today's revelation can be heard." Form should not be confused with inner content, and "therefore one should not deify form."[8] When Schmitt argued in *Politische Theologie* that "radical conceptualization" should replace the sociology of ideas about the state and jurisprudence, it was to frame political thinking as the expressionists had framed artistic perception. Beyond appearance lay, for Schmitt as for them, another reality that must be grasped in all its fullness if its concepts were to be genuinely scientific. Beyond the practical interests of law lay "a final, radically systematic structure" that informed the social world of a given epoch. Schmitt identified this structure as a "reflex" of social reality; neither did he understand it (as Foucault would later) as the construction of language. Instead, a radical sociology must push analysis to its "final metaphysical and theological consequences." Only when the interrogation is pursued with reckless disregard for the apparently true will the "substantial identities" of political institutions in a particular age and its metaphysical image of itself be revealed.[9]

The expressionist generation rebelled against its fathers and the whole of European culture. The movement made itself felt in every aspect of life: in art and literature, of course, but also in politics and moral life, in ethics and theology.[10] The radical literary style of expressionism obviously led it toward political radicalism, and figures such as Johannes R. Becher, Wilhelm Herzog, and Wieland Herzfeld took radical political positions during the Great War and the German revolution, and their antibourgeois art and commentary later came to represent the angry confusion of the Weimar years.[11] Against traditional doctrines and an encrusted, spiritless system of authority, against a mechanized and bureaucratic world of pragmatic relations, the expressionists reasserted the vision of man as more than a producer and consumer. They took up Nietzsche's questions and articulated his view of a world without the security of belief in God as an ordering force. They strove to realize Wagner's "total work of art." They thought of themselves as a metaphysical and ethical challenge to the dominant culture. Through radical vision, intense and primary perception would transcend the apparent. Image reveals truth. Looking back over a decade of expressionism, Gustav Hartlaub thought it the negation of purely formal and "extensive" or "impressionistic" art. The only meaningful conception of artistic expressionism, Hartlaub argued, grasped it "very broadly, from a general change in mentality, not as a simple formal theory."[12]

Expressionism was nothing if not the rejection of bourgeois comfort and what Henri Bergson called closed morality.[13] Kasimir Edschmid wrote that his generation came of age in a "sterile time" on the "carousel of bourgeois feelings." Against bourgeois culture and the purely economic conception of life, against a capitalist system that exploits these and the private trap of an individualist consciousness, expressionism declared: "A new image of the world must be created, one that no longer shares the Naturalist sensitivity which can be grasped only experientially, nor the fragmentary space of the Impressionists, one that simply must be, true and therefore beautiful. . . . Reality must be created by us. The meaning of objects must be chosen. No one should be satisfied with what is believed, the usual facts, the image of the world must be mirrored exactly—but only in ourselves." Art's reality can break the "bell jar that encloses one's life."[14]

Perhaps uniquely, this generation believed in the sovereignty of ideas. Their "No!" was idealist, repeating the romantic longing for harmony and unity as an emphatic rejection of everything symbolizing the fragmented self. Modern philosophy sundered subject and object; they would reunite them. Kandinsky's and Franz Marc's theoretical essays only stated what their own artistic invention had already begun to practice—an art freed of the purely descriptive and narrative forms, striving for purity in color and space. That absolute power of ideas, Marc argued in the first *Blaue Reiter*, was the secret weapon of his generation: "New ideas are the fearful weapons of the 'wild ones'; they kill better than steel and break what was thought unbreakable."[15]

Revolutionary art thrives on the shocked reactions of society, and expressionism was no exception. A conservative public willy-nilly presented its scandalized reaction to a generation looking for it: when Hugo von Tschudi lost his post as director of the Nationagalerie in Berlin because the impressionist paintings he displayed outraged the kaiser, Marc and Kandinsky dedicated the *Blaue Reiter* to von Tschudi and made his case an avant-garde cause célèbre. The resistance of society and the state to what this young generation believed true and noble proved its assumptions about a materialistic world in which everything is measured and sold, including thought and art. The form taken by the "carousel of bourgeois feelings" was utilitarianism and empiricism. Benn's contempt for the economic world of the "salesman behind the counter" is typical: "The fellow man, the middle man, the small format, the sedentary man with his comforts, the one shouting 'Barrabas' who wants to live well and proper, a satisfying pork roast on the dinner table, the dying fencer into the hospital—the great customer of utilitarianism: the measure and purpose of the times"[16]

Aesthetic impulse merely formulated the expressionist vision. Its core was "the radical perspective" that "drove ambiguities to a diachronic world vision," oppositions that cannot be mediated, contradictions that cannot be bridged. Since "all mediating instances, every realistic compromise, can be denounced as 'this-and-that,' tepid half measures, the world seen thus divides into two great areas: an absolutely negative and an absolutely positive. That is the specific and true radicalism of the Expressionist mind: he always has the outermost, the pure, the extreme case in view."[17]

Schmitt: The Early Works

All this deeply affected the young Carl Schmitt. Writing to his sister Augusta in March 1912, he offered the following definition: "A rationalist: a man who thinks everything can be explained rationally, who considers everything with a view to sober utility and as a consequence sees it all quickly and simply, as for example when someone gets into a train and says, they invented the train in order to earn their daily bread."[18] Between

1910 and 1912, Schmitt wrote a series of short stories, reviews, and commentaries that have been largely overlooked until recently.[19] A paradoxical companion to his jurisprudential works and interests before the Great War,[20] his early works are important for the formulation of his political theory. In stories, satires, and reviews, Schmitt's culture critique and antiliberal theory took shape.

Unlike his jurisprudence, Schmitt's literary work assumes a world in which there are no definitions, where everything is possible. His stories in *Die Rheinlande* explore nominalism,[21] the irrational, the apparent (but not real). "The Mirror" begins, "I am convinced, that there is nothing dead, no dead things," and tells the story of a young man who climbs into a mirror.

> The young man came right up to Mirror with his elbows. Mirror was determined not to take this. . . . Mirror gathered himself as far as possible and tried to scream; he was so upset he couldn't move. His senses failed, his heart sprung up. A moment later the young man climbed into the mirror, so that no one wondered about the broken mirror and the rationalists were apparently right. But what does a rationalist know about real life?[22]

A Kafkaesque evocation of things transformed—or realized. "Mirror" has a personality—Schmitt omits the article "der" when referring to him thus—while others "freed themselves gradually from the world of appearances and embodiment. They know the truth about the world, and themselves. They gave up the false fancy, 'I am.' The mercury peeled off; transparent glass remained. Their souls went into the world soul, where every individual disappears."[23]

"Don Quijote und das Publikum" is about reason and madness. Reality can be ignored only through indifference to "normal understanding." The public laugh at Don Quijote because the public *is* the "normal understanding": "A man who has motives other than those usual in bourgeois life will be a laughingstock. . . . the real meaning of the public has been discovered at last. The public sees quite rightly what it laughs at; the question is only whether it is right." Don Quijote demonstrates his superiority over "public opinion and its laughter" because he is "a thoroughly good and noble man; his relationship to Dulcinea is a serious one, despite the ludicrous in his situation . . . because there is human greatness in it."[24]

The "public" here is Schmitt's own time, and the transition from veiled to open critique comes in his review of Walter Rathenau's *Kritik der Zeit* (1912). Critique determines "the age," gives unity to "our" times. For Rathenau, the times are mechanical: division of labor, commerce, machines—these are the idea of the age, its expression, its symptom. Schmitt agrees that it is a time of "practicalities," of the "practical man" *(Zweckmensch).* But as such it has "only ends, no soul": "That remains as the essence of a mechanistic age, it is soulless. And Rathenau's critique makes clear that we have no soul. With that, however, the dependence of Rathenau's critique of his time on it (which he expressly denies) obvious because its description as soulless is negative and takes its content originally from a basic assumption of criticism: the soul."[25] Such a critique can be approached in two ways: under the aspect of eternity, such as that of Lao-tzu and the *Tao te ching*; or in Karl Marx's "science," which explains it "objectively" without value judgments, but unconscious of the contradiction. Rathenau's *Kritik der Zeit* is trapped within the times, Schmitt remarks, and seems "less a critique than a complaint."

A year later, Schmitt and his friend Fritz Eisler satirized Rathenau in *Schattenrisse* (1913).[26] Rathenau as aesthete and industrialist appears in the sixty-odd lines of blank verse: a study furnished in modernist style, furniture by Peter Behrens, "a carpet thick and rich as India's rice fields," canvases by Munch and Corinth but also Klinger and Böcklin, an interior made possible by the wealth of his corporation.[27] Schmitt's review had criticized Rathenau's lack of perspective on the age of mechanization. The attentive contemporary reader of this "silhouette" would know that Rathenau's own firm, the AEG, was the largest producer of electrical instruments and appliances in Europe—he was himself at the center of that spiderweb of modernity described in *Kritik der Zeit.* Ingeborg Villinger's commentary notes that Schmitt's reference to 1907 indicates Rathenau's involvement in the German colony of Southeast Africa and authorship of an article urging the expansion of Germany's colonial area in Africa: "[Schmitt] plays these two poles of Rathenau's existence against each other ironically and polemically."[28]

When Schmitt again turned his hand to satire, the playfulness of *Schattenrisse* was gone. Eisler was dead, as was August Schaetz, to whom *Der Begriff des Politischen* would be dedicated. "Die Buribunken" (1919) was a biting caricature of the boheme and of positivism. Buribunken are scribes and record keepers, who merge with the machines they use and the documents they keep. Schmitt's "Buribunkenology," a fictive science of the Buribunken and their activities, satirizes progress and rational organization, and the fragmented self of the contemporary world. The deep despair underneath the pessimism of *Politische Romantik,* which appeared the same year, is as much about Schmitt's own age as that of the romantics:

> Outline of a philosophy of the Buribunken,—I think, therefore I am; I talk, therefore I am; I write, therefore I am; I publish, therefore I am.

> What do I write?
>
> I write myself. Who writes me? I myself write myself. What is the content of my writing? I write that I am writing myself. What is the great motor that lifts me out of this self-satisfying circle of "I"-ness? History!
>
> I am a key on the typewriter of history.[29]

Before the war, Schmitt had found a genuine "Kritik der Zeit" in the poetry of Theodor Däubler, a man with a foreboding of what the age meant, and "who also knew himself as a child of the times."[30] Däubler's essays on modern art introduced the French and Italian avant-garde to a German public accustomed to the overblown style of the "Gründerzeit," whose own cultural vanguard found its form in the beginnings of modernist architecture. "The *Gründerjahre* are the expression of the bourgeois-immoral 19th century," Däubler wrote, and "the result of everything mediocre: our glorious, great Germany has suffered more through unification than in the Thirty Years' War." Like all the expressionists and like much of this European generation, Däubler conceived modernity as a conflict between matter and spirit. "Style" was not an ornamental question, not something superficial, but the necessary consequence of an intellectual-spiritual reality. "One sank ever deeper," he wrote in criticism of the "Victorian" style in Germany, "even down to an Imperial post office in brick-gothic. . . . Agents of materialism have raped the stone revelations of our mystics."

Däubler met Schmitt on his first visit to Berlin in 1912. They traveled back to Düsseldorf, where Schmitt was a law clerk, and then to Cologne for the *Sonderbund* exhibition of 1912. Kurt Kluxen, the son of a department store owner in Münster, and a friend from Schmitt's university days, bought paintings, including one by Picasso, Schmitt wrote his sister Auguste—"very modern."[31] From there they all traveled through the Rhineland, into Elsaß with Fritz Eisler and Albert Kollman. Däubler was interested in everything: Strauss's music, Trakl's and Heym's poetry, the expressionist art that "Die Brücke" had brought to the capital from Dresden. Deeply involved with the Italian futurists and French fauvists, Däubler promoted the work of leading German expressionists in Edschmid's *Tribüne der Kunst und Zeit*.[32] They understood "the new," he wrote, and Däubler especially admired Kandinsky, whose painting was "absolute color in the most radical sense."[33] What Kandinsky did with paint, Däubler wanted to do with words and language.

In the milieu of prewar Berlin, Schmitt later commented, "nothing went unnoticed, not even Däubler."[34] Johannes Schaf reviewed Däubler's epic poem *Nordlicht* for the *Berliner Tageblatt* and declared him "Europe's poet." He was, Schmitt said, "endlessly modern," his poetry "a wonder work of sound and color that completed French and Italian art.[35] *Nordlicht* had fascinated Schmitt when it appeared in 1910. Its power lay, he thought, in its dualism: it was of the age but understood it perfectly in a myth of the northern lights, whose dark and light transcended Occidental dualism. During the war, he read Däubler as a Christian poet. Only in 1938, when he found Proudhon's essays on aesthetics, did Schmitt understand that *Nordlicht* was a fantasy of the earth's fate.[36]

All that was faraway between 1910 and 1916, and Schmitt's monograph *Theodor Däubler's "Nordlicht"* (1916) remains the most influential study of the poem. Schmitt had planned to write his monograph with Fritz Eisler, but by the time it appeared, Europe had been at war for two years. Eisler fell in the first weeks, and Schmitt dedicated the *Verfassungslehre* (1928) to his memory. Schmitt brought Däubler's vision into his jurisprudence, and *Der Wert des Staates und die Bedeutung des Einzelnen* (1914) took its motto from *Nordlicht:* "First is the command, men come later." The central institution of modern life, its precondition and guarantee, is the state. No one seriously concerned with what holds together law, the state, and the individual can ignore the "spirit of the age."[37] The age thinks itself individualistic and is everything but that: the machine is its spirit; predictability and regularity are the order of the day. The Perserburg myth in the "Iranian Rhapsody" section of *Nordlicht* offered Schmitt a construction similar to the "state of nature" in the works of Hobbes, Locke, and Rousseau. It is an account of the first state, told in the building of the Perserburg. Fear of the Other and distrust lead the peasants to conclude a pact with their neighbors and enter into a political relationship in which the paradox of law and right and power reveals itself.[38] Law, the state, gold: the first state comes from distrust, not just as the striving for power but from a fundamental dualism. This, Schmitt remarks, is the soul of the Occident. In the Orient, man is outside the world as a metaphysical being. In the West he belongs to it and must be in it. This is what Däubler understood, and it is the essence of the age.[39] A time of capitalism, a mechanistic relativistic age; an age of commerce, technology, organization. Despite their material comforts, men have become poor devils in a world of mere appearances. The moral has given way to the economic; the "age of security dawns." This "eschatological outrage" was understood by Däubler: he "knows and paints the world more movingly than any critical historian could."[40] The world's misery—Schmitt mirrors Goya's *The Sleep of Reason*—comes from reason: from it comes gold; from gold, money; from money, capital. The "devastating sweep of reason" ends in "cash" *(bares Geld):* everything is for sale, everything can be bought. For the "intellectual small-capitalist" in the "ornamental garden of universal education and good taste," it is just a matter of organization. But the best organization cannot include "the only case that matters."[41]

Intermezzo: Kierkegaard and Schmitt, Entweder/Oder

"The only case that matters" remained Schmitt's North Star. The categories he used to make sense of politics and constitutions, decision and exception, came from the Danish theologian Søren Kierkegaard.

Schmitt mentions him first in a collection of religious reflections he edited in 1919.[42] It is unclear from the published work when Schmitt became interested in Kierkegaard, but he had read *Entweder/Oder* by autumn 1918, when he finished *Politische Romantik* and the Kanne collection.[43] He received Kierkegaard's *Begriff des Auserwählten* in July 1918 as a gift from the German translator, and his library contains several other volumes of works by Kierkegaard.[44] Schmitt's interest in the romantics may have come from his friendships with Däubler and others in the Berlin and Munich art scene, and *Politische Romantik* seemed aimed at what Weber called "the revolutionary carnival."[45] Kierkegaard was part of Schmitt's intense religiosity, "the inmost of all Christians."[46] Nietzsche, Byron, and Baudelaire were, compared to him, figures whose "distorted faces stare out of the colorful screen of romanticism . . . the three high priests of this private priesthood."[47]

Entweder/Oder describes to a young friend the end of Kierkegaard's engagement, and marriage appears as the moment when the ethical and aesthetic meet. Everyone, Kierkegaard writes, "feels the need to build up a life perspective, a picture of what life means and its purpose."[48] The Aesthete just wants to enjoy life. He is indifferent; life's choices appear to him from the outside as he moves from one to the other. The Ethical Man "knows himself" and recognizes the choices as his. "Who lives ethically has seen himself, knows himself, this consciousness penetrates his whole being." He does not, as the Aesthete, "live into the blue (275). Indecision distinguishes the Aesthete from the Ethical Man, and Kierkegaard constructs these characters (as Schmitt would, following him) within the images of "a parting of the path" or "the midnight hour." Kierkegaard chides his young friend, "You tell us, 'life is a masked ball,' endlessly entertaining . . . but don't you know that there will come a midnight hour, when everyone will be unmasked, do you believe that life is forever a joke, that one can sneak away before that midnight hour and escape the unmasking?" (170). Decision constitutes the person for Kierkegaard. It is not abstract; it is everything but abstract: postponed, the moment passes, and the ethical value of Kierkegaard's thought is to concentrate all the person into this one moment. Its danger is in passing "because in the next moment everything is changed" (175). By contrast the ethical life is "determined by duty and a multiplicity of rules," yet the more deeply a man constructs his life as an ethical project, the less he thinks of "duty" or "rules." These are not outside but inside him. Pleasure is always outside, and the Aesthete is thus always dependent, and therefore not free. By choice and decision, the person transcends particularity and sees possibilities as duties. This "expression of sovereignty" is never relinquished and is the security of the ethical personality: "Who lives aesthetically, always waits for things from the outside. Hence this sick anxiety" (268).

From Kierkegaard, Schmitt took the distinction between an aesthetic and ethical personality: the decision; the revelatory character of the exception.[49] These and his own culture critique in the book on Däubler opened the way for Schmitt's evolution into a political lawyer. *Politische Romantik* (1919) presents romanticism as he would later present liberalism—as a flight from the political. In *Politische Theologie* (1922), that argument is joined to Schmitt's critique of Kelsen and legal positivism. Both are antipolitical theories in different but related ways. Schmitt's critique of them opens the way for an oppositional concept of sovereignty and the exception in *Politische Theologie*, and these elements of a state theory are then transformed in *Der Begriff des Politischen* (1927) as those of a political theory in more general terms through the friend/enemy relationship.

Liberalism, Romanticism, Nationalism

Politische Romantik was written in the last winter of the war and published in early 1919—after the German revolution, just as the National Assembly began its constitutional work.[50] Compared to the Assembly of 1848, this one was more socially and politically diverse. The Paulskirche was sociologically and ideologically liberal; more than 50 percent were judges, lawyers, or professors. Its was a liberal constitution. At Weimar, workers, employees, private civil servants, writers, and journalists sat with professors, high civil servants, and what remained of the liberal classes of mid-nineteenth-century Germany. The French national assembly of 1789 and the Frankfurt assembly of 1848 were driven by powerful ideological commitments to liberty, fraternity, and equality and to the freedoms of the *Bürger* respectively. By contrast, Walter Jellinek, one of the leading legal positivists, wrote that "the mistakes of the Weimar constitution can be explained by reference to the lack of a single, unifying idea." There was no shortage in 1919, however, of political theories to which the delegates appealed.[51]

In that setting, Schmitt wrote about ontology and the romantics' tropes and conduct. These become, in Schmitt's analysis, the sources of romantic inconsequence, a disposition to avoid the legal and ethical, which he links to the political and state crisis of 1918. This apparently abstract and literary topic summarized the transition Schmitt made in his early works from conventional jurisprudence to its political theory.

The argument begins with a conventional survey of approaches to romanticism. The French think it revolutionary. The Germans think it nationalist. Both think it the triumph of individualism. Schmitt then takes aim at the most influential German work on the subject, Friedrich Meinecke's *Weltbürgertum und Nationalstaat* (1907). Part history, part justification for the German national state, Meinecke's book describes the romantic temperament. Sturm und Drang was an aesthetic rebellion against Kantian rationalism, overcoming its dualism through the individual's artistic creativity. The world becomes what it is in art, to which romantic vision sees no obstacle. Everything outside the artist, even his own feelings, can become an object of the artist's creativity. This is other and more anarchic than the idea of self-development; it is "self-invention" without an external referent. Romantic subjectivity excludes nothing, not even society and the state. Meinecke comments that Novalis ("an exaggerated cultural spirit") wanted a certain kind of beauty for all social life, all politics. For him the nation is a cultural entity that partakes of universal ideals and values, hence its "cosmopolitanism." That led not to the articulation of particular German interests but to a vision of the world *without* interests or conflict. In this world, the individual is perfectly free to realize himself and thus to overcome the second aspect of ontological dualism, that between the general and particular.[52] Schlegel's *Versuch über den Begriff des Republikanismus* (1796) took the aesthetic approach even further. The world could be governed perpetually in peace through a federation in which each nation retained its autonomy. Unlike Kant's *Perpetual Peace* (1795), whose realism is obvious by comparison, Schlegel believed his idea to be practical and important. Projecting German realities onto the scene of ancient Greece, Schlegel's was a paradoxically private notion of the political: "Do not waste your faith and love in the political world, but dedicate the depths of your being to the sacred firestorm of the divine world of art and learning."[53]

If the first romantic generation was revolutionary, the next turned their hatred for abstract reason into enthusiasm for the traditional and historical—Adam Müller's organic social theory wed to individual creativity. The literature usually ties both aspects to the theorists of European counterrevolution—Burke, de Maistre, Haller, Bonald—but Meinecke read them as elements of cosmopolitanism *and* nationalism. Through romantic political theory, he argued, attachment to language and culture (the essence of nationality) and the world of humanity as such were possible.

Schmitt does not challenge this description, but he does reject Meinecke's interpretation. The approach is tautological, defining its subject as "the political ideas of romantic thinkers" (Meinecke); as reaction against liberalism (Metzger); or simply in terms of the objects romantics wrote about or painted (moonlight and gothic ruins, classical Greece, the monarchy, feudalism, Catholicism). Noting the arbitrariness of romantic thought, they stopped there, repeating its inconsequentiality. Schmitt's animus instead targets Meinecke's "whig history" in which romanticism, liberalism, and nationalism merge as the story of Germany's unification. In that narrative, romantic harmony and unity appear the precursor to Hegel's and Bismarck's unification of the Germans in 1871. Meinecke did not get beyond "new connections, new dependencies, new sources, and new uncertainties; romanticism becomes in this way a natural philosophy, a mythology, irrationalism, without what was unique in [the romantic's] intellectual dilemma ever having been defined."[54]

Adam Müller: Romantic

Schmitt remarks toward the end of *Politische Romantik* that Cervantes's *Don Quixote* defines the beginning of an age in which "ontology became a problem." It culminates in the Enlightenment, when two philosophical revolutions, astronomy (Copernicus) and epistemology (Descartes), meet in Kant's abstract rationalism. The old teleology defined the subject in relation to a cosmic order; he was now recast as a self-defining agent whose control over nature, vastly increased by science, outpaced his ability to give the world meaning. Alone, without a priori meaning, the subject stood enmeshed in a system of rational and efficient causes that created the crisis of meaning for the individual and the "legitimation crisis" of the modern state.[55]

The similarities between the expressionists and the romantics are hard to miss. Both asserted the central role of art and feeling to overcome the lost unity of subject and object, mind and matter. But the project of overcoming modernity through emotion and subjective feeling which seems to have drawn Schmitt into bohemian and artistic circles before and during the war had, by the winter of 1918 to 1919, lost its attractions. Against that vision, his rebellion asserted the primacy of the political. *Politische Romantik* separates the political romantic from the more general type and allows Schmitt to assume the voice of realism. He might have written directly against the expressionists and the radical boheme, but he did not. Instead Schmitt displayed the contemporary predicament indirectly, as a critique both of romanticism and of Meinecke's cosmopolitan nationalism.[56]

Around the figure of Adam Müller, Schmitt constructs a gestalt of the liberal as romantic: "The deracination of the romantic, his incapacity to hold on to an important political idea from his own free decision, his inner lack of resistance against the nearest and most powerful impressions in each case have their own reasons."[57] What connects them? An intellectual situation, their metaphysical occasionalism. This explains the forms and vagaries of Müller's romantic politics. He made his reputation with lectures on "the art of the state" *(Elemente der Staatskunst)* in 1808 and 1809 and on various topics in literature, drama, and art. His means were limited, his ambitions not, and Müller became involved with a series of political projects. Urged on by his friend Gentz, later secretary to Metternich, Müller wrote a defense of nobility. As French troops neared Dresden, he fled to Berlin.[58] Once there he persuaded the liberal government under Hardenberg to finance two newspapers, under his editorship, one a governmental sheet, the other an oppositional one. While courting the liberal Hardenberg, Müller also took up with a circle of conservative agrarian interests opposed to liberal reforms, and *Elemente der Staatskunst* became their bible. For this audience, Müller railed against everything liberal—the reforms, Anglophiles in the Prussian government, followers of Adam Smith. All this time he was in the pay of the government: "In complete innocence and without any feeling for lack of political character and maneuverings, he maintained his connections to Hardenberg, collected his money further and let it be known through sudden articles in praise of the Chancellor that he would be happy to represent a different standpoint if an appropriate post in the Prussian government were offered him."[59] No post was forthcoming, and Müller left liberal Prussia for Vienna to join Gentz and work for the Holy Alliance. In Prussia, Müller kept his 1805 conversion to Catholicism a secret. It would have been awkward under Hardenberg. In Catholic Austria, it was an advantage. In his service to the provisional governor of Tyrol, the seriousness of Müller's inconsequence becomes apparent. Despite his earlier enthusiasm for the landed gentry and an agrarian economy, Müller encouraged the governor to "cure" the Tyrolians of their Italian traditions by measures so severe that both fled the province in 1815.

What Müller wrote and what he did were two different things. Being economically pressed and ambitious led him to actions that revealed his character in an especially unpleasant light. He was, Schmitt writes, "romantically impudent." Having lived for years from the tables of the aristocracy, Müller dared present himself as their bourgeois defender. A man without integrity, persistently dishonest, inconstant in private and public life, he changed his principles with the circumstances.[60] None of this was accidental. To the romantic, life is a novel, every event the beginning of a fantastic project, an imagined adventure. "All the accidents of our lives," Schmitt quotes Novalis, "are material from which we can make what we want. Everything is just the first link in an endless chain, the beginning of an endless novel."[61]

This disposition, Schmitt argues, rests on an occasionalist metaphysic that cannot explain modernity's dualism and allows it to stand as an "illusion." The romantic is an occasionalist because he avoids "a comprehensive third." To contradictions the romantic can give only literary answers that preserve those in an imaginary resolution (Aufhebung).[62] The result is that the romantic can never find reality—not in himself, in the world, or in God. He is always in the ironic position (107). The romantic perceives the either/or but avoids it. Only one of them, Schmitt writes, found its solution: Kierkegaard. "In him all the elements of the romantic were active: irony, the aesthetic perspective, the contradiction between the real and the possible, the finite and eternity, a feeling for the concrete second" (97). Romanticism subjectivized God, the central element in the system of Malbranche, replacing God with the bourgeois life:

> The solitary, isolated and emancipated individual becomes the center of the liberal, bourgeois world, its final instance, the absolute. . . . Romanticism is psychologically and historically the product of bourgeois security. One could only ignore this as long as one made the mistake of identifying it with its objects, such as chivalry and the Middle Ages—in other words, sundry themes and occasions of the romantic interest. A robber knight can be a romantic figure, but he is not a romantic. The Middle Ages is a powerfully romanticized complex, but it is not romantic. (19)

In the new foreword to its second edition, Schmitt writes that in *Politische Romantik* he sought to rescue Burke, de Maistre, and Bonald from association with romanticism and make their legitimist thought available for contemporary Europe. He does much more than that. The argument of *Politische Romantik* constructs liberalism as romanticism, the cultural product of modernity trapped within it, and fatally dependent on "the liberal bourgeois world" as its presupposition (99). Faced with an either/or, the liberal, like the romantic, avoids decision. That, for Schmitt, is the essential difference between him and the political man, and it makes the appropriation of counterrevolutionary thought by Müller and others contradictory. "The criterion," Schmitt wrote, "is whether the capability of deciding between right and wrong is present. This ability is the principle of every political energy: the revolutionary, which appeals to natural rights or human rights, as well as the conservative, which appeals to historical rights" (161).

3 Norm and Exception: Carl Schmitt's Concept of Sovereignty

Sovereign is he who decides on the state of exception.
—CARL SCHMITT, *Politische Theologie*

A "ruthless going-to-the-root-of-things" characterizes Carl Schmitt's approach to state theory and the political, as it did the expressionist approach to reality. If, as many think, Schmitt can be read as the great critic of liberal thought and institutions in the twentieth century, it was the compromising character of that doctrine, and the half measures of liberal politics, that he objected to most. *Politische Romantik* (1919) faulted conventional theories of romanticism because they were content with relative definitions that avoided the core of romantic identity, occasionalism and the evasion of decision. The new bourgeois world of the nineteenth century carried romanticism forward into its politics, making the private its primary sphere and suffering "the illusion that the world is only an occasion" for self-realization.[1] In contemporary politics, Schmitt found a practice of compromise and hesitation, and he identified liberalism as a variety of romanticism. Both aesthetic and political compromise were consequences of the Enlightenment, and Schmitt's legal and constitutional theory responds to its dualities of fact/value, matter/mind, exterior/interior. When he turned to contemporary state theory and normative jurisprudence in *Politische Theologie* (1922), the radical method with which he had deconstructed German romantic thought was applied there too with similarly unsettling results. The concept of sovereignty developed in *Politische Theologie* combined with his other works on legal theory formed the foundation of Schmitt's political science of the constitution.

Philosophical dualism presented itself with greatest force in the state and its theory as the relation of form and substance, but German legal thought largely evaded its contradictions. As the romantic imagination had escaped from reality into subjectivity, so jurisprudence sought to avoid reality through abstraction. Schmitt was not the first or last critic of legalist thinking about politics or of the tendency toward abstraction and "models" in social science. As much as the content of his critique, its context makes Schmitt's work compelling. Contemporary jurisprudence ignored this larger issue either through a pure logic of law, where it need not appear, or in the positivist emphasis on the factuality of law. Schmitt restates the problem through a radical conceptualization of norm and exception in the theory of sovereignty, a decisionist revelation of the deeper questions implied by theories of legal forms, including those of procedure and justice, legality and legitimacy. His account of the Weimar constitution presents dilemmas that are characteristic of modern political life and the rule of law not simply in normative terms but as the concrete problem of dualism in the form of the law and its political substance.[2] In myriad cases during the Republic, these issues played a role in its ultimate destabilization.

The Dream of Statute Positivism

Schmitt's theory of sovereignty and concept of the political and his constitutional theory were linked to an ongoing engagement with the varieties of jurisprudence and their relationship to specific historical events. Schmitt was neither a determinist nor a social scientist. He sharply rejected every form of technicism and sociological positivism, and his lifelong opposition to various species of analytic jurisprudence is well documented.[3] Even the most casual reader of Schmitt cannot fail to notice his frequent insistence on the "objective," "purely scientific," and "legal-scientific" intention of his arguments. Quietly and with a certain reservation, he notes in *Gesetz und Urteil* (1912) that the question of a right judicial decision is not an abstract or philosophical one but a practical matter. Nevertheless it requires that one pay attention to "particular points of view . . . whose determination is crucial" and the need for "methodological clarity and an interest aimed at the reality of legal practice."[4] Another early work, *Der Wert des Staates und die Bedeutung des Einzelnen* (1914), objects to a tendency in contemporary discussion to use "big words, such as culture, critique and life," but insists on "the fundamental contradiction between science and its concepts and the active life. The methods and the interests of a philosophy of the state," he writes, "are incompatible with those of the politician."[5] Between the two, reflection and practice, Schmitt seems to say, exists an unbridgeable gap that must nevertheless be acknowledged and somehow joined. But he also insists that abstraction simplifies the problems of law, the political, and the state. By 1921 Schmitt's tone is cool and certain: he intends *Die Diktatur* not as a history of political ideas, or as an account of how exceptional powers in the state came to be thought of in a certain way, but as the study of "systematic connections," an investigation of "central conceptions in state and constitutional law."[6] The argument would be continued two decades later in his conversations with Popitz on the relationship between philosophy and law. Schmitt never understood Popitz's concern for principles that could guide practice, nor at the end did Popitz understand Schmitt's abandonment of them. More than a decade after World War II, Schmitt could still write, "I thought that a legal science freed from the dead-end of general concepts was superior to any philosophy."[7]

Nearly half a century lay between that comment and Schmitt's first major book. The circumstances in which he wrote "Die Lage der europäischen Rechtswissenschaft" (1943–44) and those of *Gesetz und Urteil* (1912), their style, and the pitch of their arguments could not be more different. The latter was read by contemporaries as a contribution to analytic jurisprudence influenced by Kelsen and Max Weber. The former, written in the depths of World War II, was the culmination of Schmitt's long and bitter struggle with legal positivism. But his audience and themes remained surprisingly similar: a practical philosophy of law argued for the legal public.

From Kant and Hegel through the Roman Law: Nineteenth-Century Positivism

The "political lawyers" of Schmitt's generation were reacting in part to consequences of the conceptual jurisprudence on the basis of Kant's practical philosophy in civil law before 1848 and its influence on state law in the Reich of 1871.[8] The legal thinkers of that period were concerned with two questions: the relationship between law and morality, and the conceptualization of fundamental elements of the law (freedom, person, and will) on the basis of Kant's philosophy. The success of that project in nineteenth-century German jurisprudence resulted in the complete separation of legal thinking from philosophy and the creation of an independent "science" of law purified of history, politics, and economics.[9] But the beginning of the century opened quite differently. Every aspect of intellectual life reacted to an epochal political event. The French Revolution left neither literature nor philosophy, and of course not political theory, unchanged. The struggle for and against the French Revolution's doctrines and consequences defined the generation of Kant and Hegel and, to a great extent, the nineteenth century. In the area of law, there was general agreement that a satisfactory jurisprudence required an explicit philosophical foundation. The vehicle was Savigny and the Roman law. Influential jurists took up his call for a "completely philosophical and equally historical" jurisprudence and derived their material from Roman law sources. Savigny's student George Puchta gave the resulting combination of historical law and analytic method its systematic, and definitive, expression.[10]

The Declaration of the Rights of Man and of the Citizen (1789) asserted rights that are prior to political association and continue even within the state. This revival (and revision) of natural law[11] provoked enemies of the French Revolution such as Edmund Burke to denounce it as "political metaphysics," and the German reaction to the revolution, which Schmitt analyzes in *Politische Romantik,* included the startling charge by August Wilhelm Rehberg (borrowing from Burke) that its *sources* were "metaphysics."[12] Kant responded that there is no contradiction between them and that "metaphysics or *a priori* principles can be put into practice."[13] His *Groundwork for the Metaphysics of Morals* placed the self-legislation of pure practical reason at the core of a system completed by *The Metaphysics of Morals* (1797).[14] It was an entirely new justification for law that dispensed with traditional sources of legislation and political authority, replacing them with reason alone. With this, Wolfgang Kersting comments, "Kant frees us from the domination of theological absolutism and the bonds of teleological natural law; and likewise elevates us above the prosaic banalities of the doctrine of prudence."[15] But what proponents of Kant's doctrine see as a "liberation," opponents regard as the dissolution of political authority and concrete freedom. It was simultaneously a rejection of the religious foundations of authority and of early modern realism. Kant wanted none of Machiavelli's immoral politics; neither did he want a city of god (or gods) on earth. He thus reunited what the moderns had broken apart—power and right—but at the cost of any substantive reference, and ultimately the sacrifice of the political itself, in Schmitt's terms.

The formal theory of natural right assumed that there is an objective and universal principle of right valid everywhere and at all times. Earlier natural right theories made the same assumption, but by reference to empirical claims about human nature or to revelation. Kant appealed only to the legislative reason, purified of all anthropological features and excluding all elements of nature, and his metaphysics of freedom excluded every application of natural purposes and substantive ethical considerations. "Only the properties of reason itself are available to make determinate the non-empirical concept of right: lawfulness, universality, formality and necessity."[16] Right or law (*Recht*) in Kant's system is a "totality of conditions" permitting individual freedom.[17] Law maximizes the freedom of all by allowing the freedom of each to subsist with that of the other.

Kant distinguished between formal and transcendental logic in the *Critique of Pure Reason,* and the categories define "necessary and inescapable conceptual structures which the world of experience must exhibit if we are to have any experience at all": it is not an ontology. The division of phenomena (objects of experience) and noumena (things in themselves) limits our knowledge of the world to experience: since we cannot know things in themselves, ontological knowledge is impossible. If the practical fields such as law and politics require an ontological basis, then they are impossible. But a phenomenological science of these things *is* possible, Kant argues,[18] and it follows that law has to do only with the external world, in "the sphere of external social life," not with the interior or nonobjective. This was a profound break with traditional political philosophy. Law and the state were no longer to be concerned with forming the character of the citizen, as Aristotle had suggested and as had Christian thinkers for a millennium. Neither should the political world be regarded as one in which mere interest or power rules. Rather, freedom consists, for Kant, in circumstances that permit "the individual's will [*Willkür*] [to] be united with that of another according to the universal laws of freedom." The universal law *(allgemeine Rechtssätze)* follows: "Act so that the free use of your will is always compatible with the freedom of another together with a universal law."[19]

Law in this universal sense is formal. It is indifferent to the content of actions. It is concerned "solely with the formal compatibility of the external freedom of one person with that of others" and thereby limits individual action to the bounds of its "possible universalization."[20] Kant's universal principle of right is "criterial"; it seeks no specific content for the law but is intended to identify those conditions under which "law" is valid.[21] On this basis, Kant justifies absolute duty to the positive laws of the state and denies a right to resistance. His deontology leaves no room for interests or needs. The free person, conscious of his moral duty, will follow it without external sanctions. But the concept of right assumes that coercion is a priori valid against those who do not conform to the law of right. How such coercion can be justified—in this or any other system—

is the central question of political theory. Kant's answer depended on his moral philosophy, and on the claim of transcendental freedom. If these are chimerical, or "ethical ghosts," Kant's political theory and concept of right collapse into empiricism—the rule of law then becomes the dominance of the stronger or at best the result of hypothetical imperative, good grounds and shared needs.[22]

This was the modern dualism against which the romantics and Hegel reacted, the first by embedding the divine in subjectivity, the second by confronting the problematic consequences of the modern liberation from theology and metaphysics. What was entirely new in Hegel's philosophy, Joachim Ritter argues, was that he "equates traditional metaphysical theory as such with knowledge of the age and the present." The traditional understanding of philosophy as ontology (knowledge of being) is reasserted by Hegel, but as "its own time apprehended in thought."[23] The romantic impulse was a flight from the modern world; Hegel's impulse embraced the modern, in its radical rejection of the inherited and traditional, as the concern of philosophy.[24]

Hegel, by contrast, understood deduction as the development of concepts through the moments they contain. This is the "concrete" concept, one that cannot be defined in a logical-deductive analysis, and therefore has no fixed definition in Puchta's sense. Neither can other concepts be subsumed within it. Hegel's system contains little or nothing of the structure common to abstract logic but focuses instead on the image or pattern *(Gestalt)* of concepts in their relationship to each other. In the foreword to the *Philosophy of Right,* Hegel merely refers to the proof already given in the *Logic* for the dialectical method and the notion of science found there. The study of ethics and law applied this same method, the key to what Hegel calls "architecture of reason" in the life of the state. As a political philosophy—not a jurisprudence in the sense of the *Pandektenwissenschaft*—Hegel's argument tries to recover the reality and meaning of ideas and institutions. As they would later be for Carl Schmitt, the liberals are the target of Hegel's ire; as Schmitt also later argued, Hegel saw them as "romantic" people, whose confusing emotions and subjective attitudes (opinions) obscure the reality of the state. If there is a philosophy of political life, then for Hegel it will replace mere opinion with knowledge. The study of law necessarily places it within the state's "architecture of reason." This is not the "subsumption" found in conceptual jurisprudence but understanding conduct as meaningful to actors in their time. Within every legal concept there is, for Hegel, a moment of realization, an aspect of political life omitted from conceptual jurisprudence because it assumed that all legal concepts were principles in a formal logic.

By risking the identification of history and philosophy, Hegel negated the revolutionary negation of the past but retained the modern discontinuity of tradition, present, and future as its central problem—its "fate," as Max Weber would later say. In *The Phenomenology of Mind* Hegel argues that the real exists and has its structure by conceptual necessity, an argument that is more fully developed in the *Logic*. The import of his system, Charles Taylor writes, is to show that " 'form,' or the nature of thought itself, goes over into its opposite."[25] The relations between categorical concepts in a transcendental logic and the structure of reality itself can be discovered through the contradictions that are inherent in every concept and necessarily a part of reality. Hegel's dialectic moves from one level to another by discovery and identification of these contradictions. The original concept is raised *(aufgehoben)* and reconciled *(versöhnt)* with its contradiction at a higher level.

The attraction of Hegel's system for Left and Right thinkers has contributed to its misunderstanding as a *philosophical* project, but the "mistaken" reading proved to be the most fruitful since the Enlightenment for political theory. On the Left the political and historical have taken on religious substance, while reactionary idealism veils revolutionary freedom.[26] If Marx turned Hegel upside down, it must be remembered that, for Hegel, there was neither an up nor a down: thought and reality are not separate, distinct from each other. Reason as universal thought expressed itself in logical categories as spirit's *(Geist)* knowledge of itself. Reality embodies spirit and is posited by it; in this sense thought reflects a rationally necessary structure, and in grasping the categories of our thought about things, we also grasp the necessary, essential structure of the world. Hegel reasserts, against Kant, that the world posited by Geist lives in thought and that our categories are necessarily embodied in the spirit's reality in the world. Formal logic divides substance and form; Hegel defines them as a "going over" of each into the other. Hegel's image for this relationship, the dialectic of thought and objects, is a spiral, a circle moving upward. The formal-logical perspective, by contrast, builds a conceptual pyramid with a governing idea at the top, which allows those below to be seen through it and integrated into it. This governing concept is the key to all others in the pyramid. Its breadth conforms to the system's content, and its height to the reach of the governing idea. The more it gains in one, the more it loses in the other dimension. The ideal structure of this logic is so general that all subconcepts can be subsumed within it. From any place in the logical structure, one can arrive at the apex, or governing idea, but the system itself is static.[27]

The study of Roman law pandects, on which German civil law in this period was based, demonstrates the power of Kant's philosophy in nineteenth-century German jurisprudence. The Pandektenwissenschaft applied formal logic to historical sources. For Puchta, the elementary objects of legal study were not actions or institutions but legal principles (Rechtssätze), and the connections asserted to exist between those principles are purely logical. The idea at the peak of this system was Kant's concept of freedom. The free subject is the most general in jurisprudence from which, Puchta argued, all others can be derived. The relationship between concepts is interpreted not as a contextual problem but in relationship to the governing idea of freedom. They "function" not with real purpose but as part of a logical whole. The dream of this method is a complete legal system in which there are no gaps because the logic can generate new principles when needed.[28] It was a purely deductive system that assumed Kant's idea of freedom and regarded the legitimacy of the positive law as a *logical* problem—a question of subsuming concepts with the logic of law. In changing political circumstances, when legitimacy had become more than a logical problem, the deep inadequacy of Puchta's method was revealed.

The Pandektenwissenschaft received its Kantian philosophical basis from Savigny's *System des heutigen Römischen Rechts* (1840). There are many reasons the civil law became the primary field of abstract jurisprudence *(Begriffsjurisprudenz)*. Kant connected the state to private property more closely than any other philosopher, and the civil law is about contracts and exchange. It is also in the civil realm that individual freedom, as Kant understood it, most needed the protection of the state. The right to appropriate external objects is indeterminate in the rational principles of right. Positive law ends the chaos of appropriation. It is juridically necessary to enter civil society, according to Kant, indeed the duty of every person. Hobbes regarded property as the creation of the state; Locke thought government a convenience and the instrument of property; for Kant, the state is necessary to determine the right to property. His "postulate of public right" is nothing more than the creation of institutions to authoritatively interpret the rules of acquisition.

The evidence of Kant's influence on Savigny is, of course, textual,[29] but since the mid-nineteenth century, scholars have found deeper grounds for finding "Kant in the system of Savigny."[30] Person, Freedom, and Will are the nomenclature of Savigny's system of Roman law. The substance of these in Savigny's work reflects Kant's larger philosophy of human freedom and moral duty. But how did Kant's philosophy, to which he explicitly denied specific consequences, come to play such a central role in the development of German political theory and jurisprudence?

There is first the debt of German liberalism to Kant. His philosophy inspired the ideal of a "political public," or *Öffentlichkeit,* not a public in superficial terms but one free to debate and spread ideas that would eventually enlighten itself and all of society.[31] Kant thought political change would occur through enlightenment, opinion formation, and moral betterment and that this would encourage the formation of independence and "civil personalities."[32] Although he did not use the term "Rechtsstaat," it became, throughout the nineteenth century, the state theory of liberalism. During the Vormärz, almost everyone, Leonard Krieger writes, thought that the Rechtsstaat and the idea of the rule of law were crucial to making the state "mighty, powerful and rational."[33] Kant bound the ruler to respect the freedom of his subjects, but he also denied the right of resistance to authority, and in his political thought there is more than a little of Luther's quietism in the face of secular authority. The constraints of absolutism would be loosened through enlightenment, and a government with respect for persons that is based on consensus and compromise.[34] The many contradictions of historical liberalism are not to be attributed directly to Kant, of course, and his influence was more specific —in the civil law, and later the law of the state—than this ideological overview suggests. Liberals wanted a strong state under the rule of law for the sake of the nation—but they were frightened of the people's power and skeptical of a popular legislative. They wanted an enlightened ruler, guided by enlightened opinion—they did not want government by parliament alone and were generally divided over which institution, crown or assembly, could best represent their influence. Karl von Rotteck, the great liberal of Baden, worried that government might lose its independence to a popular assembly, a development that could become "dangerous and uncontrollable," even in a republic. The definition of the state offered in the *Staatslexicon* reflects these worries. It is a "sovereign, moral, personal, vital association of a *Volk,* united in a freely constituted parliament under the leadership of an appropriate and constitutionally independent government."[35]

Kant's effect on law and state theory encouraged abstraction and was the philosophical source of "conceptual jurisprudence" (Begriffsjurisprudenz) in nineteenth-century Germany. Elements of Kantian philosophy, combined with Savigny's emphasis on the historical study of Roman law, produced a jurisprudence that was synthesized in the late nineteenth century by Bernard Windscheid's *Lehrbuch der Pandektenwissenschaft* (1862–79, 1906). Although passé by the 1920s, Windscheid's work had been the foundation of the codified civil law in Germany, the *Bürgerliches Gesetzbuch* (1896) still in effect today in the Federal Republic.

The Pandektenwissenschaft applied formal logic to the study of law and that is its importance in German legal history. This "formal conceptual jurisprudence" looked for logical connections between legal principles. While Savigny—for whom Hegel reserved one of his most bitter remarks in the *Philosophy of Right* (par. 211)—still saw institutions as the object of jurisprudence in Puchta's system, these, as historically given in practice and custom, ceased to be the focus; instead, legal principles (Rechtssätze), abstractly conceived, formed the elements of jurisprudence.[36] The connections asserted between them are logical and superior as the primary source of jurisprudence that allows the system to generate further concepts and principles. Puchta still refers to the life of these within the nation, but as no more than rhetorical repetition of what had been a genuine starting point for Savigny. The further development of Puchta's system by the jurists of the Kaiserreich, notably Carl Friedrich von Gerber and Rudolf von Jhering, replaced the substance of law with logic. As formal jurisprudence developed through the last two centuries, it lost its specific connection to the Roman law and became the primary method of state law in Germany. The legal positivists of the Second Reich were modernizers who swept away the remnants of the historical school but retained its positive theory of law, and after 1871 they drew on statute law and existing state institutions for their source. Their system too was deductive, working from an a priori basis to the practical philosophy of law, but Kantian freedom and his ethics moved further into the background. Methodologically, that system could be replaced with another, and the power of this deductive system would be sustained, as long as the logical structure remained. The law still contained the concept of freedom and its subsidiaries such as "person," "rights," and "obligation, but the legitimacy of law now depended on existing institutions. Puchta and others believed a logically constructed set of opposites could be found that would exhaust all possible cases of reference. So, for example, a subjective right is either a right to a thing or against a person. With these, the concept "subjective right" is exhausted. Every other concept derived from that one can be subsumed back into the supreme concept *(Oberbegriff)* which remains constant throughout. That dream became the center of Hans Kelsen's "pure theory of law."

Hegel's philosophy of law had little influence in nineteenth-century Germany. Neither the Roman lawyers nor the positivists of the Second Reich sought a concrete theory of law in his terms; after 1871, positivism dominated state law *(Staatsrecht)* through the work of Paul Laband. His *Das Staatsrecht des Deutschen Reichs* (1876) idealized "pure thought" *(gereinigtes Denken)* and argued that jurisprudence should be independent of values and purposes, relying on formal categories and proof alone. Cultural, political, social, and economic questions—all the areas represented by the humanities and social sciences—were excluded, not because they were inferior but because the scientific character of jurisprudence could be maintained only in dogmatics. The law was discovered in legal principles and their application to existing institutions which were "constructed" through the dogmatic.[37] Logic was the means, and all other reflections—historical, political, philosophical—were "without import" for jurisprudence, a mask to conceal inadequate argument.

The consequences of jurisprudential formalism for legal practice and finally for the political culture of the Germans can hardly be overstated and was a crucial element in the phenomenon of the "unpolitical German." Franz Wieacker described it in the following terms:

> This formalism contained a fundamental decision that was ultimately tragic for the relationship of jurisprudence to its social reality. For Savigny, it remained an open question whether institutions were ideal forms of social life, but [in the work of later positivists] there is no doubt that scientific concepts had been released from their living foundations and now had a merely intellectual existence. Jurisprudence was thus finally alienated from the social, political and moral reality of the law. Formalism triumphed in a science that began as a rejection of formal rationalism and the natural law.[38]

From Legal Science to Political Theory

Abstract, distanced from politics and from the social reality of its practice, German jurisprudence by the outbreak of the Great War had become "capable of various political accommodations . . . consciously or unconsciously, it served to legitimate the status quo."[39] Theoretical interest in the state moved away from the law toward economics and sociology, literature and history. The question of what authorizes the state's power and what legitimates the positive law was left to intellectuals outside the mainstream of German jurisprudence, or outside the law altogether.[40] The beginnings of Carl Schmitt's political theory are located there, in the silence of jurisprudence on the relationship of theory to practice, and the legacy of formalism in the more unstable circumstances of the twentieth-century state.

During the years he spent as a law clerk in the Düsseldorf offices of Justizrat Hugo Lampert, Schmitt's cultural openness is striking, and from 1910 to 1915 his work is more concerned with cultural questions than with strictly legal issues. Besides his doctoral thesis on the problem of guilt in the criminal law,[41] Schmitt published the satire *Schattenrisse* (1913), *Gesetz und Urteil* (1912), and *Der Wert des Staates und die Bedeutung des Einzelnen* (1914). During this period he met Theodor Däubler and also his mysterious first wife, Papla von Dorotić, to whom he dedicated *Der Wert des Staates.* Between 1911 and 1914 there are ten articles on literary and philosophical topics, and only one on the law.[42] With Kuxen, Eisler, and Rosenbaum, his university friends, Schmitt indulged a voracious appetite for art, music, literature, and the wines of the Rhine.[43]

Schmitt's doctoral dissertation was hardly experimental and, as would be expected in that context, demonstrated a student's competence with the established discipline.[44] It did, however, address the formal and substantive definitions of a legal concept, here "guilt" in the criminal law, a theme that he continued to explore in later work. In the dissertation, Schmitt quickly dismissed the substantive concept of guilt: "what must concern us is the formal definition of guilt," not whether it is social irresponsibility or abnormality, not whether the word has a moral meaning.[45] By 1912, however, Schmitt's openness to trends in the larger culture, especially in philosophy, aesthetics, and literature, began to make itself felt in his work. *Gesetz und Urteil* (1912) took up indeterminacy and judge-made law, a central issue in contemporary legal theory, framing it as the sociological question "When is a judge's decision right?" The book was seriously received in specialist journals,[46] but only one reviewer noticed that Schmitt had gone beyond the "free-law" school *(Freirechtsbewegung).* Writing in *Kant-Studien,* Felix Halldack noted that Schmitt's critique of the free-law movement "went far beyond their fruitless critique" and sought "not only to deconstruct, but to build up" a new approach to the law and state. Much of this, Halldack remarked, was due to Schmitt's "far reaching knowledge of purely philosophical works."[47] The year he finished his doctoral work, Schmitt had read Däubler, and the following year he discovered Hans Vaihinger's *Die Philosophie des Als-ob* (1911). He saw the *Sonderbund* exhibit in Düsseldorf (1912) and traveled with Däubler, Eisler, and Albert Kollman that summer through the Alsace. Of the philosophers who appear as Schmitt frames the question of law and decision in *Gesetz und Urteil,* two transformed his thought about law and the state. From Vaihinger, Schmitt took an understanding of the hypothetical that released him from Kantian philosophy; from Hegel, he took the assumption that philosophy must apprehend its own time in concrete conceptions.[48] The first freed thought about the law and state from the grip of positivism, and the second eventually led Schmitt into the dangerous territory of a political science of the state. In this early work, the insights he gained from Vaihinger and Hegel allowed Schmitt to restate the question of a right legal decision in the larger terms he had bracketed out of his dissertation: "What normative principle is at the foundation of modern legal practice?"[49] Reason, Schmitt remarks with Hegel, can "serve good or evil,"[50] and the law's intent is not an abstract problem, nor can its determination be left to the individual judge.

Legal indeterminacy was the subject of a significant debate in German legal scholarship before the Great War. Largely framed in terms of Rudolf Stammler's influential book *Die Lehre vom richtigen Recht* (1901), discussion ran the gamut of opinion on "gaps" in the law and the sources of law, but it developed along Kantian lines.[51] Schmitt rightly saw legal determinacy as central to the Rechtsstaat theory, but he and his generation lost interest in the juristic conception of the state. "Their thought was once again either 'historical' or 'political,' or they came to refine their methodological self-consciousness in comprehensive dialogue with philosophy, sociology and psychology."[52] In the same year that Vaihinger's *Die Philosophie des Als-ob* appeared, Hans Kelsen published *Hauptprobleme der Staatslehre* (1911), his program to rid jurisprudence of all political, historical, and ethical elements.[53] As it had been for the preceding generation, the question surrounding jurisprudential debate was whether Germany could be a "national state" or a "state in an industrial society."[54] Increasingly complicated commercial exchange and industrial production needed a maximum of legal security not only for property rights but in the processes and institutions of the civil law as a whole. Amid such claims and in the circumstances of the modern economy, statute law and bureaucratic rationality seemed to offer the greatest degree of determinacy in execution and interpretation. Stammler's theory of "right law" offered a formal method that ignored the substance of the law and espoused the ideal of "absolute harmony between all conceivable appearances and relationships."[55] At this time Schmitt shared many of the dominant assumptions in jurisprudence regarding the desirability of such a legal order, but he was critical of the criterion given in contemporary jurisprudence that it must always be "in accordance with the law" *(gesetzmäßig)* because it left open whether the intent of the law should be determined by reference to legislative will or to the coherence of jurisprudence and legal thought itself.

Gesetzmäßigkeit asserted that a positive law must ground every legal decision. The German term carries various implications and combines notions for which English could employ either "legality" or "legitimacy." Depending on other conceptions within a larger theory, it could refer only to procedure or to more substantive conceptions of the right. German law resolved such issues in technical terms through the provision that cases should be subsumed within existing legal categories. Even if every decision must be able to be subsumed in that way, this did not eliminate the judge's need to make a series of decisions leading up to the final one, decisions in which the case at hand was subsumed under this, and not that, rule. To eliminate such judicial liberty, ultimately the ability to make new law by seeing the old law in a new way, jurisprudence engaged in a set of fictional assumptions, including the hypothetical decision of a hypothetical legislator: "The judge should decide as the legislator would have decided. This is a practical and valuable heuristic fiction. But it conceals the fact . . . that one has surrendered 'legality' [*Gesetzmäßigkeit*] as the criterion of a correct decision. For as the legislator would have decided, he precisely did not decide."[56] The theory, Schmitt concluded, was a mixture of theological, psychological, philosophical, and historical methods introduced into the analysis of specific cases.

If the hypothetical criterion was discarded, what others remained? Montesquieu argued that the law must conform to the general will of the people and its laws; the historical school assumed that *Volksgeist* was the criterion of right law; the free-law school tried to construct a criterion of justice relevant to legal practice. Schmitt acknowledged all of these as important but inadequate because "the question about a right law contains a completely different problem than that of a correct decision."[57] By linking the "rightness" of judicial decisions to the right law, Schmitt moved the debate radically away from questions that might be addressed formally, opening the way for political questions about how "right laws" might be recognized in modern states. Contemporary opinion focused on the legislature or "the will of the legislator" without attention to the political reality of parliamentary democracy. That problem is not addressed here, but in the early Republic he saw the new social structure of parliamentary parties as a contradiction of contemporary liberal theories of legality and legitimacy.[58] A theory that had once made substantive claims by reference to the values of a social class or a political philosophy became, in the context of democratic claims and their satisfaction, a procedure that excluded sources of law other than statute and legislation.[59] This text was the first in which Schmitt offered a "decisionist" theory of law, but it is indicative of his ambivalence about such an approach that a normative question opens the book.[60]

Vaihinger was the bridge to this transformation in his thought, and Schmitt's early works document his struggle with pragmatic and metaphysical approaches to the law. Writing for the most widely circulated law journal, Schmitt asserts that in the "struggle over jurisprudence," neither side understands the fictions on which its respective position rests. Crowning liberal positivism is the fiction of Kantian freedom; the realist critiques also rely on fictions, those of "history" or "reality." Referring to the concept of "legal persons," Schmitt writes that when critics assert that it contains nothing but is "something fabricated, not real, not actual," they completely miss the point. What matters, he writes, is "not the reality of a thought, but its practical use for jurisprudence and legal practice." Vaihinger establishes that "a fiction is not without value" and that its measure is not "proximity to reality, but its epistemological utility." Repeating the argument of *Gesetz und Urteil,* Schmitt writes that the method of jurisprudence is "to regard the results of an interpretation *as if* it were the will of the law."[61] That makes Vaihinger's philosophy particularly useful for legal scholarship because its understanding of the relationship between language and reality could break the fruitless debate between positivists and others.

That Schmitt recommends Vaihinger so warmly to a legal public indicates that he still accepted elements of a Kantian philosophy. Yet there are signs in Schmitt's earliest work of a shift away from philosophical reason toward intuition as the means to close the gulf of dualism, an approach developed through art and music. Schmitt's enthusiasm for everything modern in music and art at this time—expressionism, and the operas of Richard Wagner—drew him toward the intuitive and irrational, elements present in Schmitt's mature political theory. In early 1910, Schmitt wrote to his sister Auguste: "I've been playing *Meistersinger* all day (Kluxen gave me a nice piano version)." During the summer of the following year, he saw productions of *Tristan* and *Meistersinger* in Cologne. Later that year a piano transcription of *Lohengrin* was sent to Auguste while on holiday in Portugal. By summer 1913, he played "only Mozart, I can't stand any more of Wagner and for the last months I've been listening to *Figaro* or *Don Juan.* I'll send you the overture from *Barbier von Sevilla,* if you don't have it. . . . The introduction contains one of the most beautiful melodies ever written."[62]

Wagner's music turned Schmitt toward the aesthetic sources of truth, even in law. He would certainly have read Vaihinger's declaration that "neither life nor scholarship is possible without poetic, that is, false images" and noted his admiration of Nietzsche's revelation of this fact, "certainly in concurrence with Schopenhauer and Wagner's theory of madness."[63] The question about any work of philosophy, Schmitt wrote while under the spell of Wagner, is whether it is written for "coming generations." Intuitive knowledge and the fictional impulse of a creative will always mark great works of art and philosophy and transcend their immediate occasions and audience, and they "cannot succeed without its own madness."[64] Intuition connects art and philosophy, and their genius becomes the mass effect of popular fictions. Writing for the *Bayreuther Blätter* in the following year, Schmitt expands on Wagner's remark. Great works of art and great artists are independent of ethical questions, Schmitt asserts, but Wagner's theory of madness, read by Vaihinger in its historical context and relation to Schopenhauer's philosophy, reveals the connection between art and ethics. Wagner's mythology, read with Vaihinger, takes on a completely different meaning: myth makes the intuitive knowledge of art accessible to others. The "Wahnmonolog" of *Meistersinger* reveals an ethical process: "at first, recognition of madness comes as insight into the real relation of things, as recognition of the vanity and superficiality of earthly existence that is behind the valuation of all human deeds and striving, insight into the irrationality of all human action." Sachs sings not against himself but in astonishment at human stupidity, and his astonishment opens an objective view of his own life. Madness appears as "blind violent anger" but is carried into understanding of the human condition.[65]

Schmitt's discovery of irrational and intuitive truth found ways to incorporate the decisionism of *Gesetz und Urteil* and its normative ambivalence through fascination with language. The vehicle was an unprepossessing handbook of philosophy edited by Fritz Mauthner.[66] Mauthner's A-to-Z of concepts wants to be not only a reference book but an etymology that finds "a monograph on cultural history in the history of every word."[67] With this, Mauthner tries to retrieve the history of every word in its circumstances, a project that opposes "cosmopolitanism" and what we would today call "monoculture" but interests itself deeply in linguistic "borrowing and transfers."[68] For Mauthner, philosophy is the study of words and language, a simplification that Schmitt rejects, but the compendium of proverbs and fables prefacing the handbook would certainly have fascinated Schmitt.[69] Schmitt's review of Mauthner begins with the source of philosophy in astonishment, even at the banal: what one fails utterly to comprehend, fascinates another. "Die Philosophie und ihre Resultate" (1913) begins with that fact and moves it beyond "intersubjective" recognition—the collegial criterion of *Gesetz und Urteil*—toward the "supersubjective." Schmitt sharply rejects Mauthner's assumption that thinking and speaking, concepts and words, are identical: "the critique of language is not a critique of knowledge."[70] But this short piece moves away from the solution to gaps in the law and legal indeterminacy offered in *Gesetz und Urteil* toward "another truth, not linguistic, even if scientific truth is a kind of language."[71]

Schmitt's legal publications before the Great War all addressed topics in the civil law. The turn toward political theory and constitutional law begins with his second dissertation, *Der Wert des Staates und die Bedeutung des Einzelnen* (1914). The frontispiece carries a quotation from Däubler's *Nordlicht:* "First is the command, people come later."[72] From the perspective of his later political theory, the argument is startling: law and power cannot be combined, and what is law cannot be determined by reference to the institutions of the state that execute it, because it is more than them. Of the three concepts—law, state, and the individual—the last interested Schmitt least of all, a fact that obscures its proximity to neo-Kantianism.[73] "At the center of jurisprudential debate today," he writes, "stands a question about whether law is a valid norm distinct from facts, but not the question of the state as its reality. . . . By contrast this book is interested in the state, and touches on law only when it is necessary for the legal-philosophical definition of the state."[74] The law, he maintains, is "a pure, classifying norm, not derived from facts,"[75] but Schmitt is still interested in the relationship between that concept and practice, the realization of law. Stammler and Hermann Cohen have shown that jurisprudential questions arise from the theoretical interest in a "general theory of law," and while their work might be seen as crowning the work of the previous century, it marks a new course. Cohen's concept of action as central to the science of law is a key to the problem of jurisprudence,[76] and Schmitt's work from this point on, despite discarding Kantianism, can be seen as executing that task.

Because the state has priority over law, all states are Rechtsstaaten by definition. States are "governed into the last detail by law and the state can will only the law."[77] Schmitt consistently rejects reduction of the law to the state's execution and asserts that "the purpose of the state is to realize the law, and to work in the world toward its realization. It follows from this purpose that the state is the highest power." A metaphysical assumption governs Schmitt's thought: "The concept of the state occupies for the law an exactly analogous position as the concept of God, because of the necessity of realizing the ethical in the world, occupies for ethics."[78] From this analogy, Schmitt moves to a concept of sovereignty: "The idea of law that links it to reality must be positive, i.e., its content is given in an act of sovereign decision, it is articulated in statutes and concrete form."[79] This decision is not bound to the empirical, just as there is no bond between a norm and its practice. The language of realization suggests Hegel; the division of a pure norm from its practice that is given in the authority of the state suggests Kant. *Der Wert des Staates* and *Gesetz und Urteil* evidence the division in Schmitt's thought between a constructive theory of legal fictions suggested by Vaihinger and the desire for a truth that is more than conventional; even more than that, he is torn between decisionist and normative theory.[80]

At this time, Schmitt still phrased these issues in psychological terms that would be replaced in *Politische Theologie* by radical conceptualization. In these early works, however, Hegel appears to offer an alternative to Vaihinger, whom Schmitt reads as turning a "because" into an "as if," against which a proponent of the real (Hegel) protests.[81]

The argument of *Gesetz und Urteil* about "the will of the law" should be read against this background of concerns. He rejects both a simple empirical approach to legal interpretation and formalism, and while the formula (a decision that another judge would also have made) he suggests conforms to Rechtsstaat theory, it depends on a practice of persuasion and education and on a coherence theory of truth. The judge's decision must be demonstrably correct in given legal circumstances. The judge uses rules and norms to calculate what is correct, and in reaching his decision, the judge can be creative but never free.[82] Legal determinacy is constituted in this practice of persuasion; it does not exist outside of the intellectual work of reasoning, persuading, and deciding, which in turn depends on the coherently fictional assumptions. The law cannot be a "form" of social life, Schmitt agrees with Max Weber against Stammler; it is a valid injunction, something recognized by those to whom it pertains.[83]

Two aspects of Schmitt's early work deserve particular attention and can be found in his Weimar work. He emphasizes that a decision must be reasonable in terms of a collegial principle (it must be acceptable to a majority of the judges), but the focus here is on the personality and qualities of the judge himself. Experience is required to develop an opinion: no one can present the connections about values who has not personally experienced the issue at stake. So the personality of the judge, which is revealed with each specific emphasis, is important. "Without experience of life, or real experience of legal practice, the judge doesn't understand the values he is to evaluate."[84] Crucial are the *judgmental* powers, and although his criterion is formal—"a methodological principle for contemporary legal practice"—its reference points are broader than is perhaps obvious at first. The formal conception of determinacy *(Rechtsbestimmtheit)* used here means that certain laws, Schmitt argues, have value simply by their existence. They are useful because they determine a particular procedure, not because one way or another of doing this thing is right.[85] This part of Schmitt's argument relies on Hegel's identification of three moments in the law: abstract regulation, realization, and mediation. The judge acts in the latter moment, to mediate the law and its realization. In this specific sense, all law is "judge made."[86] Through him the dualism of law as form and content can be overcome.

Schmitt still phrased these issues in psychological terms that abruptly gave way to another language and to an approach he would call "radical conceptualization" in *Politische Theologie.* It was this language that Kant and the Enlightenment most wanted overthrown, the language of God, authority, and tradition. The early works evidenced openness to artistic and metaphysical intuition, which in the last year of the war developed in an explicitly religious direction that asserted a ground for law and the state beyond the empirical and historical. The forum was a journal of radically antipositivist thought which published work by figures as diverse as Hermann Bloch, Robert Musil, G. K. Chesterton—and Carl Schmitt. Through its editor, Franz Blei (1871–1942), Schmitt came into contact with some of the leading literary figures of the day.[87] In numerous (short-lived) journals, of which *Summa* was the most distinguished, Blei cultivated heterogeneity in opinions and political positions and mixed Left and Right political positions with gusto. Austrian by birth, Blei's own politics were social democratic–Catholic, and the journal name deliberately referred to Thomas Aquinas. Another Blei publication, *Die Rettung: Blätter zur Erkenntnis der Zeit,* carried the banner headline "Long Live Communism and the Catholic Church!" His most recognized book was the *Bestiarium Literaricum* (1922), like Schmitt's *Schattenrisse* a satire of Germany's leading literary figures.[88] The two demonstrated their regard for each other throughout the 1920s (Blei reviewed the *Verfassungslehre* for a general public in *Literarisches Welt*), and in 1931 Blei organized "a German conversation" between Schmitt and Viet Roßkopf, whom he described as "a National Socialist with great doubts about Hitler, fewer about Goebbels and none at all about Ernst Jünger."[89] Schmitt was referred to simply as "a Rhinelander," and Blei described him as a "classicist" with an aversion to everything "romantic," the defining categories of the German eighteenth century: "His education goes far beyond the empirical. . . . He is dogmatic. He regards dogma as the most rational form of thought in the sphere of the Un-Thinkable."[90] What Blei recognized in his friend was a tendency toward antiquity, dogmatics, the Latin, and admiration for the order-creating capacity of the Roman Catholic Church. Schmitt returned the compliments. Writing on Blei for the cultural pages of the *Frankfurter Zeitung,* Schmitt described his friend as "a secularized cleric" with none of the tendency toward romantic occasionalism that Schmitt so despised, "immune to militarism, pacifism, metaphysicalism"—in short, Blei had intellectual integrity and was proof against ideological fads.[91]

Schmitt's "roman, rheinisch Catholicism" made the two friends, and the most explicit statements of Schmitt's political Catholicism appeared first in Blei's journal *Summa.* The first of three articles, "Recht und Macht" (1917) addressed the question posed in *Der Wert des Staates* of how "to unite the two realms while maintaining the primacy of law over power."[92] Can law be derived from facts? "No" Schmitt answers, even while acknowledging that the exercise of power depends on various forms of law and that there is "power in law."[93] The impulse to identify the state as a "complex of norms" from which power emanates and is justified by the "relevant factual will of that state," while demanding that within the state everything should proceed juridically and "convey a rational and right will, although the ground of its legitimacy is merely a fact," Schmitt writes, is the central contradiction of contemporary jurisprudence. "A fact cannot be demonstrated away, a will is not present because it is reasonable and right. Kant's attack on the ontological proof of God is for none more important than for the jurist."[94] Contemporaries read *Der Wert des Staates* as a natural law argument, Schmitt himself as "a constructivist conceptual legal theorist [*Begriffsjuristen*] of the natural law school."[95] Schmitt shared a rejection of positivist legal theory with Catholic natural law, but he took no part in contemporary Catholic debates about whether political authority came directly from God or through the people.[96] Only when the Weimar constitution declared in Article 1 that "all state power comes from the people" did democracy interest Carl Schmitt. If questions such as those, echoing "divine right" debates in the age of the Reformation, did not resound in Schmitt's pre-Weimar thinking, the problem of *Innerlichkeit* and the form of the church that so vexed Martin Luther and the Counter-Reformation did find expression there. This theme was a touchstone of Protestant distrust of Catholicism in Germany, much as it was in the contemporary United States. The political question was simple: to which institution did a Catholic national owe first allegiance, church or state? Theologically, dualism was the problem, the inner man or soul versus the external, visible man. Luther emphasized inwardness against the Roman Catholic importance of sacraments, rituals, and the "visible" church. The true church, according to Luther, was the community of believers, a reality not perfectly in conformation with the external church of members.

Rudolf Sohm, the leading church law jurist of the time, introduced Luther's argument into a debate already in progress on the compatibility of the Roman Catholic Church with a German national state, and the place of German Catholics in that state. It was partly a reprise of the *Kulturkampf* of Bismarck's time, but no legislation followed from this tempest of religious intellectuals. Sohm argued that "the visibility of the

Church" is the fundamental Catholic dogma, and that "law" (the visible and ordered) is incompatible with the Church of Christ: "The Church of Christ is a legal organization [for the Catholic]: the Christian life is organized by Church law." This gives the Catholic a legal bond to the church, whose hierarchical authority destroys the spiritual life of the individual, and thus the essence of Christianity. For Sohm, Roman Catholicism was close to Judaism; both were legalistic and estranged from the life of the spirit.[97]

Schmitt's answer was the only publication that made "an explicitly theological argument."[98] It begins with two assertions: (1) man is not alone in the world; (2) the world is good, and whatever is bad in it results from the sins of man. These two principles contain everything meant in the doctrine of incarnation, that God became man.[99] They can be discussed only as a Christian with another Christian, not as a proposition in logic, for what matters is not "refutability" but "truth."[100] Schmitt nowhere mentions Luther or Rudolf Sohm, but the theological core of his argument here is that of the Reformation and its consequences: the life of man *in* a sinful world. Some "spiritualists," Schmitt remarks, think that one should withdraw into preoccupation with oneself—"every man is his own judge," these people say, and Schmitt concludes with irony, "and therefore his own executioner" (71). Luther thought of the political power as executive power, the power to execute and to kill in the name of righteousness. The secular authority that held this power acted for God and was set apart from other men, who owed an absolute duty to the established institutions of government. But the "inner man," Luther asserted, was completely free to see moral duty and religious truth for himself. Schmitt's approach to political power and authority is neither so dark nor so absolute as Luther's, but it does carry a profound awareness of man's solitude before God. "No one goes arm in arm with his friend before God, one meets no acquaintances in God's realm, there is no emancipation and no treaties are concluded. . . . This feeling of indescribable solitude, of unbridgeable loneliness, that no decent person ever loses, the certainty that in the most important things one cannot count on the help of others, the knowledge that no man can comfort another and that the recognition of others or any other earthly comforts are but an earthly empowerment and a dangerous illusion; this proves that the world is sinful and they are signs of longing for God, the only one who is alone" (71–72). From that explicitly theological foundation, Schmitt builds a case for the authority of offices comparable to Luther's but without the Protestant's division of inner from outer, joining the substance of law and authority to their forms.

Ernst Troelsch had seen the judgment and crucifixion of Jesus, and Christianity itself, as a historically "absurd" mixture of radicalism and conservatism from the perspective of "party politics, property, income or even education"—from, that is, the modern perspective. Against that view, Schmitt retrieves the premodern through insisting on its theology in the doctrines of Christianity, specifically Roman Catholicism's unification of the visible and invisible church. He does not try to prove this truth—it is either believed or not—but Schmitt makes the important distinction here between sectarian myth and theological truth on which his legal theory implicitly rests (75). In this early work, the categories of Schmitt's later thought are already present as a structure of opposition to liberalism and secularized Protestantism:

Recht	Macht
Göttliche	Menschliche
Sichtbare	Konkrete
Wahrheit	Unwiderlegbarkeit
"Papst"	"rechtmäßiger Papst"
Legitimität	Legalität

The dualism that came into the world through sin finds expression in law and the state, in the contradiction of what is (sinfully) concrete and what is (truly) visible. In this "outrageous confusion," the forms of authority can clothe the profoundly wrong: the Antichrist appears garbed as "the lawful pope" (77–78). The possibility that a judge's decision can be legally correct and unjust is the secular expression of that theological paradox and of what Schmitt here calls "the horrible division of power from right."

Sovereignty and Theology: Weimar

Between that argument and Schmitt's mature political theory lay a historical and intellectual abyss: war, defeat, revolution, and inflation were the background of the first German republic, based, as he would argue, on the mutually incompatible political principles of liberal representation and democracy. Although jurisprudence in the Weimar Republic stood partly in the shadow of an earlier generation's positivist methods, it did not enjoy "the normalcy of peaceful times, in which extralegal referents did not appear necessary."[101] Carl Schmitt's generation of jurists, even men such as Gerhard Anschütz, Georg Meyer's successor at Heidelberg and intellectual heir to Paul Laband's positivism, drew more explicitly on extralegal sources than the preceding generation.[102]

But Schmitt extended the intellectual reach of contemporary debates to include the classic texts of the modern state beginning with Bodin, and thought beyond the temporal and spatial boundaries of Germany after the Great War. His analysis of contemporary constitutional issues drew freely on moments of crisis in the European past, notably Rome and Renaissance Italy, the English Civil War and the French Revolution, and the constitutional crises of 1830 and 1848. The opening paragraph of *Der Hüter der Verfassung* offers a particularly striking example. "The call for a defender and protector of the constitution," it begins, "is usually a sign of constitutional crisis," and then asserts that English plans and recommendations in the period after Cromwell's death deserve special attention because they came after the first modern written constitutions and "in a time of republican disintegration, in the face of a parliament unable to take objective decisions and immediately before the restoration of the monarchy."[103] That *these* are the circumstances of his own republican constitution is silently assumed. That *he* calls for a "defender" goes without remark. The reader is meant to accept certain conclusion from those assumptions. Other historical cases follow. From all of these, Schmitt derived the polemical force of dramatic examples. Ten years earlier, in *Die Diktatur* (1921), Schmitt had derived a concept of dictatorial power from a long history of its practice, but with particular attention to the reception of Roman theory in the Renaissance and the struggle for sovereign power in the emergence of the modern state. More recent use of dictatorial offices can be found in revolutionary France and the century following. In the course of the Weimar Republic, Schmitt famously used the distinction of "sovereign" and "commissarial" dictatorship to interpret presidential power under Article 48. He understood this as part of the project of constitutional defense; many others have thought it Weimar's fatal flaw. In these texts, and in Schmitt's more jurisprudential ones, the essence of ruling appears as something to be found not in the normal practices of law but in exceptions to them and therefore in the personal element of sovereignty. All of that, contemporary theories of the state tried to eliminate. His case for the "visible church" laid the foundation for Schmitt's political and constitutional theory, and Schmitt's association of religious and political questions appears clearly here. "Die Sichtbarkeit der Kirche" lays out a line of argument that took him from the fictions of Vaihinger's philosophy to Däubler's myth of the northern lights (itself a Wagnerian theme) to theological dogma and made Schmitt fatally susceptible finally to "the myth of the state."

In the worst year of Weimar's first crisis—1923—when fiscal instability and political rebellion threatened the German union, Schmitt published *Die geistesgeschichtliche Lage des heutigen Parlamentarismus* and *Rö-*

mischer Katholizismus und politische Form. In the most influential review of the former, Richard Thoma noted Schmitt's sympathy for "the irrationalism of the mythical" and longed for "order, hierarchy and discipline." "I would hazard to guess," Thoma continued, "that there stands the unexpressed personal conviction of the author that an alliance between a nationalistic dictator and the Catholic Church could be the real solution [to the crisis of parliamentary democracy] and achieve a definitive restoration of order, discipline and hierarchy."[104] Despite Schmitt's vehement rejection of this interpretation, the two texts stand in direct relation. *Parlamentarismus* presents liberal representation as the empty formula of an exhausted ideology. The indirect democracy of the German parliamentary system, with its parties and electoral system of proportional representation, implied no substantial beliefs or politics. Rather, in this system politics appear as a contest whose outcomes are various and insubstantial, a system of interests in which questions of justice or truth play no part. "Government by talking," in the English expression, belonged to a social world that had ceased to exist and whose central belief in the rational power of discussion no longer persuaded anyone that the "outcomes" of the political "game" were justifiable. The substantial, real contents of politics became secondary, except for a general attachment to liberty. Politically heterogeneous, even inimical parties and interests were integrated, Rudolf Smend argued, only formally through the processes of elections, ministerial responsibility, budgets, and procedural regulation. In this crucial political institution, the legislative referent by which legal positivism justified itself was itself removed and abstract.

In *Römischer Katholizimus und politische Form,* Schmitt links that critique of Weimar liberalism to another, quite different theory of representation evoked by "the pathos of authority." Like "Die Sichtbarkeit der Kirche," this text too begins with the theological question of human nature—is man good or evil by nature—but in 1923, Schmitt states this as an explicitly political question, "decisive for all political theories."[105]

Form and Decision: The Personal and the Normal

Against the technical and abstract, Schmitt insisted on the reality of the political that revealed itself in exceptional times and circumstances. He rejected the primacy of the formal and the norm and seized instead on its opposite. Max Weber's sociology of law distinguished three concepts of "form." It can mean, first, "the transcendental 'condition' of juristic cognition . . . second, a regularity, and evenness derived from repeated practice and professional reasoning. Because of its evenness and calculability, regularity passes over to the third form, the 'rationalistic,' that is technical refinement, which emerging from either the needs of specialized knowledge or the interests of a juristically educated bureaucracy, is oriented toward calculability and governed by the ideal of frictionless functioning."[106]

If we ignore the first condition of knowledge, the remainder of this description perfectly captures the sociological structure of the modern state and its normative ideal. In his analysis of legitimacy, Weber had set out specific and definitive characteristics of the modern state. Of Weber's three types of legitimacy—legal, traditional, and charismatic—only the first need concern us here, for it is precisely its aspects Schmitt radically pursues via "the decision" and "exception." Weber identifies legitimacy with law, making "government" *(Herrschaft)* dependent on "the chance that a particular order will be obeyed."[107] Every type of government depends on legal grounds that shape the complex of individual motivations and social norms that constitute the "legitimacy" of rule. Modern states "rule by virtue of belief in the validity of legal statute and the appropriate juridical 'competence' founded on rationally devised rules."[108] Typical of this type of government is that "rules, not persons," are obeyed and that the officials who give orders within this system are themselves following rules according to "a formal, abstract norm." The modern civil servant works according to objective official duties, and the ideal is to act "without being influenced by any personal interest or emotion, free from arbitrariness and unpredictability, especially regarding 'personal status,' strictly formalistic according to rational rules and—*where these fail*—according to an 'objective' technical-rational perspective."[109] Not only the modern state but also the economic corporation and political parties are examples of this type of rule. Although bureaucracy is the "purest form" of legality, "no government is only a bureaucracy"; all have either monarchs (hereditary charismatic leaders) or popularly elected presidents (plebiscitary charismatic leaders) at their head.[110]

Schmitt's approach to state theory in *Politische Theologie* concentrates on Weber's observation that rules and the legal technical form of government based on them may fail. Even when they function as perfectly as possible, such governments still require some form of charisma, or "nonrational" leadership. We know that Schmitt attended Weber's *Dozentenseminar* in Munich in 1919 and 1920, and whatever their personal relationship might have been,[111] Schmitt was thought close enough to Weber's research agenda to be invited to contribute to the Festschrift Melchior Palyi edited after Weber's death. His article contained three chapters of *Political Theology* and appears first in the section entitled "Structural

Problems of the Modern State."[112] Most of the others, except for a piece by Carl Brinkmann, are descriptive historical accounts.[113] The predicament of state theory, torn between "relativistic historicism" (Erich Kaufmann) and "natural law dogma" (Kelsen),[114] exemplifies the problem of objectivity raised by Weber. He had argued that social science must avoid the reduction of evaluative and empirical work to each other and their division in simplistic causal theories.[115] The problems a causal theory raises for the state, Weber argued, cannot be resolved through psychology with its focus on the individual. The particular function of the state is to create "a higher third" above possibly conflicting social groups and thus attain its "specific mark in comparison to other associations and to other states." " 'As force,' [Weber] rightly says, 'the will of the state is not always focused on the common interest or even on the average of competing interests, but often purely physical force.' "[116]

The Definition and Problem of Sovereignty

The history of the modern state can be read as the substitution of abstract rules for personal authority, a tendency that culminates in Weber's concept of legality as legitimacy. Contemporary statute positivism and normative theories both assumed that eliminating indeterminacy from law would purge the state of arbitrariness. Both equated the personal with the arbitrary, and when they retained the notion of sovereignty at all, it remained as a systematic requirement or a logical postulate. Modern legal theory, Schmitt writes, tends to reduce sovereignty "to a textbook formula, something for an examination." But this is inadequate to its reality, "just a formula, a sign, a signal," because sovereignty "of all legal concepts [is] the one most dominated by actual interests."[117] It is also the key to a jurisprudence that is "an adequate expression of reality" and a theory of the state that is "juridically concrete."[118] As a mere formula, sovereignty depends on an assumption about the normal and expected that makes them each "causal" in their respective ways. Schmitt's reading of Däubler, and of the romantic temperament, culminates in an argument for "the only case that matters"—Kierkegaard's either/or. *Politische Theologie* begins there.

As he would do in *Der Begriff des Politischen,* Schmitt reverses the usual argument about the state. Instead of starting with the structure of law, he begins where "the law of the state stops."[119] The essential aspect of sovereignty, Schmitt argues, is usually concealed in constitutional and statute law. He brings it forward. The exception is a "boundary concept" *(Grenzbegriff)* that reveals decision, not the norm, as the specific form of the law. Schmitt's target is the contemporary legal philosophy, especially the work of Hans Kelsen. Radical as his definition of sovereignty as "a decision about the exception" was at the time, Schmitt disclaims any originality. What is new, he claims, is not his view but that of contemporary liberal jurisprudence, and he tries to locate his own theory within a tradition that includes seventeenth-century natural lawyers. Pufendorf argued that the question of a public interest turns not on a substantial definition but on "the decision about what is to count as the public interest." All claim to want "the best for the whole, law and justice for all," Schmitt writes, but Pufendorf knew that was not the question; it was rather "whose decision in the final and crucial case is decisive. Not the end, but the decision about the means to an end is what matters."[120]

The exception *(Ausnahmefall)* is not foreseen, and therefore not prescribed in the law. There is no specification of its circumstances, nor could there be. Existing law can at best describe this as "unforeseen," as an "emergency," a "danger to the existence of the state."[121] This case makes the "sovereign subject" a real question, because the emergency is a circumstance that cannot be subsumed clearly, nor can a response to it be specified in advance. In liberal constitutional terms, "there is no competence," at best the specification of who may act, not what may be done. If this competence, Schmitt argues, is not divided among state institutions, then "it is clear who is sovereign": "He decides whether there is an extreme case of emergency and also what shall be done to end it. He stands outside the normally applicable legal order and yet belongs to it, because he is responsible for deciding whether the constitution *in toto* shall be suspended."[122]

That legal theory and legal practice avoid this case, Schmitt admits, is not surprising. Both are concerned with the "jurisprudence of everyday life," not with this extraordinary case. Both concentrate on the normal and view the abnormal as a disturbance or interruption, an annoyance.[123] Liberal constitutionalism pushes back the elements of exception and decision, restraining and binding them through the ideas of "government under law" and "checks and balances." Both limit the prerogative power of the sovereign. The decision cannot have independent meaning in liberal constitutional theory. It is always an aspect of law.[124]

For Schmitt, the problem is not that such theories are methodologically unsatisfactory but that they systematically deny the reality of their own boundaries. The norm is only normal by reference to an exception. This "exceptional case" (Ausnahmefall) is an extreme; "whether it can or cannot be driven out of the world, is not a legal question." Whether one hopes and trusts that it can be, Schmitt remarks with reference to Krabbe and

Kelsen, "depends on philosophical, particularly historical-philosophical, convictions."[125]

The argument contains an implicit hierarchy of state actions to convey Schmitt's idea of sovereignty because they are all disputes over its use. At the lowest level are conflicts about competence or jurisdiction. Such specifications make up much of any constitution, and examples are ready at hand: Article 1, Section 5, of the U.S. Constitution determines that "each house [of the Congress] shall be the judge of the elections, returns and qualifications of its own members"; Article 19 of the Weimar constitution specified that "constitutional disputes within or between a Land or Länder that cannot be resolved by ordinary courts, shall be decided by the federal Staatsgerichtshof." Schmitt only mentions the next, governmental power during times of siege or war, as an illustration of the liberal inclination to specify and determine such power. But his wartime article on the subject considered its effects on the "ordinary processes" of the courts and indicated a crucial part of Schmitt's later concept of sovereignty. Prussia and Bavaria both permitted the creation of special courts when the state was besieged or at war and authorized the military command to take extraordinary measures in governing the civilian population. These effectively suspended basic rights, including habeas corpus, in constitutional and statute law. "In all such cases," Schmitt writes, "the military commander acts on his own personal accountability." Legal complaints against him can be made only to the military courts; they remain within the system of exceptional governmental power.[126] Such powers place the ordinary courts "without question" under the military commander.[127] This doctrinal article contains the central element of sovereignty for Carl Schmitt: the personal action of the commander.

This concept of sovereignty carries the early modern aspects of Bodin's argument into the public law of twentieth-century Germany. Bodin defined sovereignty as "the absolute and perpetual power of the commonwealth"—a formula that could be found in every law school textbook, Schmitt remarks. But the crucial question for Bodin in 1576, as for Schmitt in 1922, was "To what extent is the sovereign bound to the laws and obliged to the estates?" Natural law is the basis of obligation in Bodin's argument, but "in an emergency all commitments under natural law cease."[128]

The Antechamber of Jurisprudence

Nowhere in *Politische Theologie* does Carl Schmitt refer directly to the Great War and the German revolution, but the attentive reader will recognize these as the background of his decisionist argument in the second chapter. The state has not developed "logically" since the sixteenth century; rather, its development is "characterized by various political power struggles." Much of the confusion in German state theory, he observes, results from the political situation of the member states in the German Reich of 1871, a problem similar to that of the American states before the Civil War, but quite different in its solution. The American states had rights under the Constitution, but this begged the question of their relationship to the federal government by avoiding discussions on sovereignty until, by their secession in 1861, the Southern states claimed it. With their defeat, the matter was resolved by amendments giving primacy to the Union in all interstate matters and reducing the independence of the states in various policy areas. German legal theory after 1871 distinguished between the concept of the state and the concept of sovereignty. This allowed the members to retain "statehood" but denied them sovereignty. The advantage of this conception is that it is "infinitely pliable" —and therefore, depending on the circumstances, Schmitt remarks, "extremely useful or completely useless." When, as the jurisprudence of the empire commonly did, sovereignty is defined as "the highest power," that is not a theory of sovereignty or the state because no one factor is determinate.[129] "The connection of actual power" Schmitt writes, "with the legally highest power is the fundamental problem of the concept of sovereignty."[130]

Kelsen: The Pure Theory of Law. Of those who tried to resolve the empirical and normative aspects of state theory, the most important and detailed work was produced by Hans Kelsen. He assumes that the state must be a purely juristic concept, without reference to any reality or order outside itself. It is "nothing else than the legal order itself." Second, the state is "unitary"; the legal order is not its creature, nor is the state its source, but a "system of ascriptions to a last point of ascription and to a last basic norm." Third, these ascriptions are "neither real nor fictitious persons," only points of reckoning that stop at the state as their final point. Thus conceived, the state is a logic of norms, beginning with an original or fundamental norm (the highest in this system) and continuing down to the lowest. Schmitt comments that every critique of this theory is met with the assertion that a norm is valid only by reference to another norm, and that the state is juristically "identical with its constitution, with the uniform basic norm." He raises two specific objections to the normative theory. It begins with the dualism of law and social reality but ends paradoxically in a "monistic metaphysics" in which unity is purchased by excluding everything social and political.[131] It is normative because the jurist makes value decisions freely, and it is objective only because the jurist draws on positively given values. But Kelsen's theory is self-contradictory. The jurist can construct a unity objectively from any point within the system, which "he confronts with relativistic superiority." Embedded within the pure theory of law and the state, then, remains that moment of actual and personal choice.[132]

Krabbe: The Positive State. Like Kelsen, Hugo Krabbe thought of the law, not the state, as sovereign, but Schmitt pays little attention to him by comparison. Krabbe's study of the state was first published in 1906, and the second edition seems to have drawn on Kelsen to some extent, but Krabbe was far less original and systematic. His significance for Carl Schmitt seems to have been largely illustrative of a tendency to avoid theoretical difficulties in "the rule of law" by banal assertions.[133] Typical of statute positivists, Krabbe defined the state in terms of law and legislation. Largely descriptive, Krabbe's theory works through suggestions such as the state "reveals itself only in the making of law," not in its application or in "maintaining any sort of public interest at all." The state appears, finally, in *Die moderne Staatsidee,* as a means to ascertain the value of interests, which come from the popular feeling or sense of right. It thus imposes a double limitation on the actions of the state. It limits law to "declaration" of an "ascertainment" and ignores the moment of that which is constitutive. Schmitt's response is to show how "the problem of law as a substantial form lies precisely in this act of ascertaining."[134]

Gierke and Wolzendorff: Association Theory. Otto von Gierke saw the state and law as equal powers and independent factors in human communal life. He inserted the personal will of the sovereign into the life of the people, existing independently, which was the final source of the state. In Gierke's political theory, sovereignty and law are "an organ of the people convened to express legal consciousness as it emerges from the people." As Schmitt reads Gierke, associational theory appears an attractive alternative to formalism and positivism. Association theory avoids bifurcating real life and law and offers a coherent approach to the problem of revolutionary changes in the constitution. The legal breach that occurs through political revolution may be ethically required or historically justifiable and can be legitimated "through some sort of legal process that will satisfy the legal consciousness of the people," such as a constitutional assembly, a plebiscite, or reference to tradition. The tendency toward reconciliation with the past across a revolutionary breach, Schmitt comments, resolves an unbearable tension. Nevertheless Gierke's notion that law and the state are equal remains vague and seems to imply that the state formalizes political acts (such as revolutions), lending them an imprint with merely "external value." This makes the state a "proclaiming herald," not a sovereign. Following Gierke, Schmitt comments, Hugo Preuß rejected "sovereignty" with a "community" of associations constituted from below. The democratic state, according to Preuß, could not have a power monopoly, nor could "sovereignty" adequately describe its relationship to the people.

Kurt Wolzendorff took up associational theory, but unlike Gierke and Preuß, his theory retained the state's primacy. It forms national life, not as arbitrary force but as order. Wolzendorff's state theory is liberal. Its power is limited by reference to free associations and individuals in society, and the state should act only when those cannot. It is neutral toward individual interests and civil society, which must be left to self-government as far as possible. The sovereign state is an ultima ratio, the "night watchman" confining itself to the maintenance of order. It creates law, but because all law is simultaneously "a problem of the existence of the state . . . it is the 'guardian, not master,' " responsible for the law and its "ultimate guarantor."[135]

Legal Form and Decision

Weber's sociology of the state emphasized the need for predictability and its dependence on technical-rational means that exclude the personal decision. Like those he criticized, Schmitt works with the binary of form and matter, which he sometimes refers to as law and interest. At all times, he aims at the real life of the law and state, or as Weber might have said, he is interested in "an empirical science of concrete reality."[136] It is peculiar to the idea of law that its realization depends on an organization and a form. Contemporary jurisprudence, Schmitt argues, insists that the form of law must be objective and that all personal elements be removed from the state because these are "commands" rather than rules. Kelsen regards the very conception of the sovereign as a person as fundamentally wrong, "premised on the subjectivism of command rather than the objectively valid rule."[137]

What the arguments of Kelsen, Krabbe, and Preuß failed to recognize, in Schmitt's view, is that the historical connection of personality with formal authority in modern political thought came from "an especially clear awareness of what the essence of the legal decision entails." For Schmitt, there is always a moment of indifference and indeterminacy that refers to the boundary of the law itself, the exception. Kelsen's assumption that in a completed normative system, the jurist can start at any point and move up or down the hierarchy of norms contains an abstract certainty: he will always arrive at the fundamental norm from any point in the system. Schmitt's analysis of formal and material elements in law need not assume that the jurist freely chooses the starting point of reasoning, but it does assume that the decision (as the realization of a legal idea) will always contain some material indifference. The deduction that leads to one conclusion, not another, can never be traced completely. The legal system will always be incomplete; there will always be a "gap" in the law, because the individual who applies the rule or subsumes the fact is neither perfectly logical nor gifted with perfect knowledge. Furthermore, the circumstances are more or less independent of a decision. It is more important sometimes (not always) that there be a decision than that it have a particular content. Schmitt does not deny that "the certainty of the decision" is sociologically important in a "commercial age." But his argument also recognizes that certainty in the practical sense will often aim less at "a particular content than a calculable certainty." This, however, is not the theoretically interesting aspect of legal determinations. These are indifferent to content in an especially troubling way for contemporary state theory because "legal validity is attributed to a wrong or faulty decisions. The wrong decision contains a constitutive moment precisely because of its falseness" (42). It is in the context of this argument that Schmitt remarks, "Looked at normatively, the decision emanates from nothingness," because ascription is not dependent on a norm; it happens the other way around—the norm is dependent on ascription (42).

Schmitt's understanding of the relationship between legal form and decision can still be read within the boundaries of an established constitutional order. But the relation of norm to exception posited in *Politische Theologie* contains the more radical claim that sovereignty *is* order and that the sovereign decides absolutely whether there is "a normal situation." This part of the argument introduces an apparently unlimited space of legal indeterminacy in which sovereignty is that very aspect of law that is not determined. Schmitt seems to remove *all* law when he writes, "All law is the law of a situation," or "A decision is born, when considered normatively, out of nothing" (42). At every level, from the lowest normative breach to the sovereign decision, the law *is* procedure for Schmitt: it designates "how decisions should be made, not who should decide." Neither process nor competence can be determined from the "content of the legal quality of a maxim" (44). This theory has been read as "the end of law."[138] There could be no law because there are no general rules, only specific commands. But that misreads the text. Schmitt's implicit political theory—it becomes explicit in *Der Begriff des Politischen*—points to the power that creates a legal order and is always outside the law. "There are no norms that can be applied to chaos"; a normal situation must first be created. Hostile readers find in these claims a determination to destroy the normative and with it the rule of law. The sentence quoted is most often read without the phrase "considered normatively."[139] This does not mean that legal decisions are independent of statutes or other texts. But it does mean that which statute, text, precedent, or other referent will be chosen cannot be determined entirely in advance. Moreover, the power of a decision is something quite different from its justification.[140] The constitutive power of the sovereign subject, whether the people (democracy) or another (king, nobility), "creates and guarantees the situation [in which law first exists] as a whole in its totality."[141] Were the exceptional case so serious that the previous constitution of this power ceases, it would be a revolution, a coup d'état or what Machiavelli called acquisition by another.

This Mortal God

The frontispiece of Hobbes's *Leviathan* famously depicts the sovereign as "a mortal God." Early in 1938 Carl Schmitt described it thus:

> The copper-plate engraving on the title page of the first English edition of *Leviathan* (1651) together with the title *Leviathan* and the motto taken from the Book of Job, Ch. 41:33 [*Non sit potestas super Terram qua comparatur ei*, "Upon earth there is not his like"] immediately evoke in the work of Hobbes a very unusual impression: a gigantic man, composed of innumerable midgets, holding in his right hand a sword and in the left one a crosier, guarding a peaceful city. Under each arm, the secular as well as the spiritual, there is a column of five drawings: under the sword a castle, a crown, a cannon; then rifles, lances, and banners, and finally a battle; to these correspond, under the spiritual arm: a church, a mitre, thunderbolts; symbols for sharpened distinctions, syllogisms, and dilemmas; and finally a council.[142]

Had a reader of *Politische Theologie* known of Schmitt's comments on the frontispiece, this "gigantic man" would seem to illustrate the personal and decisionist in Schmitt's theory of sovereignty. What attracted him to Hobbes in 1922 was quite different than the use he found for *Leviathan* in 1938. In the early 1920s Hobbes offered a state theory characterized by an "abstract scientific orientation," which retained the concrete sovereignty of the state. "Autoritas, non veritas, facit legem" meant that no abstractly valid order can be substituted for relations of power in which one is subjected to the other: "To speak of superior and inferior and attempt to remain simultaneously abstract is to [Hobbes] incomprehensible. . . . 'For Subjection, Command, Right and Power are accidents not of Powers but of Persons.' "[143] If the problem of sovereignty is the relation between legal form and decision, then it could not be solved, Schmitt argued, by bracketing out the decision as the moment of the personal and the political within the state.

Why did such abstraction seem obvious to his generation? Schmitt's answer was more radical than the sociology of ideas might suggest and depended on an implicit but far-reaching philosophy of history. The modern constitutional state depends on metaphysical assumptions that appeared in the late Middle Ages. "Legal and constitutional problems concerning the structure and interpretation of the bodies politic" determined a "field of mutual influence" between church and state in the thirteenth century.[144] Hermann Kantorowicz traced the constitutional doctrine of the king's two bodies to the church doctrines of transubstantiation and the church itself as the mystical body of Christ (Aquinas). The term *corpus mysticum* acquired sociological and ontological connotations that permitted identification of the clerical legal corporation with the mystical body of the church. This "secularization" continued in church claims for temporal authority while from the other side, the secular state itself "strove for its own exaltation and quasi-religious glorification" (207). Theorists of the early modern state "quarried the wealth of ecclesiastical notions, which were so convenient to handle, and finally proceeded to assert itself by placing its own temporariness on a level with the sempiternity of the militant Church." When, during the Investiture Controversy, Vincent of Beauvais called the body of the state a *corpus reipublicae mysticum,* it was to borrow supernatural values from the church, "to raise the state beyond its purely physical existence, and to transcendentalize it" (208). The corporation law of this period and the recovery of Aristotle made possible the development of the church doctrine of a mystical body—and a state theory of "the Prince as the head of the realm and the realm as the body of the Prince" (218). The metaphor grew in succeeding centuries until James I, speaking to his first Parliament, declared, " 'What God hath conjoined then, let no man separate.' I am the husband, and all the whole island is my lawful wife; I am the head, and it is my body; I am the shepherd, and it is my flock."[145] The modern state emerged, Kantorowicz suggests, on the foundation of a community endowed with a mystical character; from James's claim to "be" England, it was not so far to Hobbes's declaration in *Leviathan* that the sovereign is "the real unity of them all."

When he writes that "all significant concepts of the modern theory of the state are secularized theological concepts," Schmitt means that they not only follow a certain path of development but share "a systematic structure." In that structure, "the exception" is to the normal as "the miracle" is to the laws of nature. As political thought moved from an assumption that the world is governed by an all-powerful God intervening directly in the temporal to a deistic philosophy expressly denying the Creator's interference with the laws of nature, the theological models and analogies on which jurisprudence and political theory had formerly been based lost their foundation.

After the Enlightenment, reason became the basis of the state. Before then, political argument had tried "to justify the ways of God to man" (Milton); it demanded justice and articulated political ideals. The advance of scientific method eroded the basis of such questions, turning political thought away from questions of purposive ends toward technical or instrumental means. This rationalization created the dilemma of sovereignty in contemporary state theory because it turned justice into a technical question. Contemporary state theory asserted that only if we accept that assumption can a "positive jurisprudence" develop—that is, a jurisprudence of technique, not decision. This argument, Schmitt contends, not only wrongly defines the substance of law; its proponents adhere to it *despite* contradictory empirical evidence. Neither a logical form nor a neutral instrument vis-à-vis society, the state "intervenes everywhere":

> At times it does so as a *deus ex machina,* to decide according to positive law statute a controversy that the independent act of juristic perception failed to bring to a generally plausible solution; at other times it does so as the graceful and merciful lord who proves by pardons and amnesties his supremacy over his own laws. There always exists the same inexplicable identity: lawgiver, executive power, police, pardoner, and welfare institution. . . . the state acts in many disguises, but always as the same indivisible person.[146]

The jurisprudence of the empire contained a unitary concept of sovereignty—"the sole supremacy of the state"—that made it an abstract person a *unicum sui generis* with a "monopoly of power 'mystically produced' " absent in the Republic. Hugo Preuß rejected that theory as "a legal disguise" of divine right. Of his contemporaries, only Hans Kelsen stressed "the methodological relationship between theology and jurisprudence," but its conclusion does not follow from Kelsen's epistemological assumptions. The latter are unitary and (so Schmitt's argument here implies) should lead to a unitary state "person." Instead Kelsen asserts democracy, the opposite of the unitary, authoritarian state,[147] as "the expression of political relativism and a scientific orientation . . . liberated from miracles and dogmas and based on human understanding and critical doubt."[148]

Schmitt and Kelsen represent polar opposites in the intellectual circumstances of early Weimar, and it is perhaps surprising that Schmitt thought their views of the relationship between jurisprudence and theology compatible. What one sees as the problem of state theory, a premodern remnant to be disregarded and where necessary replaced by the popular deity of the electorate, the other follows into the most disturbing recesses of modernity. Marx, Hegel, Weber—all were wrong about the sociology of ideas, and especially Weber, who thought legal ideas were the result of training, a concept Schmitt's early work *Gesetz und Urteil* (1912) accepted. When is a judge's decision right? Schmitt asked there, and he answered, "A judge's decision is right today when it can be assumed that another judge would have decided the same way. 'Another judge' means today the empirical type of the modern jurist."[149] Reviewing this early work, Walter Jellinek noted Schmitt's "strong desire" for a determinate concept of the right decision; his aversion, that is, to the legal indeterminacy of legislative sovereignty. But the elegant argument failed to persuade Jellinek that the young author had overcome the difficulties inherent in legal positivism's notion of "lawfulness" (*Gesetzmäßigkeit*), but merely replaced one hypothetical subject (the legislator) with another (the judge).[150]

In succeeding works, Schmitt refocused the argument of *Gesetz und Urteil* until, by 1922, the solution to the jurisprudential question of a "right decision" was formulated as a "radical conceptualization" of sovereignty. As *Politische Romantik* opened the way for Schmitt's rejection of liberalism after the Great War, *Politische Theologie* developed a different kind of sociology, one that allowed incorporation of irrational and mystical elements into Schmitt's political theory though an image as fantastic in 1922 as Hobbes's "gigantic man" was in 1651. His sociology of concepts, Schmitt claims, transcends the "immediate practical" interest of jurisprudence to "discover the basic, radically systematic structure and to compare this conceptual structure with the conceptually represented social structure of a certain epoch." We might call the "idealities" that result from Schmitt's method "constructs," but that would mislead: these are not constructed by human reason; rather, they are "spiritual" and "substantial" conceptualizations that dissolve the boundaries of norm/exception, procedure/substance, lawful/personal. They are the foundation of all political organization, of *constituting* the political itself: "The metaphysical image that a definite epoch forges of the world has the same structure as what the world immediately understands to be appropriate as a form of political organization. The determination of such an identity is the sociology of the concept of sovereignty."[151]

Conclusion

The first decades of the twentieth century were surreal (Apollinaire): art and literature, "reflexes of society," became fantastic expressions as shocking as modernity itself. Against the background of war and revolution, Weimar Germany "hungered for wholeness," and its culture represented the trials of modernity.[152] The grotesque, the crippled, and the bizarre were juxtaposed with the rationalized and antiseptic architecture of the Bauhaus. Against those pristine walls, George Gross and others placed the maimed survivors of the Great War, beggars in Germany's great cities.[153] Next to the Bauhaus, the most celebrated artifacts of the 1920s were its films and photographs. In *The Cabinet of Dr. Caligari,* many have seen a prophecy of Germany's fate under Hitler. But the most powerful evocation of Weimar's modernity came before the war:

> In their structure and mechanism all the great cities of the world are alike. From the middle of a spiderweb of rails they shoot out their stone threads of streets over the land. Visible and invisible networks of rolling traffic run through their canyons, burrowing underneath, and twice daily pump human bodies from the extremities to the heart. A second, third, fourth network distributes water, heat and power, an electrical nervous system that carries the movements of the spirit. Food and entertainment glide by on tracks and canals. It is everywhere the same, this stone image.[154]

When Fritz Lang made *Metropolis* (1927), unease already shadowed the wonders of technology. Would it liberate mankind? Or as the film suggests, can only the heroic figure of a woman release these automatons?

Schmitt regarded the monster of modernity within the state much as Rathenau had described the network of the *Großstadt:* its structure corresponded in Schmitt's political theory to the jurisprudence of the modern state. As roads, canals, and power lines enabled *any* purpose, all ends without difference, so legal positivists created a state in which anything was possible, a technique instrumental to any purpose. In 1917 Schmitt argued for the primacy of law, which "may not be derived from power." If it could be, "there would be no more law," and Schmitt even understood the state as the rational opposition of "interests."[155] In 1922 Schmitt still clung to the belief that, by revealing the personal and indeterminate in law, sovereignty could be restored not for the sake of "decision" alone, but for reasons Hobbes too advanced: outside its boundaries—in the state of nature—the laws of nature are not binding. By 1938, the original meaning of the state had been neutralized, and the content of its concepts emptied. It was as a technical apparatus

> the "milieu" of the metropolis [that] activates fantasies about the technical and extrapolates the conception of the state from [that] visionary conception. With the incredible development of the technical means of disseminating communication, information, and weaponry, the power of the state's command mechanism grew in a manner that was astonishing. . . . the exact functioning and the inner precision of modern technology appear to be independent qualities—independent of all religious, metaphysical, juristic, or political considerations or aims. This is obvious to everyone. How futile and fuzzy are theological, juristic or similar arguments. How "clean" and "exact" is the machine in comparison!

As a machine, the state assumes the "truth and value neutrality of a technical instrument."[156] That it was not always so can be demonstrated by the image of Leviathan itself. The symbol evoked God's power, and Hobbes took it from the Book of Job, making of the great fish a "mortal God" at once both the representative-sovereign person and a huge machine. Mechanism, organism, and the work of art are still parts of it, Schmitt writes, "products of the highest human creativity." The image, however, belonged to a mythical world, a premodern magic—not the rationalized world of the modern. In that world, only the state as an irresistible but empty command structure remained. Was Schmitt's interpretation of Hobbes an act of resistance to the Nazi regime, as some have claimed? Perhaps—but it was certainly a justification of his chosen path in 1938, for the state machine cannot be resisted. Even natural law does not require futile sacrifice, a course that would seem to Carl Schmitt, as the war against internal and external enemies began, increasingly senseless. When he wrote *Der Leviathan,* the Nazi state discriminated and excluded, but the "total domination" of the camps lay in the future. The world did not know that "everything is possible."[157] Even Schmitt, who read the circumstances of the time through Hobbes, did not image the total horror possible through the modern Leviathan, only that its command, and therefore his obedience, was total.

4 The Political and Its Theory

The specific political distinction to which political actions and motives can be reduced is that of friend and enemy.
—CARL SCHMITT, *Der Begriff des Politischen*

The middle years of the Weimar Republic had "the appearance of normalcy." *Rentenmark* reforms stabilized the currency and ended the Great Inflation, the Dawes agreement modified the reparation terms of the Versailles treaty, and votes for the antirepublican parties declined in the Reichstag elections of December 1924. Between the beginning and the end of Weimar lay the "golden years" of the German 1920s.[1] After the German revolution, the ideological problem of the new republican constitution was manifest in persistent cabinet instability,[2] a widespread crisis of belief in Weimar's liberal-democratic principles and institutions, a general alienation from the new social order, and far-reaching debate about the central concepts of modern political theory.[3] The intensity of the debate and its immediate relevance to the success of the Republic make this one of the great periods in the history of political thought. Chief among its theoretical concerns was the relation of the state to the law it made, and of the political to the state, a complex of questions ignored by the jurisprudence of the empire, whose approach reflected the dualism of that political system.

The Weimar constitution replaced the German monarchy with a political system based on parties and parliament. This was entirely new: the role of parties after unification in 1871 was held to a minimum through a combination of Bismarck's leadership and the federal arrangement of the

Reichsverfassung, giving Prussia hegemony over the other member states. It was a "restless" empire. Beneath the Wilhelmine order, an expansive new industrial society developed, burgeoning with interest groups and political parties. A vibrant bourgeoisie grew rich and comfortable in Germany's belle epoque as it did in France, and the cities were transformed by the new electrical and chemical industries, as well as the older ones, coal and steel. It was also a period of mass migration, from the farms in Germany's East and South to the industrial core in Berlin and the Ruhr, a mobility made possible by the extraordinary expansion of the railroads.[4] German naval power challenged British supremacy at sea, and the "delayed nation" acquired its first colonies in the imperial race among European Great Powers.[5] Above this newly industrial, urbanized society stood a political and cultural facade and the politics of "notables" in the Second Reich. Constitutional stability in the empire depended on acceptance of Prussian hegemony (dominant in representative institutions, in the executive and bureaucracy), and an antidemocratic elite consensus ("open yet authoritarian"); both elements were guaranteed by a military loyal to the old regime. Its constitution was, as Carl Schmitt later remarked, "a truce" among the parties representing the domestic balance of German states in the 1860s.[6] Its politics were cut to the outlines of "Great Power" questions "as these have ever been: military, foreign and economic policy, and domestic emergency powers."[7]

The constitution said little about the democratic element that found expression in political parties, elections, the public sphere, basic rights, and military conscription. Their formal representation in these institutions was accompanied by direct and populist elements that Max Weber described in 1895 as "Caesarist, not cut from bourgeois wood,"[8] and the relation of friend and enemy that defines Schmitt's concept of the political ran like a red thread through the politics and discourse of the period. Concern with European balance-of-power politics and containment of enemies within the newly unified Reich dominated Bismarck's chancellorship. The Kulturkampf against Catholics and socialists shaped the attitudes of the bourgeoisie toward democracy and colored opinion about the rise of political parties. "Beneath the roof of the constitutional state and the legal categories of the Reich constitution there was a charismatic and populist undercurrent that influenced the variables of power and consensus."[9] The bourgeois elites of this generation sought "a new Caesar to protect them against the rising classes below and against the dynastic powers above."[10]

None of these dramatic transformations found expression in German legal theory, which removed itself from the political culture through statute positivism and the exclusion of "political questions." Its effect, however, was deeply political, preserving the constitutional position of the monarch and the classes represented by him in two respects. National unity, the objective of liberal politics in Germany for more than half a century, had been obtained through war, not through politics. Bismarck's Germany joined the remnants of the Holy Roman Empire to Prussia after victory over France in 1871. His decision for the "small Germany" solution to the national question (unity without the Austrians) emptied the ideas of the Vormärz and of German liberalism itself. The liberal middle classes had their national state, but not political power within it. While the Land constitutions of the mid-nineteenth century contained various bills of rights, the Reich constitution of 1871 did not, and the leading state lawyer, Paul Laband, explicitly rejected the concept of "subjective" rights: "Rights to liberty or basic rights are norms for state power, which the state gives itself; they form limits for administrative authority, they secure for the individual his natural freedom of action within a certain parameter, but they do not establish subjective rights of the citizens. They are not rights because they have no objects."[11] This conception reflected the development of legal thinking about rights since the middle of that century but became untenable in the twentieth-century context of mass democracy—as did its state-centric definition of the political.

Sovereignty, Identity, and Democracy

Der Begriff des Politischen opens with a dramatic reversal of the assumptions of German state law that also acknowledges the new constitutional circumstances of the Republic: "The concept of the state presupposes the concept of the political."[12] Although consideration of the technical difficulties of state theory immediately follows,[13] Schmitt radically opens the standard definition by declaring that "in the decisive case [the state is] the ultimate authority."[14] *Politische Theologie* established this "decisive case" as the sovereign moment, the exception where the norms are suspended, a theory of sovereignty further specified in *Der Begriff des Politischen* as the *political* moment. This theory leads Schmitt to address the state as a *problem* in its democratic constitution, and the consequences of the Republic's entirely new constitutional circumstances for German jurisprudence. Only "radical conceptualization," Schmitt had argued in *Politische Theologie* (1922), can clarify state theory and its jurisprudential definitions.

The problem of form and substance addressed in Schmitt's early work structures his analysis of the Weimar constitution. He rejects methodological formalism on more than logical grounds: by bracketing out political elements in the law and "purifying" it of all such questions, positivists such as Anschütz or Kelsen missed the reality, the substance of the state. Schmitt's vision of that reality emerges dramatically in works from 1919 on, first as a description of the political activism of his times, next as the relationship of what is constituted in the state as "the political unity of the people," then to an intensity with no definite substance.[15] Like Sigmund Freud and the crowd psychologists, Schmitt assumes that human beings are motivated by fundamentally irrational passions and desires that can be governed rationally but never eliminated entirely.

Sovereignty as Constitutional Power

By reversing the usual relationship of norm and exception, sovereignty appears as the decision about the exception, the moment outside the normal in which the political appears. The political in this sense is unpredictable; it is not specified in the state's institutions, or in competition for power within the state. Schmitt's reading of modern European history suggests three loci of the political: (1) the moment of indeterminacy contained in all law, (2) revolution and civil war, and (3) war between states. The political in the first sense appears in the discretionary powers of bureaucracy and legal "gaps" in which elected officials operate. Both are residuals of the freedom inherent in human organizations, the ultimately indeterminate quality of human actions. *Der Begriff des Politischen* and *Verfassungslehre* concentrate on the political as an ever-present possibility in human existence and the sovereign moments in the recent German past and its present. Schmitt's definition of sovereignty transforms its political theory from one located in a person or institution (Hobbes and Bodin) into a moment of existential intervention in a process over which the sovereign in that formal sense does not preside as creator and controller.[16] It is significant that Schmitt does not write a "general theory of the state" *(allgemeine Staatslehre)* in the style of the previous generation, nor is the *Verfassungslehre* a positivist commentary such as Anschütz's *Die Verfassung des Deutschen Reiches.* Instead, it analyzes the empirical elements of "political unity" within a theory of the modern constitution as a type.

Schmitt's dictum that the political is "the distinction of friend and enemy" was formulated simultaneously with the *Verfassungslehre* (1928) and is directly related to it.[17] What *Der Begriff des Politischen* understands as a problem, *Verfassungslehre* attempts to resolve, relating the political to the constitutional, framing them as reflection moves from the simply empirical toward a question about the internal coherence of reality. The intellectual grounds of this argument were laid in Schmitt's criticism of Kant's deontology. There was no more important task for the jurist, he argued, than the development of a position beyond Kantian dualism, a theory that would relate the empirically known to the real and thus remove jurisprudence from the "dead hand of abstraction."[18] This deeper structure can be known, Schmitt argues in agreement with Hegel and Marx, not as a logical structure but in history. That radical epistemology generates Schmitt's sociology as a "radical conceptualization" and his critical theory of politics and institutions.

The *Verfassungslehre* is a theory of constitutional power in relation to the rule of law. After setting out a typology of constitutional theories (absolute, relative, positive, and ideal), Schmitt moves to demonstrate that only the positive theory is a political science of the constitution and its laws. "Every legal order is in some sense a concrete order . . . one in which some individuals rule over and subordinate others,"[19] but in Schmitt's view, this is not just a material analysis of class structure, such as Marx's *Critique of the Philosophy of Right,* and representation is central to creating political unity. Liberalism sought to incorporate that power, but in order to subordinate populism to particular interests: property especially, but also the bourgeois culture of education and "public opinion." This struggle defines the history of nineteenth-century constitutions everywhere on the continent and in Britain during the 1830s.[20] In Germany after 1848 constitutional monarchy was a "dilatory and formal compromise" between two competing representatives of political unity, the people and the king.[21] The liberal assembly at the Paulskirche compromised the political ideas and objectives of the Vormärz and failed to achieve national unity. This dualism (Robert Mohl) meant only that a decision had been postponed: "Within each political unity, there can be only one subject of constitutional power."[22] The real circumstances of such compromises affect their stability, and in Schmitt's analysis, the Reich constitution of 1871 survived only because "favorable political and economic conditions made it possible to ignore the decisive alternative."[23]

Identity

The "fact" of the republican founding did not generate "norms" for Schmitt,[24] but it identified the German people as the real subject of sovereignty. By foregrounding constitutional power, Schmitt can read the theory and reality of the empire critically; the liberal idea of representation survived formally after unification, but in actuality, the Kaiser was not a "constitutional monarch" as nineteenth-century theory presumed, but had recourse to state (executive) power when necessary and thus "remained the subject of constitutional power."[25] The decision might have fallen to the people after 1871, but it did not. Only in November 1918 "did the democratic theory of the constitutional power of the people triumph."

Schmitt's account of the German revolution weaves together representation and direct action to present a political account of events strikingly different from that given by the Reichsgerichtshof in cases arising from the revolution. While it could not be denied, the court said, that a new Reich government had been established on November 10, 1918 (the reference is to Ebert's appointment by Prince Max of Baden), and that this government was based on the power of the workers' and soldiers' councils, and although violence had been used to effect this change, neither could it be denied that there had been little resistance from the "previous Reich authorities." This new government established itself without serious violence and "stayed in power until it freely gave over power to the National Assembly."[26] The thrust of the court's decision was to minimize the revolutionary break and emphasize the continuity of state institutions.

The reality of constitutive power was inscribed in the first article of the Weimar constitution, and even legal positivists acknowledged "the basic decision for democracy."[27] But what kind of democracy, and what kind of constitution—those questions were not answered in the common acceptance of the fact of democracy, and the relation between popular sovereignty and the rule of law was a persistent source of disagreement among constitutional lawyers in the Republic. A single-chamber Reichstag and a strong presidential branch were created by the constitution. The emergency powers of the president in Article 48 were held over from the Reich constitution of 1871 and the 1850 Prussian constitution. Of the two elected branches, only the president was directly chosen by the people; Reichstag members were elected in a complicated system of proportional representation that allowed voters to cast a ballot for a party, but not a person. The parties then selected representatives from their lists; there were no local representatives, in a system that represented parties, not geographic districts. The parties themselves were highly organized, with various associations (men's glee clubs, hiking clubs, women's associations, youth groups), and party allegiance was based on class or religion. There were no *Volksparteien,* parties that recruited across class and religion, before the National Socialists, and democracy in the first and final years of the Republic failed to meet the fundamental requirement for "the government and opposition game": the system included from the start participants and parties that were not loyal without reservation to the government of the day and the military.[28] What had been a logical problem for the constitutional law of the empire became in the Republic an actual one.

Der Begriff des Politischen is most concerned with revolution, war, and civil war as loci of the political, and its emphasis on enmity provokes the most virulent criticisms of Schmitt as reducing politics to war. But this reading unbalances the arguments of these texts, in which "political unity," not antagonism, is the ordering concept. "Enmity" marks the extreme of dissociation that appeared in the revolution and mass movements of the 1920s. The violence in the winter of 1918–1919, when bloody reaction followed revolution, was mirrored in the struggle of parties offering dramatically different Weltanschauungen. *Der Begriff des Politischen* emphasizes the potential fragmentation of political unity, while the *Verfassungslehre* bounds and harnesses its active reality in constitutional power.

This analytic sets democratic elements of the state in opposition to liberal elements; the former are its "political" component, the latter its "legal" *(rechtsstaatliche)*. By considering these in concrete historical instances, their dynamic relation emerges explicitly in the identity of a sovereign people within their constitution and implicit in normal governmental processes. Liberal constitutional theory understands the latter as a delegation of sovereign power; the electorate is seldom, if ever, conceived as potentially revolutionary—capable of retrieving its constitutional power. Schmitt focuses on precisely that experience and possibility.

Democracy

The dilemma of the Weimar constitution turned on the contradiction between representation and identity. The former was the normal governmental type in which the latter appeared as an exception. But if, as Schmitt argued with Rousseau, democracy assumes an identity of governing and governed, where is the democratic component in representative democracy?[29] Schmitt answers with a historical overview of the origins of modern European constitutions. Its dynamic relation to political and national identity overcomes the binaries direct/indirect, democratic/legal, and democratic/representative. The immediate democratic power evidenced in November 1918, like that of France in 1789, was an actual moment of sovereignty that could be preserved only by being constituted. Here "representation" refers to a really existing power, a "fact with normative power." It requires no justification, and its legitimacy cannot be queried. It is the subject from which values and norms derive their existence, a subject that is constantly reproduced through institutions that represent its original substance as an identity: these create "the actual object of modern constitutions, the existential type and form of political unity."[30]

The analysis focuses less on "rights" as the key element in democracy than on identity and its various instances. Although the English Magna Carta is often seen as a precursor to modern constitutions, Schmitt considers it only as an example of English exceptionalism in which a specific class challenged the king and received in return a bill of rights and parliamentary privileges: "The English Parliament appeared in its struggle with the King as the bearer of national, i.e., political unity, while in other European countries it was the absolute prince who achieved political unity in the face of the medieval *Stände.*"[31] The circumstances of English history enabled a smooth transition between a national unity represented by the king and one in which parliament took on that role, Schmitt remarks, but in the continental states, the transition from monarchy to some form of popular representation was more circuitous. Modern political unity was achieved first through princely absolutism. The history of German constitutions in the preceding century is a case in point; before the final dissolution of the Holy Roman Empire of the German nation in 1806, all that remained of a state, Schmitt agrees with Hegel, was "nothing more than the sum of rights which the various Länder had taken from the whole," and their constitutions were nothing more than the guarantee that a "state" no longer existed. Pufendorf described the condition of Germany in the eighteenth century as "abnormal," a "monster," but it was also the perfect example of a Rechtsstaat on the basis of *pacta sunt servanda:* the "constitution" was a conglomerate of treaties, pacts, agreements, capitulations, all of which were legally guaranteed.[32] In the other European states, by contrast, the state as "political status" was sovereign in an absolute sense: its power was undivided, and characteristics of the modern state such as territorial boundaries and impenetrability appear in consequence of this absolutism. The modern state, Schmitt comments with reference to Bodin, also had a "world historical importance in overcoming the legitimacy of the feudal and estate-based constitution.[33]

While these early modern constitutions transformed the fragmented societies of their time, the first constitution to contain the typically modern "mixture of liberal and democratic elements" was the French constitution of 1789.[34] With it the question of *pouvoir constituant* appears. No longer the power of a king, this concept must take account of the multiple subjects who enact it. *Politische Theologie* noted the origins of jurisprudence and state theory in theology and referred the legitimacy of early modern states to their metaphysical foundation in a divinely ordained order. The *modern* state begins with this secularization of the "higher" power and the law. Rousseau's *Social Contract* and the French revolution brought down the heavens, in theory and in fact, transforming the theological grounds of the state and legitimacy. In place of God as the original power there now stood the people. Monotheism had provided the metaphysical basis of the early modern state and its sovereign subject in monarchical constitutions. These were constitutions without the people, and even Hobbes, who recognized that new power in the English Civil War, revised divine right more in method than in substance. The "real unity of them all" remained, as it had been in the later Middle Ages, the figure of kingship, and the liberty of subjects consisted in the silence of the law. Hobbes's civil liberty divided public from private; the subjects of this sovereign could still be free even if the laws under which they live are not made by, but given to, them.[35]

In the French Revolution and its constitution, two distinctive elements are visible, one democratic, the other liberal.[36] The French people demonstrates that it carries the *pouvoir constituant;* it is "aware of its ability to act politically and explicitly affirms its political unity and ability to act and under those conditions gives itself a constitution."[37] Remarkable and definitive of the modern in politics was the self-consciousness of the revolutionary French, who "constituted themselves" in that moment. Another definition followed: the constitutional decision about the type and form of their further political existence. Schmitt holds tightly to the real subject in this analysis, the actual "people" who made themselves a nation. This actual constituting (in revolt and in self-consciousness) precedes the writing of a constitution: "Political existence comes before constitution making" (50).

The second is the liberal rule-of-law element in the new French state after 1789. State power is limited and constrained, giving the French state a new form that replaces the old absolutism of the ancien régime. In this, the political power of the people is clearly visible, an absolute power, Schmitt argues; just as the power of the absolute princes was without bounds, so is that of the people. This produces an "intensification of state power, to the most intense unity and indivisibility" that is then "balanced and limited" in the Rechtsstaat elements of the democratic constitution. However, "all distinctions, divisions, constraints and controls on the state power remain within the boundaries of political unity." The constitutional laws are thus, Schmitt argues, relative, not primary. "The constitution was not a contract between people and prince or among various organizations, but a political decision made by a single and united nation to determine its own fate" (51).

The November revolutionaries created a new state when they destroyed the old Reich, and made visible the constitutional power of the German people. That power was represented first in the Council of Peoples Commissars (the provisional government from November 1918 to February 1919), based on the workers' and soldiers' councils organized in the course of the revolution, and then in the National Assembly. Neither the council nor the assembly, Schmitt argues, were legally bound in any way, and they were provisional governments in the purely democratic meaning of a constitution:

> They were not the subject or bearer of constitutional power, but its representative. Until the promulgation of constitutional law, they were not bound to any law other than those proceeding from the constitutional power of the German people that was expressed in its comprehensive decision about its own political unity. Ultimately they were the single constitutional power of the political unity of the German people. As long as their commission was not completed, they were constitutionally unconstrained. . . . The unique circumstances of this "constitution-giving" assembly that gathered after the revolutionary destruction of the previous constitutional laws can best be described as a "sovereign dictatorship." (59)

The Other and the Political

The opening paragraphs of *Der Begriff des Politischen* tersely assert that the idea of the state has become problematic. Not the state but the political exists independently. As have many political theorists, Schmitt begins with human existence but deduces no content or purpose from it, and man's existence as a conscious and embodied individual is silently assumed here as a "concrete existent" possessing all the qualities of mind associated with time, reason, and the passions. He undertakes no original theory of human nature, nor is there a fundamentally new philosophy. Given Schmitt's purpose, it would have been unnecessary. Every political theory has some vision of the human predicament. Concern for its contingencies marks it, and the reach of its vision can be measured by "revelation of the universal predicament in the local and transitory mischief."[38] Carl Schmitt was by no means a master of political philosophy. But he was a master theorist of the modern state and its difficulties, and one whose vision, if not novel and masterful, included those who were.

Der Begriff des Politischen explicitly assumes consciousness of the other as a concrete and existential given. This "I" implies a "you," and the plural, "we," implies "them" in a structure that draws on Hegel's analysis of consciousness and self-consciousness in the *Phenomenology of Mind*.[39] There the self-consciousness that is primarily a simple existence for self by exclusion of every other and every thing appears for others "in the manner of ordinary objects." But confronted with the "bare, negative fact of self-identical consciousness," each remains conscious of itself only until recognition that "as the other is for it, so it is for the other." In this recognition, self-consciousness shows itself as pure negation, unfettered to any determinate existence, not bound by particularity and "*not* tied up with life." In this process, Hegel argues, the subject discovers that his own and the action of the other aim

> at the destruction and death of the other. . . . The relation of both self-consciousnesses is in this way so constituted that they prove themselves and each other through a life-and-death struggle. . . . And it is only by risking life that freedom is obtained; only thus is it tried and proved that the essential nature of self-consciousness is not bare existence, is not the merely immediate form in which it at first makes its appearance, is not the mere absorption in the expanse of life. . . . The individual who has not staked his life, may, no doubt be recognized as a person; but he has not attained the truth of this recognition as an independent self-consciousness.[40]

Hegel's philosophy moves that moment of recognition toward the relationships of master/slave, but also through need and desire for the other, into moral and ethical relationships from the family to civil society to the state. The existential moment in which the other is recognized by Hegel's subject becomes, through Carl Schmitt's reading, a public moment of the political. "The political enemy need not be morally evil, or aesthetically ugly; he need not appear as an economic competitor and it can even seem useful to do business with him. He is the other, the stranger whose essence it is that in cases of conflict he means the negation of one's own kind of existence and therefore will be resisted or fought in order to preserve one's own way of life."[41]

Much later, in a postscript to the reprint of *Land und Meer* (1942), "a world historical reflection" told to his daughter Anima, Schmitt refers the "attentive reader" to paragraph 247 of *The Philosophy of Right*. He intended in *Land und Meer* to develop Hegel's thought in that paragraph, as Marx had developed the ideas of paragraphs 243–46. The theme is bourgeois security versus the political life, already the subject of Schmitt's earlier work. In *Die geistesgeschichtliche Lage des heutigen Parlamentarismus*, what is "new and fascinating" about *The Communist Manifesto* was "the systematic concentration of class struggle into a single final struggle of human history, into the dialectical peak of tension between the bourgeoisie and proletariat."[42] By contrast with Marx's vision of final, decisive struggle, contemporary liberalism avoids all finality. Discussion in the liberal system of representation is romantic, an "endless conversation," because, as a political doctrine, it avoids decision. This is the "metaphysical" ground of the liberal system of individual rights and freedoms, that there should not be a decision that ends discussion. Instead all questions are endlessly considered and discussed in a consequential system of balancing and dividing. Faced with the question "Christ or Barabbas?" the liberal bourgeoisie either adjourns or appoints a committee to consider the question.[43] By contrast, representation "in Hegel's system is the self-development of consciousness out of positions and negations to always new syntheses."[44] *Politische Theologie* and *Die geistesgeschichtliche Lage des heutigen Parlamentarismus* present liberalism as a culture of willful evasion that culminates in escape from the most important decision, the political distinction of friend and enemy. Schmitt's reference to Hegel authorizes this perspective. In *The Philosophy of Right,* paragraph 247, Hegel contrasts the "pursuit of gain" characteristic of the bourgeois to "industry," which, when exposed to danger, rises above it. As the earth, "the *firm* and solid ground," is the precondition of the principle of family life, so "is the *sea* the natural element for industry": "for the ties of the soil and the limited circles of civil life with its pleasures and desires, [the sea] substitutes the element of fluidity, danger, and destruction." Seagoing, Hegel concludes, gives industry its world historical significance. Not comfort and pleasure but risk and danger, not the bourgeois but the political life, Schmitt means to say by invoking Hegel, make human existence significant. Against the world historical view that he claims for himself, Schmitt contrasts the Marxist concern (par. 243–46) for welfare, "a certain standard of living" for the large mass of people who are denied, Marx would say in unison with Hegel, the mediation of work and thus "the feeling of self-sufficiency and honor" characteristic of the bourgeoisie. Marxism makes of the bourgeois a caricature for Baudelaire or Murgur's *Bohème,* a world historical figure "by means of Hegelian dialectic." Dialectic intensifies "all the emotions of hatred and contempt," and in the conflict of proletariat and bourgeoisie, it becomes "the last representative of a prehistorical humanity . . . the very last enemy of mankind."[45]

The Criterion of the Political

Der Begriff des Politischen assumes that realms of human activity are constituted by specific distinctions. In morality, these are good/evil; in aesthetics, beautiful/ugly; in economics, profitable/unprofitable. "The specific political distinction to which all political actions can be reduced is that between friend and enemy." None of the life spheres are necessarily related, but they may be so contingently.[46] That psychology and ordinary language often associate the enemy with the ugly or evil or unprofitable changes nothing, Schmitt remarks, and the possibility of separating this negation from all others proves its objectivity and independence. It is neither normative, nor an intellectual contradiction, but a given reality. Every normative or intellectual position has its friends and enemies, even liberalism,[47] which tends to mix political and other distinctions. Its enemies are conceived as economic competitors or as opponents in a discussion, and its polemic brands the other as morally inferior, or the political as immoral.[48] By excluding such normative judgments, Schmitt intends to refute liberalism. Whether someday there will be no enemies, whether it is advisable to educate people away from thinking in those terms—this is beside the point. What matters is that "today this is a real contradiction and confronts every people that exists politically."

There is no definition of "politics" such as those found in many other works. For Schmitt, it is not necessarily about anything substantive, and it is sufficient to distinguish between friend and enemy—recognition of the real existence of a friendship community and of the real possibility of war (26). The latter is the most intense case of dissociation, the former of association in the political sense. Between these, a variety of associations and dissociations appear. A polity does not constantly face the question "friend or enemy?" nor does it mean that political existence is nothing but bloody war. Schmitt does not idealize war, nor does struggle appear as a virtue: "War is just the extreme realization of enmity. It need not be a common occurrence, nor something normal, neither must it be an ideal or something to be longed for; but it must persist as a real possibility, if the concept of an enemy is to retain meaning" (34). The primary meaning of the political is given in the possibility of war, and from that "most extreme point" of enmity, Schmitt distinguishes political actions according to their intensity. The primary form of the friend/enemy decision is made by "the state as an organized political entity" *for itself*. This decision cannot be delegated or abrogated.[49] What one normally thinks of as politics—the maneuvers and tactics of parties and politicians in parliament or dirty business, influence peddling, or logrolling—are secondary forms. Finally there are forms of politics so banal that they seem a "parasite and caricature configuration" in which there is only "some sort of antagonistic moment that manifests itself in all sorts of tactics and intrigues."[50] All these reflect the ordinary language use of "politics" to mean "polemic."

In *Der Begriff des Politischen* Schmitt establishes the political as (1) an intensity of identity/negation, the friend/enemy distinction; (2) an independent sphere; and (3) one without any necessary content. The political is not *for* or *about* anything, not determined before it appears, but always concrete and existential. Only the subject can recognize the political and decide who is the enemy. But who is this subject? On one reading, there is none. Ernst-Wolfgang Böckenförde correctly notes that the friend/enemy distinction is a phenomenal criterion not of politics or the individual but of an aggregate condition, "the political." It is a reference point of the state and of political prudence; sound judgment and appropriate action necessarily have the extreme case *(Ernstfall)* in perspective.

Schmitt qualifies this aggregate by reference to "the public." The distinction between a "private opponent, whom one might dislike personally," and the "public enemy" *(öffentliche Feind)* of an entire people already appears in the first version of the text, and Schmitt comments that most languages, including German, do not distinguish clearly between the private and public enemy. The scriptural verse "love thy enemies" (Matt. 5:44 and Luke 6:27), accurately understood, means "love thy *private* enemy": "it does not mean the political enemy."[51] In 1927 Schmitt already used the Latin words *hostis* and *inimicus* to distinguish between the two conceptions, public and private, and in subsequent versions that distinction is made more forcefully in references to the digests of Roman Law and Plato's *Republic,* and the history of Christian crusades. The latter suggests the political theological underpinning of the text and introduces the extreme case of war elaborated in *The Philosophy of Right.* There Hegel referred recognition of the other to life-and-death struggle and the risk of self. In *The Philosophy of Right,* the individual has "a substantial duty" to the state that must include sacrifice. Here as in the *Phenomenology,* this duty recognizes risk, death, and war as ethical moments that demonstrate the ultimate seriousness of life: "War is that condition in which the vanity of temporal things and temporal goods—which tends at other times to be merely a pious phrase—takes on a serious significance."[52]

The mood and structure of *Der Begriff des Politischen* reflect a political temperament and expressionist style at odds with Schmitt's insistence on the amoral, empirical character of the political and with his frequent claim of objectivity. One cannot reasonably deny, he writes, that "even today the nations are divided by the friend/enemy antithesis, that it remains actual today and is an ever present possibility for every people that exists politically."[53] This is not an evaluation, he maintains, but a "simple fact," a reality—this is how the political world organizes itself, which only the foolish ignore. The crucial passages in section 3 of the 1927 and 1932 texts present the political as an existential criterion—the real possibility of killing. It is about life and death. But *Kampf*—struggle, fighting, battle—is not an ideal sought through politics, and the most extreme form of struggle, war, is not "a mere instrument of politics" (Clausewitz) or its goal and purpose. Rather, war is the reference point for the politically serious, "an ever present possibility that determines human conduct in a specific way and gives it political significance." Politics can aim to avoid war, and Schmitt asserts emphatically that "the definition of the political given here is neither militaristic nor imperialistic nor pacifistic."[54] A series of "not-that" statements specify it further. The political is not an everyday relation, nor is it the normal; it is not an ideal, and it is not the constant confrontation of one people by another. The question "friend or enemy?" is not asked all the time, and there is no sense in which a nation is the "eternal enemy" of another, an ironic rejection of the nationalist cliché "France, the hereditary enemy" (*Erbfeind Frankreich*). The central elements of the political can be found in this important section of the text. The friend/enemy distinction is (1) public, (2) collective, (3) an affair of sovereignty, (4) real, (5) a matter of combat and killing, (6) a constant possibility, not a constant occurrence; and finally, "the political" is a criterion, not a substantive definition. It is a quantitative, not a qualitative, factor of human life, measured in the intensity of association and dissociation.

Of State and the Political, War and the Enemy

The first "crisis of the state" was, for Carl Schmitt, the critical position of the German Reich under the Versailles treaty that had made it "an object of the politics" of other European states.[55] Threatened by internal rebellion and separatism, carrying a heavy burden of war reparations, Germany was not only a "debtor nation" but also an "outlaw" state. The terms of peace limited German sovereignty as punishment for the Great War, and French policy actively sought division of its western territories from the Reich. Schmitt's critique of liberalism and liberal state theory starts with a polemic against the ideology of "national self-determination" and "freedom" that cloaked Allied policy toward his own country, and seemed to prove the criterion of the political as a decision on the exception. Liberal proclamations asserted those rights and liberties—but not for Germany and the Germans, who were not "enemies" in Schmitt's sense but something worse: an "outlaw" nation without rights.[56]

The argument of *Der Begriff des Politischen* was the culmination of a view about Germany's position under the Versailles treaty that Schmitt developed in the middle years of the Republic, often in a party-political context, but also in lectures and seminars at the University of Bonn. One of these, "The Rhineland as an Object of International Politics" (1924), was originally delivered as an address to the Center Party in Cologne on April 14, 1925. When it appeared in print, the lecture was renamed "On the Fate of the Political."[57] Although sketchy, this article makes a claim that would be expanded in *Der Begriff des Politischen* and *Verfassungslehre:* "the state is a political unity, and the decisive unity rests on its political character."[58] The crucial aspect of "political unity" for Schmitt in 1925 (and still in 1927) derived from international politics and not only the possibility of war but the reality of the Republic's limited sovereignty. Later versions refine this perspective to emphasize the existential question of whether a state can defend its people's "own proper way of life" from subordination to others, and ultimately extinction. Schmitt's publications and lectures at Bonn, where he accepted a chair in 1922, reflect his varied interests in constitutional law, political theory, international law, and political economy. In the academic years 1924–25 and 1925–26, Schmitt and his colleague Erich Kaufmann traded lecture duties, with Kaufmann (a specialist in international law) lecturing on the Weimar constitution and Schmitt taking over International Law.[59] During 1925–26 he offered a seminar called "*Homo economicus* and Politics" and, in summer semester 1927, one directly related to the development of *The Concept of the Political,* "The Unity and Impenetrability of the State" (Einheit und Undurchdringbarkeit des Staates). From 1921 onward, "democracy and the state" are constant themes in his work, concerns linked in *Der Begriff des Politischen* through his analysis of the state's internal and external political unity.

The first (and subsequent) versions of the text introduce the concept of unity via the friend/enemy criterion as the necessary basis of a constitution and a political response to "the real possibility of conflict." The state is "the decisive unity" in which its members are commanded to kill and be killed. During the Republic, Schmitt still thought of this as an authority belonging only to the state, its *jus belli:* "the real possibility that on the basis of its own decision in a given case the enemy is identified and resisted."[60] This command is *independent* of other states, based on an independent decision about an existential threat to the state as constituted, and cannot be delegated to another state or suprastate organization. When it is, that state ceases and becomes a proxy for the power of a real state. New military technologies appear to have reduced the sovereignty of the state; only a few states can now wage war with any prospect of success:

"smaller nations must freely or by necessity try to maintain their independence through the politics of advantageous alliances." This argument was applied to the major foreign policy questions of the mid-1920s: the Rhineland and the Balkans, the League of Nations and the Treaty of Versailles, and in a critical defense of *raison d'état* against Meinecke's *Idee der Staatsräson* (1925). Schmitt's harsh analysis of the League of Nations, *Die Kernfrage des Völkerbundes* (1924 and 1926), coldly rejects the optimistic expectation about the League expressed by Hans Wehberg that it is "an association of peoples, not of governments."[61] Elements of that argument appear later in *Der Begriff des Politischen.*

Die Kernfrage des Völkerbundes follows Bodin, defining the marks of an institution in its social function and power. As Bodin removed theology from questions about secular authority, enabling one to see the state in early modern Europe as a social order, so Schmitt will remove the pieties of liberalism. Allied hegemony over defeated Germany was the primary source of Weimar's domestic crisis, which the major foreign policy questions of the Republic's middle years intensified. The demilitarized Rhineland and Germany's exclusion from the League of Nations were threats to German territorial integrity and unity,[62] the classic locus of realist state theory: as the preservation of a state's territory from external intervention and the domination of other states; and the primacy of foreign policy, especially the pursuit of self-interest in international relations.

Germany's international weaknesses are presented in *Die Kernfrage des Völkerbundes* as more than just defeat in war. Attention to the "higher values" of liberal imperialism and its radical conceptualization frame this text of political realism. The Versailles treaty and the Weimar constitution of 1919 are artifacts of a thoroughgoing metaphysical transformation: with the destruction of the German empire and the breakup of the Austro-Hungarian empire, liberalism is established in Europe as the only political system. It is, he comments, "an astonishingly consequential system."[63] Liberal hegemony is significantly challenged only by communism, which alone among contemporary ideologies confronts it with the instruments of class warfare.[64] This conflict between liberalism as "Americanism" was immediately apparent, Schmitt argues, in Wilson's policy toward the civilian population in Germany by making assistance dependent on a communist government not coming to power. The resulting market economy and liberal constitution were not an American *diktat* but the decision of Weimar's constitutional fathers as representatives of the German people. Should the *Rätebewegung* succeed, Hugo Preuß wrote in November 1918, there would be "Bolshevist terror" in Germany as there had been in Russia.[65] Such an "upside-down authoritarian state" would foreclose Germany's political development and exclude the German middle classes from participation in government. German self-determination and preservation of a unified national state were embedded in the Weimar constitution from the outset, which Schmitt formulated as the question of constitutional power in the *Verfassungslehre.*

Liberal Imperialism

Allied policy at Versailles broke with nineteenth-century practices of annexation and imperialism only in style, not in substance. Earlier methods of conquest and incorporation were replaced by others in which the fact of domination is itself denied. Versailles and the policy statements of the Allies after 1919 obscure their political ends, presenting these as neutral administrative measures or as instances of freedom and self-determination. Those key words of liberal ideology suggest that "no people could be the object of international politics" and that "every people is now the subject of its own political and state existence."[66]

However, the foreign policies of England toward Egypt, the United States toward the Caribbean, and France in the Middle East demonstrate that the Great Powers continue to exercise control over the internal and external policies in those places. After the end of England's mandate over Egypt in 1922, and its declaration as a free and sovereign state, the British retain their control through prerogatives to protect the Suez Canal, to defend Egypt against foreign threats, to protect foreign interests there, and to take measures necessary for the colonial administration of the Sudan. Such "intervention rights" allow the intervening power, Schmitt argues, to decide the meaning of "concepts such as protection of foreign interests, defense of independence, public order and other indefinite, but crucial aspects in the political existence" for the subjected country. What interest do the Great Powers have in this new form of domination? Primarily that no "legal consequences," such as the extension of citizenship to colonial peoples, follow from their domination.[67]

These new world politics cause core ideas in modern political theory (freedom, independence, sovereignty, self-determination) to "lose their meaning." Those under liberal domination have less protection than foreigners. Although these territories have been declared "sovereign states," their natural resources remain available for exploitation through a set of treaties and international organizations such as the League.[68] It is even suggested by its proponents that the League is an association not of states but of peoples. Such generalizations, Schmitt argues, permit the League's proponents to claim a universalism and federalism for it that contradicts its statutory definition, as even they understand it.[69] Its text begins with a clear identification of its subject: not the "idea" of a league of nations but a specific institution is the subject. *Die Kernfrage des Völkerbundes* and other articles on international issues and on Weimar's institutional problems challenge the legitimacy of liberal institutions with the same argument: their theories are not their reality.[70] The problems of the state among other states, the state at war and in crisis, link sovereignty to *Der Begriff des Politischen* and indicate how intimately Schmitt's thinking about the political developed through the experience of war and its aftermath for Germany.

Excursus: Kerensky and Lenin

Der Begriff des Politischen carries the following dedication: "In memory of my friend, August Schaetz of Munich, who fell on August 28, 1917, in the storming of Moncelul." The engagement in which Schmitt's friend fell occurred in what Churchill called "the unknown war,"[71] the war on the eastern front. By the time Schaetz was killed, the February Revolution had overthrown the czar. In the summer of 1917, Russia's provisional government formulated an aggressive plan to confront the German armies along the southern part of the front that stretched from the Baltic to the Black Sea. They were initially successful, but the better-equipped and more mobile Germans counterattacked with a relentless shelling of Russian emplacements and broke through their lines on July 19. Disillusioned and angry about political events at home, Russian soldiers mutinied and began to desert.

After a lull, German forces in an area southeast of the Siebenbürgen in the Transylvanian Alps were attacked on July 22 outside Focsani by a combined force of Russians and Rumanians. General August von Mackensen counterattacked but could not break the enemy. Just west of Focsani, both sides dug into trenches in an area the Slavs called Muncelul. Fighting had been heavy for nearly a month when on August 28, 1917, Schaetz's Bavarian regiment again stormed the Rumanian lines in a failed attempt to break through. Schaetz fell as he went over the top toward the enemy.[72]

Only a few weeks remained for the Russians in the Great War. Kerensky's plan failed in every respect. It was an attempt more to secure Allied finance for the provisional Russian government than to break the Germans. Heavily indebted and dependent on foreign capital, Kerensky and others in the provisional government were pressed on both sides: by reactionary interests that profited from the war and by the Marxist Left. For different reasons, both wanted to keep the peasants who made up the bulk of Russia's army at the front. The counteroffensive that summer was a ploy, part of the domestic intrigues preceding the October Revolution.[73]

Ten years almost to the day August Schaetz fell, Schmitt was writing the lecture that would become *The Concept of the Political.* That the Great War was the formative event of Carl Schmitt's political thought is evidenced in the work's dedication, and the centrality of war to its argument.[74] The state at war and the domestic and international predicament of the Germans after 1918 occupy the immediate perspective of *Der Begriff des Politischen*—its larger horizon, political modernity itself.[75]

Days after the revolution of 1918, Hugo Preuß described the political choice facing Germany thus: "Either Wilson or Lenin, either the democracy that developed out of the French and American revolutions or the brutal form of Russian fanaticism. One must choose."[76] Preuß, the father of the Weimar constitution, grasped the predicament clearly, and his "either/or" in this historical moment helped defeat bolshevism in Germany after the Great War. This article for the *Berliner Tageblatt* on Armistice Day was "one of the most important documents in German constitutional history."[77] Preuß opted for Wilson and the West, but for Schmitt, that was only a superficial alternative to Lenin. Kerensky embodied liberal indecision when faced with "the decisive case" of political survival that haunted Schmitt throughout the Weimar Republic. As the situation at home and on the front moved toward disaster, Kerensky and others in the interim regime hesitated, reacted, and failed to master the moment. As the Bolsheviks gained influence over Russian troops, Kerensky feared both a revolution and a German offensive, and like many others in the government, he placed all his hope in a successful offensive. Early on they pledged "peace without annexations or contributions." The German government largely ignored these feelers. With Ludendorff poised to invade Russia, the provisional government in Russia left power with the generals. On the home front, they hoped that bankers and industrialists could keep the economy from collapse. Mensheviks "found themselves striving to suggest to their followers that they should obey the prescriptions of a regime that they had themselves been elected to repudiate."[78] After the fall of Nicholas, Kerensky became minister of war, not because he was expert in military matters but because he appealed to the masses of peasants and ordinary people who made up most of the army. Elected to the Duma and to the Soviet council, Kerensky tried to play on both sides, appearing as a revolutionary in one place and as a parliamentary operative in the other. By May 1917, he thought that Russia must either "accept the consequences of a virtual demobilization of the Russian army and capitulate to Germany, or assume the initiative in military operations."[79] Kerensky urged General Brusilov to attack and, acting against the advice of his field commanders, formulated a plan. In the course of its execution, Schmitt's friend August Schaetz was killed.

If Kerensky stood for everything Schmitt despised about liberalism—its half measures, its contradictions, its compromises, its pallid vision—in Lenin he saw the embodiment of the *Weltgeist.* After 1840, "Hegel wandered to Moscow via Karl Marx and Lenin," he wrote in *Der Begriff des Politischen.* Lenin and Russian bolshevism transformed the dialectic into "a new concrete-enemy concept . . . the international class enemy." Through Lenin, everything in Western political thought, everything in the theory of the state, was transformed into "weapons in the battle with this enemy."[80] Hegel's definition of the enemy, Schmitt remarks in that context, is "a negated otherness." The relation of enemies is mutual negation, and each has its own existence; but their relation carries the danger of war. Quoting Hegel's *Natural Law,* Schmitt writes, "This war is not a war of families against families, but between peoples, and hatred becomes thereby undifferentiated and freed from all particular personality."[81] Lenin's theory of imperialism and his understanding of classes make the role of the state in Hegel's philosophy of history appear outdated. It is not states that act in history but classes, according to Lenin. In this Aufhebung the dialectic of the other reveals itself inside and outside the state's boundaries. War, the political, and illegality are all instruments of a struggle that transcends the limitations of state or national boundaries. If the enemy is a class enemy, he must be confronted and destroyed wherever he appears. This is the seriousness of the political. Unlike Kerensky and the liberals of the German republic, who ultimately shared the Russians' fate, Lenin was ruthless. Persons "who think of politics as small tricks which sometimes border on deceit must be decisively refuted. Classes cannot be deceived."[82]

Democratic Wars

The Great War was the first of the "total wars" of the past century in which entire societies and all their productive powers were mobilized to defeat an enemy. It was a war conducted with the instrumental rationality of cost-benefit analysis. War economics were "maximum slaughter at minimum expense," as Bertrand Russell once said, and while analysis of the war economies of the combatant states reveals their isolation from the actual business of killing, the ultimate objective was "slaughter of the enemy."[83] Still, in this war, all the states involved ran their war making as businesses, through the free market; everything used—materials and weapons—had to be paid for, a fact that led John Maynard Keynes to predict confidently to Beatrice Webb in August 1914 that "the war could not possibly last for more than a year." The world, she noted in her diary, "was enormously rich, but its wealth was, fortunately, of a kind that could not rapidly be used for war purposes: it was in the form of capital equipment for making things that were useless for making war. When all the available wealth was used up—which he thought would take about a year—the Powers would have to make peace."[84] The forecast was off by a factor of three, and while these states did not yet behave as if they *owned* everything (not just their conscripts), they not only financed an extended conflict but *borrowed* on the capital markets to do so. It cost roughly twice as much to win as to lose the Great War. "The Central Powers [Germany, Austria-Hungary, Bulgaria, and Turkey] were significantly more successful at killing, wounding and capturing the enemy than the Entente Powers [Great Britain, the British Empire, France, Russia, Italy, the United States] . . . whereas it cost the Entente powers $36,485.48 to kill a serviceman fighting for the Central Powers, it cost the Central Powers just $11,344.77 to kill a serviceman fighting for the Entente."[85]

As the war bogged down into a conflict of attrition, and those who survived described the entirely new annihilation made possible by poison gas and heavy artillery, one might ask why the armies kept at it so long. Advance over the trenches was suicide, and even when not going over the top, men were vulnerable to machine guns and snipers and to air bombardment. A British officer described losing three-quarters of his company at Passchendaele thus: "Poor old Pepper had gone—hit in the back by a chunk of a shell; twice buried as he lay dying in a hole, his dead body blown up and lost after Willis had carried it back to Vanheule Farm. Ewing hit by machine gun bullets . . . Chalk had been seen to fall riddled with bullets; then he too had been hit by a shell." On the other side of the lines, it was no different. Ernst Jünger described the feeling of being shelled: "It was as if one were tied to a post and threatened by a fellow swinging a sledgehammer. . . . The brain links every separate sound of whirring metal with the idea of death and so the nerves are exposed without protection and without pause to the sense of absolute menace" (340–41). There is no doubt that coercion was one reason men kept fighting in those conditions, but carrots were added to the sticks. Creature comforts (yes, even in the trenches), home leave, drugs (the rum ration), and male bonding—all these kept men going (350–55). They kept fighting, too, because they liked it. Men at war, Freud had argued in "Thoughts for the Times on War and

Death," could reassert all the primitive instincts repressed in society. "In our unconsciousness," he wrote, "we are like primitive man, simply a gang of murderers. . . . Our unconscious is just as murderously inclined toward the stranger, as divided or ambivalent toward the loved, as was man in earliest antiquity. War . . . strips us of the later accretions of civilization and lays bare the primal man in each of us" (357). War, Schmitt would argue, lays bare that primal as the political: "the stranger, the other" is so different that it is possible to kill him. In normal times, we need not think about this possibility—just as we need not think constantly of death—but political prudence necessitates that it not be completely repressed.

For some, higher values motivated sacrifice, whether these were "love surpassing the love of women of one pal for his half section" and the desire not to let down a comrade, or the transcendent values of religious belief in the higher justice of an afterlife.[86] The ecstatic, breaking up the routine of everyday life, also played its part, and Freud's explanation (for all its fall from intellectual fashion) "better explains the readiness of millions of men to spend four and a quarter years killing and being killed" than today's biological behaviorism.[87] Before the war began there was ample evidence of the breaking down of civilization in Freud's sense. Georges Sorel yearned for the cleansing power of violence to break the hypocrisy of bourgeois life in Europe. Men killed themselves from fear that they would not be accepted for military service. The poet Robert Graves superstitiously preserved his own chastity during the war; "by suppressing the sexual impulse, Graves sought to ward off the suicidal one." And for many there was a thrill in battle, "not to be missed" as a shell whizzed by.[88]

After the war Jünger described its horror as a kind of numbness, at once strange and beautiful: "It was a weird sensation to look into those dead and questioning eyes. . . . We had to stare again and again at these things we had never seen before, without being able to give them meaning . . . we walked in a dream through a garden full of strange plants."[89] Killing took on an aesthetic quality: men wanted not just to kill; they wanted to do the job "beautifully." There was also a violent hatred of the enemy—Germans were "unutterable vermin"—and a gradual detachment from any moral compunction.[90]

The scope of the Great War, its comprehensive inclusion of all members of the state, was the most democratic experience of all. Far from ensuring peace, democracy made possible the total mobilization of men in a war that was more the product of European imperialism than an existential necessity. In *Der Begriff des Politischen,* Schmitt compares the international law and practice of limited war, fought only when necessary to preserve a nation's own existence against this total war and enmity

(Feindschaft) to the old state system. Those gave the enemy a certain standing in the *jus publicum Europaeum,* in contrast to the total mobilization of the Great War. But his iteration of this older law of nations would be hollowed out by the practices of states after 1918. Demobilization was a temporary phenomenon, soon giving way in the interwar period to continuous mobilization. That did not cease, Ernst Jünger argued in 1930, with the Armistice but became possible through the technologies of mass culture and in the reality of state policy. A total mobilization of social energies can only be achieved "when the image of war is prefigured in the condition of peace." In the postwar period, "new methods of armament are already designed for a total mobilization," and "not only the attack, but *defense* demands the most extraordinary efforts." It followed for Jünger that "individual freedom" was significantly limited; "there should be nothing that cannot be understood as a function of the state."[91]

The Storm of the Political

In the last year of peace before the outbreak of World War II, Schmitt expanded on Jünger's argument, drawing specific conclusions about the character of wars in a fascist age. The fascist theory of the "total state" yields "total war," a conceptual pair that expands the argument of *Der Begriff des Politischen* to the triad "total enemy—total war—total state."[92] That Schmitt could write on this subject a year after attacks on him in the SS journal *Das Schwarze Korps* indicates the ambiguity of his position in the Third Reich, and the argument is a nuanced acceptance of the fact that fascist wars will be total. Such wars will be characterized by the following: (1) every reserve will be applied to the fullest extent; (2) geographic position and war technology may determine the particular effect of total war;[93] (3) the character of the war may change in its course, and the will to fight can ebb or, as in the Great War, increase; (4) total war may be developed in conjunction with new methods of "total opposition and trials of strength." These "intermediate stages" of war, as evidenced by the examples of Corfu (1923), Japan-China (1932), the League of Nations' use of economic sanctions against Italy (1935), and intervention by Great Powers in civil wars (Spain, 1935–36), are attempts to mitigate the risks inherent in the possibility of total war, which "everyone wants to avoid."[94] Before the twentieth century, only Britain, as the dominant sea power, could make total war, and Schmitt derives the tactics of total war from the English model.[95]

In this passage, Schmitt's original conception of enmity as hostis, with its appeal to limited war and honorable treatment of the opponent, breaks down completely. Air power, he argues, will soon effect a total "three-dimensional" war—war at sea, on land, and in the air—that will completely destroy the remnants of limited war. Schmitt's radical conceptualization of this new total war acknowledges two aspects of European fascism, whose political theology sets the soldier in the center as an instrument not of religion (as in the sixteenth century) but of the economy: "The economy stamps itself into total war, which it makes possible, and turns war into an instrument of power elites." The soldier of these wars will be, moreover, a figure who embodies the extreme of the common man, "the expression of *völkisch* identity."[96] The liberal-democratic constitution of a political unity that had been Schmitt's theme in the *Verfassungslehre* appears here as the result of the "Versailles diktat . . . down to its last roots a foreign thing imported from England, directly or via France and Belgium."[97]

This reversal of Schmitt's understanding in 1927 of the democratic sovereign as a constitutional power startles and unsettles. The reality of total war from 1939 to 1945 was preceded, however, by a populist enthusiasm missing from the Republic, which Schmitt on the afternoon of January 30, 1933, had so bitterly regretted. The Nazis crushed every element of representation that was indirect and rational—parties, interest groups, elections. What was left was acclamation and referenda and the myth of unitary representation possible in one man. The age of "state wars" was a wonder of political order, Schmitt wrote after World War II, in which war was a matter exclusively of states and the arts of war products of human reason. The result, he wrote in 1950, was that no wars of extermination were fought in Europe during that period.[98] That this was possible, Schmitt's philosophy of history implies, was not due to human will alone, and this aspect of his political theory is the most radical rejection of Kantian dualism in the invocation of a Providence that brings forth the dialectic of opposites which is reality.

Nearly a decade before *Der Begriff des Politischen*, in *Die geistesgeschichtliche Lage des heutigen Parlamentarismus* (1923), the dialectic had been "an important intellectual factor," but "only an intellectual instrument for what is really no longer a rationalist impulse." In *Der Begriff des Politischen* communism appears as the authentic version of Hegel's dialectic. Enlightenment philosophy taught that the other (the irrational) should be educated—this is the meaning of Fichte's "educational dictatorship"—but in Marxism, "the bourgeois is not to be educated, but eliminated." Its material philosophy sees every intellectual discovery, all ideas, as secondary to a deeper, more vital "course of events." Schmitt understands "the absolute rationalism" of the Enlightenment as a kind of "force," against which another more direct force arose, not as a philosophical position but as a *political* position. Marxism acts directly against the "relative rationalism" of liberal political theory, attacking the rational foundations of parliamentary government and its democratic elements: "As Trotsky justly reminded the democrat Kautsky, the awareness of relative truths never gives one the courage to use force and to spill blood."[99]

The essence of contemporary politics in Schmitt's view was such confrontation between men who see the world in relative terms by those who are absolutely certain of their own truth. "It is a matter of life and death. Marx understood his enemy—the bourgeois liberal—better than he understood himself."[100]

By the time Joseph Goebbels spoke to a carefully selected audience at the Berlin Sports Palace on February 18, 1943, Europe had already experienced total war for nearly four years. The Germans were now asked to mandate an even more total war that erased the distinction between civilian populations and combatants entirely: "We enter thereby the path of final victory. . . . Now let the nation rise and the storm break!"[101] For the Allies too, total victory in a total war had become the goal. Nearly two and a half years would pass before Goebbels's final victory turned to total defeat.

Conclusion

The essence of the political is *more than* the struggle of powers for domination, Schmitt had argued in 1924, but he left this "more than" undefined.[102] *Politische Theologie* supplied the conceptual framework of Schmitt's work in the 1920s, not as a normative structure but as an increasingly radical rejection of legal formalism and statute positivism. What mattered in Weimar was not the constitutional document so much as the search for the real political forces that informed it, giving its provisions their immediate and concrete meaning—and the possibility of governing those for the sake of Germany's self-preservation. At stake was neither a norm nor logic:

> About an abstract concept there will in general be no argument, least of all in the history of sovereignty. What is argued about is the concrete application, and that means who decides in a situation of conflict what constitutes the public interest or interest of the state, public safety and order, *le salut public,* and so on. The exception, which is not codified in the existing legal order, can at best be characterized as a case of extreme peril, a danger to the existence of the state, or the like. But it cannot be circumscribed factually and made to conform to a preformed law. It is precisely the exception that makes relevant the subject of sovereignty, that is the whole question of sovereignty.[103]

This description is evidence that Schmitt still thought in terms of the state and its order. But the sovereign moment was also revelatory and therefore capable of transforming the empirical.

Schmitt and Kelsen agreed that law must work within a structure of norms, but for Kelsen, legal norms were self-justifying, while for Schmitt they required a political reality. He brought this into the center of jurisprudence in the question of legitimacy. The "hard case" could be found in moments when there *were* no rules to govern a case but only its decision, a perception that appears in Schmitt's earliest work. In *Gesetz und Urteil* (1914), Schmitt struggled with the principle of legal determinism as the question of how a judge can be bound to the law and independent and answered in technical-rational terms. *Der Wert des Staates* (1916) developed that problem in larger terms. The state is valuable because its power makes law "predictable," creating bonds in the ordinary law. Before 1914, the question had been academic. Afterward it was not. The space of the exceptional expanded in Schmitt's political theory until it became the most important reality. In *Politische Theologie* he asserted that "all law is situational," a phrase repeated in *Die Kernfrage des Völkerbundes:* "No law is valid in a vacuum, all law is situational."[104]

The international conflicts of intrawar Europe, like the domestic crises of the Republic, left both "lawless" in those terms. If peace, security, and order were goods sought from the state, neither its domestic nor external reality achieved that goal. The criteria of a "genuine federation resides in a minimum of security and homogeneity" that the League of Nations fails to meet. The "central question" referred to in Schmitt's title issues from that fact: "The problem of its legitimacy in international law is the central question of the League of Nations." This in turn arises from problems that Schmitt would make the core of his analysis of Weimar's constitution as it failed in 1932, legality and legitimacy.[105]

5 Constitutional Theory

A concept of the constitution is only possible if one distinguishes between constitutional laws and the constitution.
—CARL SCHMITT, *Verfassungslehre*

The years from 1929 to 1933 were decisive for the Weimar Republic, and Schmitt's constitutional theory framed his response to them. The *Verfassungslehre* (1928) was unlike any contemporary work on the Weimar constitution. Its analytic power and persuasion came from the fact that it was not an interpretation of that one constitution, nor was it a general theory of the state, but a political science of the dominant constitutional type of the twentieth century, the *bürgerliche Rechtsstaat*. In the transitory mischief of the 1920s, the crisis of parliamentary democracy manifested itself in polyarchy and antagonistic pluralism. The theoretically sovereign demos that had "given itself this constitution" confronted an array of special interests and vested minorities.[1] A shorthand of the Republic's immediate problems records them as the failure of proportional representation and the corruption of executive privileges. They were more than that, but the crises that opened and ended Weimar lent themselves to an understanding in which the presidential powers of Article 48 at first seemed the only hope of saving the new constitution and at last the cause of its downfall.

Exceptional Times

The end of normalcy began with "Black Friday" on the New York Stock Exchange. The collapse of American stock values on October 25, 1929, affected all the European markets, but in Germany it led to a crisis of the state. Before the crash, a now familiar politics of expanding state services in response to voter demand had appeared. Two of the parties most committed to the Republic, the SPD and the Catholic Center, were also committed to moderating capitalism through various social and welfare provisions. It was a politics that economic science seemed to justify. The modern state had so thoroughly "organized" capitalism, Rudolf Hilferding declared to party members at the SPD congress in 1927, that socialism was no longer about changing the economy but about winning elections. The point was not "class struggle" but voter turnout. As society organized itself more completely through the state, justice would be achieved by reform and redistribution, not revolution. Hilferding was not the only optimist. The economist Bernard Harms explained in a 1928 lecture that the world's economic system had attained such stability that there could be no serious crises in the foreseeable future. Government and economy, so was the contemporary sentiment, could be steered toward any goal: "even if we cannot bring the stars down to earth," Harms declared, "at least we shall try."[2]

The optimism seemed warranted at first. The elections of May 1928 "relegated the Nazis to the status of a minor curiosity on the radical fringes of German politics" and gave the country its first SPD chancellor since 1923. Hermann Müller was able to form a broad-based coalition after an election that one contemporary called a positive plebiscite on the republican form of government by the German people.[3] Yet there were signs of fragmentation. The radical parties retained their share of the vote nationally and even gained in the provincial parliaments, while the liberal parties (DVP and DDP) seemed to lose appeal among the middle classes, a decline exploited by the DNVP. In 1928, German voters were "turning increasingly away from both liberalism and conservatism toward special interest alternatives." Splinter parties outpolled the two liberal parties and almost matched the conservatives, with the result that the "Reichstag election of 1928 reflected a fundamental breakdown of voter identification with the traditional parties of the bourgeois center and right."[4]

When the unexpected happened, crisis replaced optimism. The radicalization of German politics after 1929 has been a central topic of political history since Hitler came to power. No single factor, no individual's action, explains the triumph of "the Bavarian lance-corporal," but the failure of the elected and appointed governments to master the effects of the depression must surely be a key to the constitution's failure. And the important happenstance of persons in places of crucial importance who were unable—whether by accident or willful intent—to sail the ship of state past its final shoals should never be ignored. The Federalists wanted a constitution that would survive those in power, and it is the happy story of American constitutional history that, by and large, they got it. The same cannot be said of the Germans—and had the Americans tried to write their own document in those circumstances, they might not have succeeded nearly so well.

Total industrial production remained steady in 1929 but fell sharply in the following three years.[5] Real wages increased slightly in 1929, but they too fell in that period.[6] After the start of the depression, unemployment nearly doubled (from 9 percent to 16 percent within half a year). Müller's government protected social benefits at the beginning of the depression, and unemployment insurance and wages remained steady. When a more conservative coalition under Heinrich Brüning (Center) replaced Müller on March 3, 1930, policy on wages and prices shifted dramatically. Increasing unemployment, failing businesses, and falling prices traumatized the German electorate until by autumn 1930 "the social bases of Weimar democracy appeared to be shrinking ineluctably." The pattern had appeared once before, in 1924, but dissolved in times of prosperity and economic stability. Those would not come again soon, and the elections of 1930 marked the end of Weimar's "transient stability."[7]

The shock of the Reichstag elections in September 14, 1930, was as great as the crash of 1929 had been, and politically more important: the National Socialists won a spectacular 18.3 percent of the vote, boosting their seats in the federal parliament from 12 to 107. After their electoral breakthrough, Colonel Ludwig Beck, who would become one of the July 20 conspirators against the Nazi regime in 1944, led a celebration in the officers' mess. Beck was an exception among officers who had seen active duty; they tended to old-fashioned conservatism, "black, white, and red," not revolutionary National Socialist élan. But the Nazi success created a kind of fatalism. The British attaché in Berlin, Colonel J. H. Marshall-Cornwall, was told, "It is the *Jugendbewegung,* it can't be stopped." For many young people, not just some in the military, National Socialism seemed to offer "a means of escape from Germany's financial and political troubles."[8] Before the Great War, organizations of young people tended toward the romantic and unpolitical, a culture of "Peter Pans" (Peter Merkel) that was transformed during the Republic. This recollection in the late 1930s is not untypical:

> One often hears the question why it was that youth spontaneously rallied to Hitler. But the experiences of war, revolution and inflation supply an explanation. We were not spared anything. We knew and felt the worries in the house. The shadow of necessity never left our table and made us silent. . . . Misery, shame, hatred, lies, and civil war imprinted themselves on our souls and made us mature early. So we searched and found Adolf Hitler. What attracted us like a magnet was precisely the fact that he only made demands of us and promised us nothing. He demanded of every person a total commitment to his movement and therefore to Germany.[9]

At the beginning of his chancellorship, Brüning had hoped to revive the center-right *Bürgerblock* and broaden his parliamentary base, but the September 1930 election created a new political landscape. Sensing the possibility of coalition with Hitler, Alfred Hugenberg's German Nationalist Peoples Party (DNVP) moved even further away from the parties of the Weimar coalition. Three antiparliamentary parties (NSDAP, KPD, and DNVP) controlled 255 of the 577 seats, not enough to carry a no-confidence vote, but enough to block constitutional reforms. Under those circumstances, Brüning could not get passage of an "Enabling Act" that would have allowed the government to function while parliament was gridlocked. Numerically the remaining parties might still have formed a comfortable majority in the Reichstag, but no consensus emerged.[10] Chancellor Brüning resorted increasingly to government by decree under the presidential powers of Article 48. The Social Democrats, the largest faction in the Reichstag, "tolerated" Brüning's fiscal policies for the next eighteen months, while anticonstitutional parties on the extreme Left and Right waited for their moment. Justifying this position to the SPD congress at Leipzig in 1931, Rudolf Breitscheid declared, "We only tolerate the violation of democratic forms in order to save the substance of democracy."[11]

Political Constitutional Theory

Schmitt's *Verfassungslehre* was written simultaneously with *Der Begriff des Politischen* during the spring of 1927,[12] and both texts make a common argument: the phenomena of the political appear in degrees of association and dissociation that theoretically must include "the real unity of them all" and its opposite in war and civil war.[13] The *Verfassungslehre* was intended as neither "a commentary nor series of monographic studies" but aimed to found a new science of constitutions, their law and politics.[14] Schmitt's approach tests a constitution against its origins and founding intent, their development and the substance of the constitution, and argues for incorporating political questions (such as "sovereignty") into a reading of the constitution. Only a political science of law and the state can demonstrate their relation to "political unity," and Schmitt's critique of positivism and liberalism culminates here in the "legal-critical" analysis of the Weimar constitution, "the typical constitution today." Like Machiavelli, Schmitt too argues with historical examples that reveal the origins of the bürgerliche Rechtsstaat as the Florentine had demonstrated the origins of principalities. "Historical contingency and political relativism" determine the fate of constitutions, and Schmitt opens the horizons of constitutional possibility by rejecting the liberal Rechtsstaat as an "absolute dogma." Its importance lies not in philosophical doctrine but in the fact that such states became the norm after 1918.

Liberty and Constitutional Theory

The centerpiece of the *Verfassungslehre* is Schmitt's demonstration that central concepts of liberal theory are embedded in the class struggles and intellectual positions of the European bourgeoisie. "All the demands of the liberal bourgeoisie in Germany from 1848 and from the period of conflict between 1862 and 1866 were realized in half a century," Schmitt writes, "but in the meantime, the political and social circumstances had changed completely, and what was realized took on another meaning than it had fifty years earlier." The introduction of parliamentarism, which the German liberals of 1848 sought and failed to achieve, occurred in the Weimar constitution, but now as something "posthumous."[15] Detached from their earlier context, these concepts live on in entirely changed social and economic circumstances, as substantially different, often contradictory political theories and institutions. Every modern constitution, Schmitt writes, is "a mixed constitution," and his analysis of the Weimar constitution as an example of "the modern constitution"—the bürgerliche Rechtsstaat—divides it into legal *(rechtsstaatlich)* and political elements. In the course of the argument, the organizational principles of liberalism are shown to conflict in specific instances with democratic equality.

Kant defined the civil condition *(bürgerliche Zustand)* as "a legal condition that rests a priori on these principles: (1) the freedom of every member of society and a person; (2) the equality of each as a subject with the other; (3) the independence of every member of a community as a citizen." This formulation is, Schmitt comments, "the clearest, final expression of the principles of the bourgeois Enlightenment, and has not been superseded."[16] This theory assumes that individual freedom is prior to the state.

Liberal constitutionalism further assumes that the freedom of the individual is in principle unlimited, while the authority of the state is in principle limited. The division and balance of power inscribed in liberal constitutional documents proceed from that theory of freedom with the intention of limiting state authority over the individual through circumscribed competencies.

Kant's political philosophy inspired German liberalism, and its elements are present in the rule-of-law provisions of the modern constitution. The Weimar constitution contains these as fundamental rights and the division of powers, and in various organizational specifics characteristic of the Rechtsstaat.[17]

Such organizational criteria define liberal constitutional theory. They specify procedures or rules that must be followed for an outcome or the application of a law to be "legal," but legal thought separates this formal designation from specific qualities on which the larger theory of law is based. Schmitt's critique of Kelsen and the statute positivists brings it, and its practical consequences, forward, concluding that a formal or "quantitative" understanding empties out the meaning of "the rule of law" and the Rechtsstaat. Law must retain its connection to "the principles of the Rechtsstaat and bourgeois freedom," Schmitt asserts, if the law is to rule in the manner and with the results this theory intends. Laws are made and laws rule in a monarchy and in the Soviet Republic, he notes, but this "rule of law" is not the one intended in Rechtsstaat theory. Only if "certain qualities that distinguish a legal norm from an arbitrary command or a measure" are retained can one speak of "the rule of law" in the specific understanding meant by phrases such as "on the basis of law." Within the framework of liberty, the state may encroach on individual freedom only "on the basis of a law." This formula (the expression varies; in the United States it is "in the name of the law") was intended to ensure that intrusions into the sphere of liberty should be administered in accordance with the "provisions" and "priority" of law, and it originates in nineteenth-century claims against the king's bureaucracy, police, and military. The legality of administration is the hallmark of the rule of law in this sense, and only in this sense does it guarantee bourgeois freedom. Consistent with legality in this sense, the Rechtsstaat is one whose entire activity is thoroughly comprised in "exactly prescribed responsibilities." At base this notion describes a kind of functioning or "instrumental rationality" that is measurable and definite, not in its substantive dimensions but in its procedures. All powers within the state are prescribed legally, even the making of laws, their administration, and enforcement. The constitution thus appears as the "fundamental law" of a closed system of laws and lawmaking or administration conceived as norms alone, never as "the fullness of state power." The system is "sovereign," not penetrated by the needs or necessities of political existence.[18]

For Schmitt, *ratio* is the defining characteristic of modern political theory and liberal constitutionalism. The organization of state power and its institutions is justified by reference to a specific concept of reason. Early theories of government presented law as the result of "will," anathema to legal theorists of liberty in the modern period, who assume that law "is not the will of one or many men, but something rational-general; not *voluntas,* but *ratio.*"[19] Constitutional schemes such as the division of powers are valuable not in themselves but as techniques that protect this idea of law from particular orders or measures.[20] German state theory retained this concept as long as it remained conscious of the "principles of the liberal Rechtsstaat." For Kant, a government whose power is not divided is "despotic"; for Hegel, "a law is truth existent in the form of the universal."[21] There are other kinds of states or governments, but the constitution of liberty intends to bind individuals and institutions to higher values and virtues: appropriateness, reasonableness, and justice.[22] All these assume that "a law" is a general norm and that the bond that ties legislator, judge, or administrator to "the law" is its generality.

Democracy

The modern constitution is, like Aristotle's polity, a "mixed constitution" containing elements of the three classic forms of government. Schmitt divides it into "legal" (rechtsstaatlich) and political parts, further identifying the first with liberalism and the second with democracy. Both are conceptualized without regard for the practical consequences of such an approach: its purpose is the definition of concepts that have maximum analytic power. Given the mixture of ideas and their complicated history,[23] the compromises and combinations that shaped the Weimar constitution, the impact of Schmitt's approach is sharply critical.

That principles of equity such as those noted earlier have "become problematic," Schmitt argues, follows from the fact that "natural law has lost its evidence." The dualism of formal and material law is the result of that transformation in consciousness and beliefs. It has also made the hierarchy of values within which liberty emerged now unrecognizable. Schmitt reads the history of rebellion and resistance to state authority from the Reformation onward critically, and always with a view to higher values that might make constitutional forms and modern jurisprudence coherent through their justification. Individual liberty and privacy are the higher values of liberal constitutionalism, but Schmitt regards them as inadequate, because "posthumous," to constitute the political. Although they appear in the constitutional text of the Weimar Republic as rights and the rule-of-law organization of state functions, their contemporary understanding and practice have made them disintegrating factors.

Schmitt resolves the constitutional dualism of public and private through radical separation of its liberal forms from Weimar's democratic substance. In this project, he confronts a question posed by Sieyes more than a century earlier, and implicit in every democratic constitution: "Who *are* the people?" That a "German" people exists is obvious but is not sufficient to answer the question intended by a political theory of democracy, nor is the empirical history of this democracy adequate. The people are neither particular actors (in the revolution) nor the National Assembly; they are not "the voter" casting a ballot, nor are they the respondents to surveys of opinion. The people in their natural existence as actual individuals are different from "the people" as the constituting power of democracy and its focus. So much is clear from the first pages of the *Verfassungslehre.*

The primary conceptions of "the people" developed here draw directly on Schmitt's argument in *Der Begriff des Politischen.* The people is a subject capable of decision, specifically capable of the political decision that distinguishes friend from enemy. What tended toward a negative reading in that text—jus belli and the real system of international relations based on "politically existent nations"[24]—addresses the positive implication of the political: that peoples constitute themselves politically as friends. This boundary includes and excludes, and Schmitt's analysis of its inclusive dimension is consistently developed against the possibility of the exception in war and civil war. The people of a democratic constitution are present as "a political unity," and the character of a constitution is given in the active voice: the constitution does not give itself but is given by a political actor who includes and excludes in that act. The primary concept of democracy for Schmitt, here as in the *Parlamentarismus,* is identity manifest in "a concretely present people identical with itself as a political unity."

Democracy can be thought of in two ways, as a procedure or a substance, and both appear in Schmitt's theory of the Weimar constitution. Substantial conceptions of democracy are based on identity, which Schmitt constantly develops as the pairs ruling/ruled, governing/governed, and commanding/obeying, and his theory is explicitly based on Rousseau's *Social Contract.* Like him, Schmitt thinks of democratic identity in terms of "a general will," the key to forming a people into a nation and a state.

For a theory of the state in those terms, Schmitt must divide liberalism from democracy as he had previously done in the analysis of parliament and its theory. "Equality and freedom are often referred to together as a democratic principle," Schmitt notes, "but in truth these two principles are often contradictory in their assumptions, their content, and effects."[25] Freedom is the domestic content of the bürgerliche Rechtsstaat in whatever political form (monarchical, aristocratic, or democratic), and liberal freedom assumes that individuals are "naturally free," an idea relevant, he argues, only for the legal, not for the political, part of the constitution.[26] For its political part, equality is the decisive aspect of a democratic constitution. This analysis has many precursors in the history of political thought, in addition to Rousseau, beginning with the English Levellers, and continuing through the Left and Right students of Hegel. It is always implicit in the disjunction of legal persons "equal before the law" and the substantive inequality of real persons. Radical democrats such as Marx believed that changing the social and economic bases of the modern state (capitalism) would cause the law to "wither away" with the state. Rousseau's "social contract" would realize a complete identity of its members through their education away from "particular wills" ("they shall be forced to be free"), and the circumstances of inequality would cease as a result. In Schmitt's reading, democratic equality is the foundation of "a strong state" in a political world, which may preserve freedom domestically through the rule of law but will act to preserve "its own particular way of life" and existence externally and, if necessary, internally.[27]

Procedural theories of democracy refer to a "method of exercising state activities,"[28] and most definitions specify democracy as "majority rule," Schmitt comments, but that leaves open the where and when of "the majority": a majority of all those voting; a majority of all citizens whether they vote or not; a majority of the population.[29] Such qualifications are secondary to the substance of democracy and can even be parasitical and destructive of it, and Schmitt is particularly critical of two liberal elements in "liberal democracy": liberal equality and privacy.

The first assumes a bland and vague equality—whatever "bears the human face" is equal—and insufficient to generate "specific distinctions and limits." No "legal, political, or economic criterion" can be derived from liberal equality. Its constitutional importance is that equality in this sense is part of a larger idea, "individualism," grounding fundamental rights.[30] Every equality takes its meaning and importance from an inequality; human beings think of themselves differentially, imagine themselves as more or less than another, but this is not liberal thinking, which *must* disregard all such discriminations, whatever the content. That political theory can and must take those into account offends the "ideal, beautiful, and sympathetic" notion of democracy. This "limitless expansion of the concept of democracy," Schmitt notes, can be found among liberals and social democrats, that is, among those whose opinions would lead to very different politics.[31]

A rigorous concept of democracy, "like any genuine political concept," must be able to produce distinctions. Thus "political democracy does not rest on mankind undifferentiated, but only on membership in a particular people, whereby this membership in a people can be defined through various moments (the notion of a common race, belief, a common fate and tradition)."[32] Equality, Schmitt argues with reference to Husserl's *Logische Untersuchungen,* can only appear in relation to difference and acquires its meaning first in relations of subordination. Schmitt's theory of democracy assumes that it will include some and exclude others, and that as a political concept it is territorially situated: "democracy" describes the constitution of a people substantially equal, who live in a bounded place. Whoever does not belong to the people as a political unity is outside political equality, although they may receive equal treatment in other spheres as the result not of the requirements of democratic principles but of "universal liberal rights of freedom" within "unpolitical areas" such as "private property and legal protection."[33] The Weimar constitution defined equality in these terms.[34]

As a political theory, democracy looks for equality within, and difference (or inequality) outside, its borders, Schmitt concludes. Political equality is, furthermore, the basis of all other kinds of equality: equal voting rights, universal conscription, equal access to offices, equality before the law. Only if all citizens are really equal in this political sense is democracy more than "a fiction"—to presume otherwise imports an unpolitical "as if" into constitutional theory.[35] This argument undermines the notion of universal human equality as unpolitical, and a paraphrase of Schmitt's argument in *Der Begriff des Politischen* applies in this context as well: the foreigner need not be morally evil or aesthetically ugly, and he need not be an economic competitor; it can even be profitable to do business with him. But he is "other," "different" to a degree that conflicts with him are possible, which cannot be resolved legally or by arbitration.[36] In political theory, the other is so defined, and in Schmitt's constitutional theory it follows that the state lawfully excludes foreigners from membership.

Substantial Equality

Democratic equality, Schmitt argues, is "substantial equality," and because all citizens share in it, they can be treated equally. When Schmitt excoriates the positivist theory of democracy as merely formal and empty compared to a substantial theory of the constitution, this concept of substantial equality or, as he further refines it, "homogeneity, and specifically the homogeneity of a people," is what he means to evoke.[37] The idea had preoccupied him for nearly half a decade. It can be found in the first version of *Der Begriff des Politischen,*[38] and in *Die geistesgeschichtliche Lage des heutigen Parlamentarismus* (1923 and 1926), where he denied that parliamentary government was a democratic form at all.[39] Rousseau's influence is obvious in those works, as well, where democracy is defined as "the will of the people" in legislation; their will is identical to the will that makes the law.[40] In his 1927 lecture on "Der Begriff des Politischen," the friend/enemy distinction is followed immediately by the statement that these concepts "are to be understood in their concrete and existential sense, not as metaphors or symbols," and that "the concern here is neither with abstractions nor with normative ideas, but with an inherent reality and the real possibility of such a distinction."[41] Hermann Heller's lecture "Political Democracy and Social Homogeneity," in the same Berlin series, attacked Schmitt's concept of the political on grounds that have become a familiar reading of it. The "political," Heller argued, is more than the determination of an enemy; to define it in those terms leaves out of account "politics inside the state as a process of building unity."[42] It is that dimension of equality taken up in the *Verfassungslehre.*

The question of democratic equality appears in the *Verfassungslehre* as part of a theory of nationality and the nation, as the social basis of modern democracy.[43] There is no single, exclusive, or necessary basis for democratic equality, Schmitt argues, but it is determined by reference to a "higher third" whose substance might be religious (the Reformation and English civil wars), racial (the British Empire), or common tradition and destiny. Wherever the nation-state could be found as a democracy, its constitutional forms were based on national homogeneity:

> In contrast to the general notion of a people, nation refers to a people individualized through its political consciousness. Various elements contribute to the unity of a nation and consciousness of that unity: a common language, shared historical destiny, traditions and memory, common political goals and hopes. Language is a very important factor, but not decisive. Decisive is the commonality of historical life, conscious willing of that commonality, great experiences and purposes. Genuine revolutions and victorious wars can overcome linguistic differences and found the feeling of national fellowship, even if the same language is not spoken.[44]

This modern conception of nationhood and membership in a national group grounds democratic equality for Schmitt, and its absence in a state is something "abnormal," even "dangerous."[45] Among the means of increasing homogeneity discussed here are peaceful resolution of differences, separation, and gradual assimilation of one group within the other; a variety of legal means can be and were used at the time and still today to regulate this political problem of heterogeneity.[46] There is, however, no significant engagement with the creation of "unity from diversity" in Heller's sense, as the result of politics below the distinction of friend and enemy—with "secondary" kinds of politics according to Schmitt's criterion. Liberal equality envisions a world of "universal human rights" in which nation-states gradually give way to supranational entities. In other words: a world without Schmitt's political. This perspective is dismissed as a fantasy that ignores the real world of conflicts, and the political as the human condition.

The concepts of democratic theory are intended to realize "an identity of governed and governing."[47] Specific democratic procedures, such as elections, are not its substance and can even produce inequalities when their purpose—reproduction of democratic identity—is understood in simply quantitative terms. Constitutional substance exists beyond the technical questions of electoral systems and voting, beyond the legal norms of a constitutional text: "The word 'identity' signifies the existential in the political unity of a people in contrast to some kind of normative, schematic or fictive equalities. Democracy assumes in the whole and every detail of its political existence a homogeneous people, that has the will to exist politically."[48] Homogeneity and political will—these are the two substantial qualities that make up democracy for Schmitt.

State and Constitution

From democracy in that sense, he identifies the constitution as "an inclusive decision about the type and form of political unity," and further, the state *is* this unity.[49] These relationships can be schematically figured thus:

people	=	political unity (substantial equality or homogeneity)	=	state

These equivalencies lead back to the concept of a people in its dynamic political reality, not in a static legal definition. Schmitt's analysis of the modern constitution focuses on the variety of "wills" expressed in its law and institutions, its liberal element, and the substantive will of the people as its sovereign. In each category, aspects of the people in and above their constitution can be found, but the mixture of forms obscures sight of the *whole* constitution in its democratic essentials. "The people" has various constitutional meanings. "The people" within the constitution as a legal entity is of interest to Schmitt only in relation to the realization or absence of democratic equality. Within the constitution, the people exist through provisions specifying the participation in government. Through voting, the people determine those who will perform state activities, but this activity has two different meanings. Elections determine representatives; the president of the Reich was elected directly by the people, the members of the Reichstag, and other legislatures indirectly through votes for party lists, not individuals. If democracy is "government by majority," it is unclear who or what the majority is, Schmitt argues. Such institutions falsify the "substantial equality" and political unity of the people because "in truth it is not das Volk [the people] who is formed and organized, but the procedures for voting or for presenting a vote, and the will of the people is just the result of a system of equivalencies or even fictions. The people is then a simple or qualified majority of the participating voters or those entitled to vote."[50]

The Weimar constitution also included direct democratic provisions, permitting various referenda and initiatives.[51] In these provisions, "the people" takes on a different meaning than an electorate, and while the majority usually decides the outcome, a minority could initiate a question to be decided directly. In all these, Schmitt argues, the same fiction is at work, namely, that the outcome is "the will of the people."[52]

The substance of democracy is drawn from the people as "not formed" and "not constituted." The people "above" and "next to" the constitution is the politically real subject of constitutional power, the source of public opinion and the subject of acclamation, and those capable of putting questions in the direct democratic institution of an initiative. As Schmitt's account of equality had been existential, so too is his conceptualization of the people "next to the constitution." In this aspect, the people continues to exist beyond its constitutive moment as the pouvoir constituant, as the real sovereign above the law into which Schmitt's constitutional theory introduces a material, physical quality. The people are "present" in democracy, as Rousseau too suggested. "The people," Schmitt agrees, cannot be represented but can only be present: "as present, really assembled people it exists in pure democracy with the greatest possible identity: as εχχλσια in the marketplace in Greek democracy; in the Roman forum; as an assembled team or army; as the Swiss *Landesgemeinde*" (243). Public opinion is not a constitutional-legal institution, but that does not make it any less important for Schmitt's theory of democracy, and its recognition that the sovereign people are "outside of and above every constitutional norm"—not bound by law—tends to give this form of participation greater weight. The people are always immediately present, Schmitt writes, a "real existence," and even when not voting or taking part in the constitutional procedures of a democracy, the people are still present. "The people is a concept that comes into existence only in the public sphere. It only appears in the public, it acts only in the public. People and Public exist together; no Public without People, and no People without Public" (243).

Öffentlichkeit: The Public against the Private

Presence and acclamation are the criteria of democracy, which Schmitt deploys critically against the indirect methods of democracy in the modern state. Their organization (i.e., the people within the constitution) seldom attends to the people "assembled"—impractical, Rousseau knew, in large states—and the practice of indirect democracy "ignores the people as such . . . because it belongs to the bürgerliche Rechtsstaat as such to ignore the sovereign, whether that is a monarch or the people" (244). Elections, and even institutions of "direct democracy" such as referenda and initiatives, are "private" in substance, transforming the *citoyen,* "the specifically democratic, i.e., political figure, into a private person from the private sphere" (245).

Rousseau distinguished the sum of particular wills ("the will of all") from the General Will. The latter is a homogeneous will that achieves substantial identity in the public reality of a people. As citoyen, not as Bürger/bourgeois, this "public" is the reality of the political. From it follows, for Rousseau, the just state and, for Schmitt, the legitimacy of the law and constitution. Both theories are built on the model of the polis or the local assembly in which a people gather physically. The institutional arrangements of modern constitutions are designed to ignore that people, even to prevent "assembly" as a political concept by making it the private right of an individual.[53] Voting too is privatized as a secret ballot cast by individuals, "not a democratic procedure, but the expression of liberal individualism." It is justified as a protection against improper influence and other abuses, but its intellectual justification is liberal, not democratic: in transforming the citizen into a private man, the secret ballot expressed "the private, not the public," concerns, whether these are "religion or economic interests."[54] The people vote not as a people but as individuals, even in the processes of direct democratic initiatives or referenda, and the complex of constitutional provisions and electoral law is intended to keep the people divided into a sum of particular wills, arithmetic and counting one by one, "the will of all."[55] The absurdity of these methods, Schmitt argues, is obvious when one acknowledges that the "secret" is not a secret at all: the voter can do what he wishes with this secret, a fact all the more striking when one considers that "the voter" is exercising a public state function. "The secret ballot is the point at which this transformation of the citizen into the private man takes place" in a modern constitution, Schmitt argues, and "democracy is changed into the liberal protection of the individual." Here, perhaps, he concludes, are the arcana of modern liberal democracy.[56]

Against this private, particular function Schmitt sets Öffentlichkeit, as public opinion, "the modern form of acclamation."[57] As in the analysis of elections and voting, Schmitt here too dismisses the concept of public opinion as "survey" or the arithmetical tabulation of responses. In acclamation, the people as sovereign exercise their political freedom, not as individuals with rights but as citizens with an opinion. There is no democracy and no state without public opinion, which "originates and exists 'unorganized,' " and when it becomes (as voting) an "office," it no longer exists. It must be free, unorganized, and outside the constitution, or it is not the substantial expression of the democratic will. Schmitt is certainly aware of modern techniques to influence and steer public opinion: "There are parties, speakers and demagogues in every democracy, from the Athenian to the bosses of American democracy, also the press, film and other psychological techniques to handle the masses. There is always the danger that invisible and irresponsible social powers will direct the public opinion of the people."[58]

Democracy, however, has its own answer to that danger. As long as the substantial equality that defines a democratic state is present, and the political will of the people is vital in their consciousness of themselves as a political subject, able to distinguish friend from enemy, "there is no great danger." Should this democracy decay, "then no organization and no legal norm will help."[59]

Representation

The Weimar constitution, like that of the United States, made no mention of political parties; the word "party" appears only once, and then as a pejorative: "Professional civil servants serve the whole, not a party" (Article 130). The parliamentary rules of the Reichstag acknowledged political parties in various specifics of its business, most significantly their role in the legislative order. The formation of a *Fraktion,* or party, must be reported to the president of the Reichstag, and its rules further define a party as a minimum of fifteen. Bills could be introduced according to Article 68 by the government or "from the middle of the Reichstag" if fifteen members sign the proposal, whether from one or more parties. Schmitt objects to this rule as transforming the legislative as a representative of the people into a forum for party business. Through the organization of parties into permanent institutions for contesting elections, "representation" loses its substantive meaning.

Many others have made a similar argument, including Burke and the Federalists, and Schmitt's critique of political parties in the modern state looks back to an eighteenth-century view of them. The Enlightenment thought public opinion and the public sphere an essential factor in the state, decisive for the realization of public virtue and good government. Most were proponents of enlightened despotism, who believed that "enlightened public opinion" was the best safeguard against misuse of power, and in this way, freedom of press and speech became political institutions in Europe.[60] The belief in public opinion was particularly strong in England and France, less so in Germany, but with the coming of mass democratic states, the meaning of this concept shifted from a philosophical to a sociological one.[61] While Germans regarded "public opinion" with skepticism—Hegel refers to it as "two-faced"—A. V. Dicey claimed a direct and intimate connection between it and parliamentary legislation, a condition, Schmitt remarks in passing, that obtains only in the English-speaking world.

As class consciousness developed, the figure of public opinion as "a man in the street" became more problematic: "as soon as this man became a class-conscious proletarian, his nature changed"; and as a reference point, "the simple worker" or "Jacques Bonhomme" becomes a romantic trope—and thus unpolitical.[62] The contemporary sociology of public opinion and its importance in positivist theories of democracy lead only toward the same political arithmetic of fictional equations. His model instead is "the public" as acclamatory, and the example given is "public outrage" over the extradition of war criminals in 1920.[63] At least one type of public opinion in democracy is protest, and for Schmitt, public assemblies, demonstrations, and other spontaneous expressions of political views are democracy above the constitution.

This theory conflicts sharply with the liberal concept of law and legislation, and as Schmitt applies it in the *Verfassungslehre*, it undermines the legitimacy of parliament. Contemporary legal theories of the constitution focus on law as norms and rules, or a determinate system of constraints and injunctions whose content varies. Here he turns the principles of the bürgerliche Rechtsstaat in classical liberal theory against itself. The people of a liberal state are not those of a democracy, and its intentions are not the same as a democracy: one aims to realize freedom, the other is a condition of equality. The Weimar constitution contained both principles, and its organization of offices, rights, and duties was complicated and often self-contradictory. Positivists such as Gerhard Anschütz read the text literally and treated every article as being of equal importance. Kelsen achieved an absolute theory of it, but in purely logical terms. Schmitt wanted a theory that was absolute and that grasped the constitution as "a unitary whole" in terms of democratic sovereignty, reinstating a personal moment of decision in the constitution and making the willful character of sovereignty its core through explicitly decisionist language. Constitutions are valid and effective because they are given by a constitutional power ("a force or an authority"): "The word 'will' refers, in contrast to mere norms, to an existing power as the origin of an ought. The will is existentially given; its power or authority lies in the fact of its existence" (9). The democratic people had given itself a constitution whose whole was more than the parts, Schmitt argued, and whose core decisions were for democracy (Preamble, Article 1, section 2); for a republic and against monarchy (Article 1, section 1); for federalism and the retention of the Länder (Article 2); for a fundamentally parliamentary-representative form of government and legislation; and for the bürgerliche Rechtsstaat with its principles, division of powers, and rights. These founding decisions are for a "constitutional democracy" (23–24).

Parliament against Democracy

Such decisions are political, not legal or normative, but liberal theory avoids the question of where the democratic sovereign "is" within the constitution. Normativism separates norms from will in a manner parallel to the distinction of is from ought. Normative theory can approve or disapprove but can give no account of why a constitution is valid and effective. Such judgments function to insulate the constitution as law or norm from the political. Kelsen and the positivists agreed that the Weimar Republic was a democracy, and they argued that the democratic will informed the Republic's liberal institutions. When government or parliament or the courts act and decide, they do so on the basis of law that is "the will of the people." Schmitt's political theory of the constitution denies this account and turns its normative justification upside down by contrasting *ratio* as the ground of law with the practices of political bargaining and interest representation.

An "educated and propertied" class that could be represented in a parliament that was "an assembly of educated persons, that represented education and reason and even the education and reason of the whole nation," had been the social foundation of nineteenth-century German liberalism (310–11). For the *Bürgertum,* Schmitt argues, even the concept of a nation belonged to that of education, because it stood for specific qualities. In this sense, parliament gathered reason from the whole people and brought its particles into the discussions of a parliament. Schmitt's reading of classical liberal theory owes much to Guizot, but it would not be an unorthodox reading of Mill's *On Liberty* and *Representative Government.* Education is a quality that can be represented; property cannot. The *interests* of property can be advanced, but when the legislature becomes a forum for interests, it has lost its character as a place of reason: "Parliament ceases then to represent a certain education. It becomes partly a committee for the exchange of interests, partly a means to express public opinion, and therefore becomes functionally dependent on the voters. It becomes what one called the English parliament of the last century: simply an accounting machine between the electorate and government" (312). Since the beginning of the Republic, Schmitt had defined the parliamentary system as "discussion": "in public speeches and counterspeeches the true inclusive will of the people comes as a *'volonté générale'* " (315). In this analysis, it is clear that "the people" of Schmitt's democracy, whose will might be expressed under such ideal circumstances of communication, are different from the demos, who "cannot discuss . . . but only acclaim." The advantage of parliament in this ideal sense is that it mediates between the people and the government (based on civil service and the military) as "a place of rational discussion."[64]

Liberal political theory assumes that reason is the principle of legislation and parliamentary institutions. Schmitt rejected this theory early in the Weimar Republic, and *Die geistesgeschichtliche Lage des heutigen Parliamentarismus* separated "liberalism" from "democracy" on grounds that Rousseau offers in *The Social Contract.* Representation intervenes between the democratic will and law; it is a mediating factor in the theory of law, legislation, and constitution. Political theory gives different judgments on whether such mediation is good or bad, but Schmitt is less concerned with such normative questions than with analysis of the empirical foundations of the modern constitution. Instead, the constitutional theory presented here identifies two distinctive sources of "law," representation and the will of the people, which are categorically different and therefore in uneasy relation to each other.

Law, in the formal sense, is "that which is undertaken by an office charged with legislation."[65] In no area of the law are the resulting "abbreviations and fictions" more important than in constitutional law, where the identity of governed and governing in a democracy has removed the original meaning of the phrase "on the basis of a law." Representation of the people before a monarch required the consent of parliament (the popular assembly) to all significant legislation—taxation, the budget, declarations of a state of siege or of war, appointments, pardons—and it has become, Schmitt asserts, "nothing more than an artificial expression when such things are done 'on the basis of a law.' " Form loses its meaning here; nothing substantial is given a form. Rather, such usage is "an abbreviated description of the extraordinarily extended competence of a particular instance."[66]

Schmitt returned to this theme in his Festschrift article for Johannes Popitz, setting it in the wider horizon of a general crisis of legality that reaches its peak in the twentieth-century legislatures, institutions he calls "the motorized legislative," the result of "increasingly simplified and increasingly accelerated" legislative procedures. These are far removed from the idea of rational deliberation and defined competencies, and they produce "enabling" legislation rather than law in the Rechtsstaat tradition.[67] Schmitt was writing against the background of a Nazi Reichstag, but he had made the same argument in the crisis of 1932 about the Weimar Reichstag. In the liberal-democratic legislatures, not just under fascist dictatorship, decrees, orders, and measures supplant law.

The Concrete Constitution: Society, State, and Economy

While still in Bonn, Schmitt began to take an interest in fiscal and economic questions. His move to Berlin's Handelshochschule and subsequent friendship with Johannes Popitz accentuated the economic elements in Schmitt's account of the concrete circumstances of the constitution,[68] and some of his most influential work in these years developed in close collaboration with Popitz. As state secretary in the Finance Ministry, Popitz knew firsthand the technical and administrative details of managing fiscal and economic policy, and through him Schmitt began to elaborate a political economy of the constitution as the continuation of a critique of liberalism. Adolf Wagner, one of the founders of the *Verein für Sozialpolitik und Sozialwissenschaft,* had discovered the "law of increasing state activity" at the end of the nineteenth century, with its state-socialist purpose clearly visible in his theoretical work on finance. This perspective looked back to Hegel and forward to Keynes. The classical economists had seen the state only as a cost to the economy. Hegelians of the Left and Right, most notably Lorenz von Stein, countered that theory with one giving the state an active role in providing for the welfare of its members and securing substantive justice. From Hegel, these social scientists derived their justification for this new and not liberal state, a view Popitz also espoused and developed in the context of financial administration. Only the state represented "the whole" and "the common interest," and therefore its boundaries could not be determined abstractly or in advance, as the classical liberal division of state from society implied, but only in response to given circumstances. Wagner's law was less an empirical model than a justification for an increasing state share of the national product and increasing public expenditures. Nevertheless, in circumstances of "economic emergency" and greatly increased demands on the state, it became almost as obvious as the laws of nature.[69]

Economic liberalism had dominated German thinking before the crash of 1929, but after it even the most decided liberals revised their view. Wilhelm Röpke called it "a secular catastrophe" which the economy could not survive without state help.[70] In a flood of popular articles, leading economists steered opinion toward accepting intervention either on the grounds that it was necessary to master the current crisis, or as a step toward socialism, or as the way to a new and better capitalism, a third way between liberalism and communism. Others understood the dramatic structural transformations of the state within the frame of "freedom and community." A stronger economy could develop, Hans Ritschl argued, through the dualism of a social economy and the market.[71] Ritschl assumed that the social economy would increase at the cost of the market, and he based his argument on a philosophy that placed the state and its political subject above the market economy and its subject, the exchange society. Here the state appears as the legal organization of this new society.

Some, Popitz included, saw the growth of the state within the economy more ominously. When its share of the national product reached 53 percent, Popitz thought that the "noneconomic factor of the state" suspended the laws of the market. For others, this new state activity promised to activate the political will of the people, binding it more closely to the Republic and its constitution. Even Carl Schmitt thought "financial dictatorship" might spur the growth of "neutral powers" to counterbalance party-political forces in Germany. The citizenry, however, saw themselves in "a relatively helpless passivity in relation to the modern Leviathan 'state' into whose care one surrendered and learned to trust the 'freedom' of the welfare state."[72]

John Maynard Keynes, whose critique of classical liberalism became the new ideology, put the issue raised in these German debates as a question about reforming the agenda of the state. In the English context, it was approached by asking what could best be done by the individual and what could only be achieved socially, but the Germans situated it in the realm of state theory.[73]

Carl Schmitt's view of these questions combined preferences for a strong central state with the maximum freedom for the markets compatible with political order and stability. The development of his constitutional theory through the concept of democracy was not just an alternative to normative and statute positivist constitutional law but a response to the economic state. This is particularly striking in his interpretation of articles in the Weimar constitution that provided for direct democracy. Legislative power belonged to the Reichstag (Article 68), but provision was also made (Articles 73, 75) for popular initiative *(Volksbegehren)* and referenda *(Volksentscheid).* A direct initiative was possible if one-tenth of those entitled to vote demanded it, but the constitution limited that process procedurally and substantively. No referendum could take place if the proposed legislation was "accepted by the Reichstag without revisions" (Article 73, section 3), and there could be no initiative on "the budget, spending bills, or wage policy."[74]

The *Verfassungslehre* (1928) distinguishes democratic power before, over, and in the constitution. As constitutive power, it could not be limited, nor did it require justification, and the power of the people in that sense stands *over* the constituted power of the state.[75] Democratic power expresses itself within the constitution through national and local elections and beside the constitution as "public opinion." In the direct democratic provisions of the constitution, Schmitt saw "an extraordinary legislature," but one limited specifically with respect to finance, a limitation he justified in 1926 by reference to "the monetary sovereignty of the state." "Money laws" provide the state with new sources of income and direct new expenditures for which the state alone is responsible.[76] Only the state can balance and plan expenditures: "The budget is not merely a statistical collection, but an orderly and balanced whole. It determines a balance that unifies the plan and makes it coherent, so that direct intervention or disturbance of this balance should be a matter for the budget itself to determine" (24). It was an interpretation that seemed to undermine Schmitt's theory of democratic identity.

Toward the end of *Volksentscheid und Volksbegehren,* Schmitt returns to Rousseau's theory of democracy in *The Social Contract,* setting his argument into the context of the modern state with radical effects. Rousseau had asked whether there were any men fit to receive laws and had concluded that *The Social Contract* would suit few, if any—Corsica and Poland, perhaps, but certainly not Paris or London. In the "true state," the people were excluded from finance questions because these were corrupting, and furthermore, perfect equality would ensure that financial questions were only administrative, not political. There could be no genuinely political questions (financial or otherwise) in a "true state." But how impossible it would have been to expect democracy in his sense from the citizens of Weimar, and how different the effects of their exclusion from "the monetary sovereignty of the state." The people are to be excluded from finance because in a mass society, representation and taxation lead to redistribution of wealth; the less well off would be more represented in parliament than the wealthy, on whom the burden of taxes would fall most severely:

> According to received doctrine, partly from the Estates, partly liberal and bourgeois, that those who are taxed should be represented and also control the use of their taxes. "Popular representation" was formerly a representation of those who contributed or who paid taxes, and what it approved was also carried out by their representatives. This firmly connected taxation and representation. The famous liberal dictum "no taxation without representation" only has meaning if it also holds in reverse. In the mass democracies of modern industrial states, such simple calculations can no longer be maintained. The "people," i.e., the majority that demands expenditures, does so for the out-voted minority too. (53–54)

Pluralism

Robert Dahl defined "antagonistic pluralism" as a condition in which fundamentally opposed political forces compete through formally democratic institutions to pursue their own specific interests by means of state power. In the most extreme cases, these groups are willing to dismantle the procedures of formal democracy once they have achieved power within the state.[77] There is no more vivid example of antagonistic pluralism than Weimar.[78] Like Schmitt, Left theorists of law and constitutions such as Otto Kirchheimer and Franz Neumann wanted to "put the state back in credit," much as opponents of neoliberalism in Europe and America today.[79] Carl Schmitt was the first German to take an interest in the pluralist theories of G. D. H. Cole, J. N. Figgis, and Harold Laski—and Schmitt was the first anywhere to notice Weimar's antagonistic development and to argue for "an ethic of state" to overcome it.

Pluralist theory conforms to the empirical world as many experience it, and that explains its attraction, Schmitt argued in 1930.[80] The individual lives in a complex of diverse and disordered associations, religious groups, trade unions, professional associations, clubs, and the family and is bound to each of them in their particular ethics. This pluralism of loyalties discredits the state as an association with a paramount claim to loyalty. That is the philosophical frame of its crisis, whose clarification, Schmitt argues, is necessary for its solution. Only if the state is grasped as "political unity" and the consensus necessary to maintain "the substantial democratic homogeneity of the people" is achieved can the crisis of the republican constitution be overcome.

In "Staatsethik und pluralistischer Staat," Schmitt sets out a conception of the political as *inclusive,* "an intensity of unity" with "various content." From the most intense degree of unity, "the most intense distinction, the grouping of friend and enemy," can be determined: "Political unity is the highest unity, not because it is an omnipotent dictator, or because it levels all other unities, but because it decides, and has the potential within itself to prevent all other opposing groups from dissociating into a condition of extreme enmity—that is, civil war" (36–37). Pluralism is important and modern, Schmitt notes, because it "conforms to the empirically real situation" and is philosophically interesting because of the application of William James's pragmatism to state theory (31). But Cole and Laski misunderstand that problem and work with an outdated and unrealistic concept, the absolutist state of the seventeenth and eighteenth centuries. This is wrong, Schmitt argues, not only because that state did not exist as the lawyers conceived it—Bodin's "sovereignty" is not an empirical description but a criterion of analysis—but also because this is a concept of government, not of the state. For Cole and Laski, the state is the government, an apparatus or administration, "only something instrumental" (35–36). The powers in society, Schmitt concedes, rightly look at government as something they can divide among themselves and as a source of power. In any case, an instrument cannot be the object of loyalty and duty; it cannot be part of an ethic. The state so conceived is just a word, the object of pluralist polemic that obscures the situation.

Schmitt analyzes this crisis as something factual and existential that leads to the destruction of ethical distinctions and obligations. The contemporary crisis of the state is not just a crisis of government (although it was a crisis of parliamentary government) but also a crisis of political unity and therefore of democracy.[81] The disintegration of political unity causes the crisis of government, and it *is* the crisis of the state. As he had argued in *Politische Theologie* and in *Der Begriff des Politischen,* the political creates the normal through sovereignty: "The most intense unity is either there or it is not there; it can dissolve itself, and then the normal order falls away." Schmitt's argument here follows Hobbes implicitly. Sovereignty and law obtain only in the commonwealth, not in nature; and without political unity there cannot be a normal situation: sovereignty reappears in the exception to the normal (37).

The political world is pluralist, Schmitt argues, but not in the way Cole and Laski think it is. Their conception, apparently based on social groups, is radically individualistic and answers the question of conflicting loyalties by reference to "the individual," a double contradiction, Schmitt argues, because a "social situation encompasses the individual, but cannot be changed at his will." The question of the state concerns "a *social ethic,* not the inner autonomy of the individual" (33). Moreover, it is false to think that the individual decides for himself; the group decides, and its decision is motivated by interest: "When the unity of the state falls away, different social groups will probably make the decision on their own accord—that is, on the basis of their group interest. . . . When social pluralism is opposed to state unity, it means nothing other than abandoning the conflict of social duties to the decision of social groups. And that means the sovereignty of social groups, but not the freedom of the individual" (34–35). Only the state can guarantee "the freedom of the individual," because a strong state guarantees the space of his liberty.

The state as a unity capable of preserving individual liberty within the nation in an international system of states is not a simple entity, a formula left over from the age of absolutism. Modern society has changed rapidly, and new technologies have accelerated those changes, but the state has always been the creation of unity from social diversity. The modern democratic state is the product of consensus, as every state has been. There have been two roads to unity historically: through power and order from above; or unity can be created from below as the substantial homogeneity of a people (35). As the latter, unity must constantly be reproduced, Schmitt argues, in the dynamic of compromise and agreement among social groups, and their balance; through a more static and functional unity; in a domestic unity called forth by external threats; and finally in the power and unity that comes through consensus. To say, as the pluralists then and proponents of "civil society" today, that left to free play, social diversity will create political unity, or that such unity is unnecessary, denies the political and the reality of unequal social power. Power creates consensus that is often rational and ethical. The opposite is also true: power creates consensus that is often irrational and produces an ethically despicable consensus (35). The means of creating consensus are economic, educational, and psychological, and these means are not free floating in society but in the hands of interested parties. The political world is not an ideal seminar, any more than the market is a place of free exchanges.

Toward the end of "Staatsethik und pluralistischer Staat," Schmitt returns to the plurality of national states, with an argument for their diversity. In the modern world, only the nation-state offers an arena in which an ethical ordering of obligations and rights is possible, because only there is substantive equality possible. Laski's pluralism ends in a disordered monism, Schmitt charges, because its final referent is "humanity." But concepts such as God, the World, and Mankind are "supreme and sit enthroned high above the plurality of concrete reality. They retain their dignity only as long as they remain there. When they become part of the scuffles of political life they are transformed immediately, lose their meaning and take on a false power and a false proximity." Schmitt concedes that ideals such as "humanity" and "mankind" belong to a human life, but "they constitute nothing, at least no differential society" (38). They are regulative ideas. When turned to political use, these higher values become instruments of repression and of "murderous imperialism."[82]

For Schmitt the political, conceived jurisprudentially as legal indeterminacy and sociologically as an independent decision, is necessarily part of the reality and theory of the state, and *prior* to it. This argument counters liberal theories that separate law from politics, and it takes aim at Weber's definition of politics as "striving for a share of power or influence," whether within the state or between states,[83] an argument, Schmitt notes, that depends on the state's being a fixed point in terms of which the fluid content and purposes of the political can be determined. Schmitt knew that legal practice demonstrated the connection between law and politics in any state, and he believed that universal suffrage and mass political mobilization transformed that relationship utterly in the liberal Rechtsstaat.[84] It is because the state has become problematic that all relative definitions of the political, such as Weber's, are now inadequate. The concept of the state and its reality are no longer "a clear and definite authority."[85] This reverses, Schmitt asserts, their relationship: what is obvious is "the political," so that the state appears dependent on it, and not the other way around.

The crisis of the later Republic was parliamentary and economic, and its effects made a crisis of the state. Both Popitz and Schmitt sought escape from Weimar's predicament in the state, not as an abstraction or a logical theory, and not in the text of its constitution. The state that could resolve this crisis was not the product of electoral politics, nor would the necessary policies come from the floor of the Reichstag. It had become the locus of "tightly organized" parties without "representative character" whose business was not discussion and the search for a common good but "mutual calculation by power and interest groups." From that body there would be no resolution of the crisis, only its intensification. Even before the economic crisis and the electoral triumphs of the Nazis, Schmitt regarded the German parliament as fragmented and incompetent. "Parliament represents political unity less and less; it is becoming an exponent of interests and the votes of a mass electorate, and a parliament of a few hundred party functionaries cannot be justified by the idea of 'leadership selection,' which instead leads to the search for leadership based directly on the trust of the masses."[86]

His argument for "an ethic of state" characterizes the unity that rests on agreement among a multiplicity of groups who recognize a constitution as their common basis as "an ethic of the constitution." This consensus is not simple acceptance of "the rules of the game" but a constitution of the state as political unity and the realization of substantial homogeneity.[87] The agreement of parties cannot be *pacta sunt servanda,* a framework to be changed at will, according to shifting patterns of interest. While no constitution can exist that does not enjoy a common recognition of the rules of political participation in the struggle for power, according to Schmitt, that recognition *presumes* a real political unity that is its actual basis. Diversity and difference do not make the state as political unity obsolete, on the contrary: the more diverse and different the political world is, the more necessary the state.

Polyarchy

As the decade of the 1930s opened, "pluralism, polyarchy, and federalism" defined the concrete constitutional circumstances of the Weimar Republic, a reality that undermined the ethic of the constitution and made urgent the question of how it might be defended.[88] Many factors brought this predicament on the constitution, which Schmitt called "the pluralistic party-state" and "polyarchy."[89]

Der Hüter der Verfassung (1931) applied Schmitt's constitutional theory to the legal and political conflicts of the Republic and offered a series of novel categories for analysis of the economic and social dimensions of the modern state. Here as elsewhere, Schmitt sets the theory of the liberal Rechtsstaat against its reality, but the political conflicts of the Republic and its constitutional fragmentation are explained here, as they were in "Staatsethik und pluralistischer Staat," from the horizon of classical liber-

Carl Schmitt. Photograph taken November 11, 1926. Gift from Schmitt to the author.

Carl Schmitt. Photograph taken in 1930. Gift from Schmitt to the author.

alism. Moreover, Schmitt's history of state and society is a construction, not an empirical reality; the criteria of analysis are drawn from that necessarily present "parliament" as "no longer what it was" and whose "disintegration" empties out the central concepts of law and the state, and the political theory of free individuals. The center of those ideas and theories does not hold when "state" has become "the mere product of compromises among many conflicting groups, at the very best a *pouvoir neutre et intermédiaire,* a neutral mediary, an arbitrator of struggling groups, a kind of clearing office, a troubleshooter, that holds itself back from an authoritative decision."[90]

Der Hüter der Verfassung elaborates the empirical and constitutional causes of the ethical crisis of the state presented in "Staatsethik und pluralistischer Staat." Pluralism has made the German parliament "a showplace of special interests," dominated by political parties. Their reality as "tightly organized" corporations whose business is to win votes stands in stark contrast to the constitutional text and the intent of the framers. Hugo Preuß conceived them as "pillars of public opinion" completely in the tradition of classical liberalism, "incapable of organization, 'an undefined fluid.'" Instead they are permanent institutions, with vast staffs penetrated by complexes of vested interests, with an array of suborganizations to which "their intellectual, social and economic clientele" is bound.[91] This elevates and destroys the liberal notion of a "party" that forms occasionally within an otherwise politically neutral society, and at this moment, the state/society division presumed by liberal theory is transformed into the reality of a total state. In the Weimar Republic, that total state is a "pluralistic party-state," but that does not make it any less total than the one-party states of soviet Russia or fascist Italy.[92] But it is not qualitatively total because it has no unitary purpose or idea. It is quantitatively total, intervening everywhere in a society not really separate from the state, but penetrating and part of it. The result is a weak state, honeycombed by special interests and their parties; and "the state ceases to be a sphere of objective reason and all the means of creating a political will lose their content."[93]

The reality of parliament in a pluralistic party-state caused the governmental instability of the Republic and changed the substance of legislation from the product of rational discussion into the calculus of interests: "In this respect the change since the nineteenth century is fundamental. [It] is concealed by the screen of words and formulae, old ways of thinking and speaking and the formalism that serves them. One should not deceive oneself about the implications of this for attitudes toward the constitution and state."[94] On the analysis of those changes in the institution of parliament, and the organization of political parties, Schmitt asserts that the thick concept of legality has given way to a diluted understanding of the law which separates it from the substantive concept of legitimacy.

The constitutional text defined Weimar as a "unitary federal state,"[95] a formula that avoided irreconcilable positions in 1919.[96] Left to the practice of the Republic, its circumstances produced further fragmentation as special interests and the demands of social policy in an industrial society created a "vertical division of powers."[97] The polyarchy of economic interests forms the real boundaries of the state, according to Schmitt, and through them, the state is being transformed into "an administrative state," actually "a taxation state."[98]

The Reich, indebted by the costs of the Great War and reparations burdens, made deep inroads into the finances of the Länder, reversing their previous relationship. Instead of taking income from central tax funds, the Länder now found themselves contributing to it. The development of central bureaucracies to administer various programs (such as the railways and veterans' benefits) began to impinge on the relative independence of the Länder, and their relationship with Berlin was further irritated by the central government's leading role in the national economy.[99] Between Carl Schmitt and Johannes Popitz, a mutually influential analysis of these issues developed in the later 1920s that is obvious in *Der Hüter der Verfassung.* As state secretary in the Reich Finance Ministry, Popitz had a leading role in creating administrative techniques to alleviate these burdens through their redistribution across all the member states and was an important advocate for tax reform.[100] Popitz was an early critic of Weimar's "administrative confusions" and "complicated structures" and a proponent of rationalization. After his resignation as state secretary, Popitz felt free to advance broader, more political arguments about the constitutional dimensions of administrative and fiscal issues. Pressures from within the private sector and the party politics of the Reichstag had created, he argued in 1927, a "polycratic" system that displaced parliamentary democratic political will formation. Popitz's concept of polyarchy drew on Schmitt's critique of pluralism in *Der Begriff des Politischen,* but Popitz focused on the modern forms of interest representation within the state, not the political parties:

> The will representatives are the Reich, the 17 Länder, 65,000 communities and communal organizations, social insurance funds—there are 7,427 medical insurers, 106 professional organizations, 35 invalid organizations, the Reich insurance office for government employees, the miners pensions insurance fund, and the office for employment

> and unemployment insurance—and further the Office of Public Economy which has its own budget, above all the Reich railways and post, the Reichsbank and in addition to these, multiple other, more or less independent public offices and undertakings.[101]

In unison with Schmitt, Popitz called this "the power of the many" that made escape from the economic depression more difficult and undermined the federalism of the constitution.[102] He had in mind here, Lutz-Arwed Bentin notes, not only the complicated independence of the social insurance offices to the Reich but the administrative responsibility to supervise expenditures from Reich to Länder to the communities.[103] A "unitary" solution was Popitz's preference, although he remained ambivalent, even in July 1932, about reforms that could destroy the historical and cultural inheritance of the Länder for the sake of administrative efficiency.

Civil Law and Private Property: The Constitutional Effects of Polyarchy

The constitution drafted at Weimar, like all liberal-democratic constitutions, was a compromise among the parties. This fact, which contemporary lawyers and political theorists tended to see as exceptional and its major fault, was neither when viewed in a comparative perspective.[104] The constitutions looked to as models by Hugo Preuß in drafting its first part and by the delegates to the assembly at Weimar embodied significant compromise: the English compromised elements of monarchy and popular government, as did the French. In a compromise that would become typical for the nineteenth century, the United States compromised equality and property rights, in an arrangement that created the "working tension between democratic rights and the privileged status of private rights."[105] Madison's political theory assumed that property was connected to other basic human goods, especially liberty, and that the link between liberty and security could be made most effective through property rights. Property was not only a symbol of autonomy for the eighteenth-century Federalists but the actual means of having control over one's life, expressing oneself, and protecting oneself from the encroachments of others.

Although its protection requires involvement of the collective, one of the basic purposes of private property is to shield the individual from collective power. It defines what the society, or its representative, the state, cannot touch (in the ordinary course of things).[106] Madison and the other founders of the U.S. Constitution recognized that property, because it is unequal, must distort democratic participation. Their tack was not to make shares of property equal, thus offsetting its undemocratic effects, but to limit democracy through minority rights.[107] Property rights thus became a key to American constitutional history, their interpretation shaping its culture and politics. For most of its two centuries, the U.S. Constitution has proved flexible enough to accommodate changing views of them without major conflict or recourse to extraordinary governmental means.[108]

Their status in Weimar Germany was more contested and more confused than in the United States. However, as for critical periods of America's constitutional history, the debate over property in the Weimar Republic determined how that country's political institutions were understood. In 1923, 1925, and 1927, three cases arising from property rights claims defined the issues that came to a head in the last year of the Republic.

At the start of the Great Inflation, German courts held to the principle of "mark equals mark." Whatever the real value of the currency you had saved or borrowed, the formal value of what you had or owed remained the same. It was a devastating interpretation of contracts for the traditional German values of thrift and saving, and it hit the middle classes hardest of all. A variety of interest groups clustered around the issues of *Aufwertung,* or the revaluation of "paper mark" debts, and the government's view from 1923 to 1925 took shape within the context of the wider issues of financial and currency policy during the economic crisis.[109]

The government of Wilhelm Marx (Center Party) formed on November 30, 1923, initially opposed the revaluation of debts, continuing the policy of its predecessors,[110] but a decision by the Reichsgerichtshof on November 28, 1923, concerning the value of a prewar mortgage repaid in "paper marks" during the Great Inflation was instrumental in reversing the position of the Marx cabinet. The key figure in shaping policy on this issue was Hans Luther.[111] Former chancellor Gustav Stresemann (foreign minister under Marx) set the issue with the context of Germany's international political and financial circumstances, and his arguments turned the cabinet around. First among them was concern for the success of Rentenmark reforms, introduced six weeks earlier under his own government,[112] which were now threatened by stock market speculation after the court's decision. The reforms, Stresemann told his colleagues, were crucial to the German position in diplomatic negotiations with the Allies over war reparations. Finally, Stresemann expressed his concern that "precisely those classes of the population on which the state had earlier been based should not now be proletarianized by legislation."[113]

The constitutional crisis that enveloped Germany during 1923 had begun with the French occupation of the Ruhr, which Reich president Friedrich Ebert met with a call to "passive resistance," a campaign supported by the government of Wilhelm Cuno and the near unanimous support of the Reichstag. The pattern of financial crisis and its management which dominates the last years of the Republic was already present that winter: economic chaos combined with serious political threats, domestic and international, produced a situation that could not be governed by the normal means of parliamentary democracy. Beginning in late September 1923, when an *Ausnahmezustand* was declared for the whole of the Reich, and continuing through the first *Ermächtigungsgesetz* of October 13, 1923, and the second Ermächtigungsgesetz of December 8, 1923, until the dissolution of the Reichstag on March 13, 1924, the usual channels of legislation were suspended in favor of the "commissarial dictatorship" of the president in Article 48.[114]

Judicial Politics and Constitutional Claims

It is an irony of German politics that the need to end financial speculation set off by the court's decision on November 23, 1923, and thus secure the basis of the Rentenmark reform, had already led the cabinet to opt for a 15 percent revaluation in the third Steuernotverordnung (February 14, 1924), when the Richterverein beim Reichsgerichtshof made its dramatic intervention in the scramble of interest groups coalescing around the issue of revaluation. Just as the court's decision on November 28 set the stone rolling for some kind of revaluation, so the judges' intervention six weeks later set in motion the German judiciary's claims to review ordinary laws and executive decrees in accordance with their constitutionality.

Although there was opposition to a broad interpretation of the courts' review powers, the judiciary had its way in winter 1923.[115] By spring, mark was no longer equal to mark. A revaluation of debts had been achieved de facto through the courts, and the groundwork had been laid for wider claims by the judiciary. Rumors in the German press over Christmas 1923 that the government would act to prevent revaluation despite the court's decision provoked a political response from the judges. In a public letter to Chancellor Marx, Walter Simons, president of the Reichsgerichtshof, warned against legislation of this sort. It would violate the basic principle of contract *(Treu und Glauben)* and infringe property rights guaranteed by Article 153. Further, the judges claimed, "Treu und Glauben stands outside an individual law, outside legal-positivist determination. No legal order that deserves the name can survive without this fundamental principle." Continued application of the principle "mark equals mark" would result in a level of injustice "unbearable in a Rechtsstaat."[116]

Simons's letter of January 8, 1924, in the *Juristische Wochenschrift* not only defended the Reichsgerichtshof's use of equity arguments ("Treu und Glauben") in its decision the previous November but also asserted the court's right of judicial review.[117] To the controversy over revaluation was now added that of the court's role in German politics. In July 1925 a federal law revalued preinflation debts by 25 percent, settling the material question of equity raised in the Reichsgerichtshof decision two years earlier. But constitutional debate was fueled by the court's decision in November 1925 of a case whose circumstances predated the Weimar Republic and whose details were a paradigm of the civil law conflicts over property that followed the Great Inflation.[118]

Having decided in favor of the plaintiff, the Reichsgerichtshof expanded the parameters of its decision by asking, "Are the courts entitled to review the constitutionality of federal laws?" and turned to the Revaluation Law of July 1925. Commenting on public challenges to its validity, the court acknowledged that provisions of the national law, "statutory as well as common," which directly or indirectly apply to the question, must rule, but then asserted that "where such provisions are lacking, it will be necessary to go back to the general principles which may be derived from the nature of the legislative or judicial power and from the activities emanating from these powers as well as their interrelationship."[119] Not only had the Reichsgerichtshof reviewed the constitutionality of a particular law, but it used this occasion to claim that the courts are the final interpreters of the constitution.[120]

Judicial review was the specific issue raised by the Reichsgerichtshof decision on November 4, 1925, but it belonged to the wider problematic of "constitutional jurisdiction" *(Verfassungsgerichtsbarkeit)*. What does the constitution mean, and who decides in cases of conflict such as those in the winter of 1923 to 1924? When the Staatsgerichtshof declared itself to be "the defender of the constitution" in a ruling on October 15, 1927, the lines of constitutional conflict were complete.[121] Controversies in the civil law led to constitutional claims by the judiciary and ultimately to a conflict that was more political than legal: who should defend the constitution?[122]

Constitutional Defense

The Vienna conference of constitutional lawyers in 1929 took place after the German court at Leipzig had asserted its claim to review all laws and state acts for the conformity with the constitution. Both speakers, Heinrich Treipel and Hans Kelsen, agreed that the main question in contemporary jurisprudence concerned the relationship between politics and law in the area of constitutional jurisdiction.[123] Participants in the discussion, including Hans Thoma and Rudolf Smend, agreed. In his paper, Kelsen argued that judicial review completes the ideal of the rule of law, and concluded by advocating a system of constitutional judicial review that far exceeded those specified in Article 19. Judicial review of the constitutionality of governmental acts should extend, in Kelsen's view, to include not only the ordinary law but also treaties with other states, administrative decisions, and executive decrees. "All general norms" should also be included within the purview of a constitutional court, but Kelsen specifically excluded reference to "natural law" principles such as Treu und Glauben from the argument. Nor did Kelsen limit the criteria for the court's decision to the constitution alone; legal precedent, executive decrees, and administrative practice, as well as the rule of international law, were valid points of reference. The institution of judicial review should, Kelsen concluded, "serve as an objective and neutral instance" for the resolution of all constitutional conflicts.[124] Political disputes would in this way be neutralized, appropriate for judicial decision.

The competing constitutional theories of Schmitt and Kelsen shaped the debate about constitutional defense. The determination to reach past legal positivism and Kelsen's normativism led Schmitt to a forceful presentation of the elements in modern society as disintegrative factors within the constitution. More than that—the elements of pluralism, polyarchy, and federalism characteristic of contemporary Weimar belonged to political modernity *as such* for Schmitt. Rather than the constitution of political unity within which socioeconomic forces can be governed, the institutions of Weimar were their object. *Der Hüter der Verfassung* links his argument *against* courts as "defenders of the constitution" to the case *for* the Reich president because those factors exist as part of the state. The state's redistribution of wealth, its creation of work, and its use of labor in the national economy make the state today "the self-organization of society": "In such circumstances, the demand for 'non-intervention' [by the state] is utopian, even a self-contradiction."[125] When so much materially is expected, even demanded, of the state by its subjects, constitutional interpretation cannot assume that political, economic, and social realities are "extraneous" matters. Their governance is, on the contrary, what the law *does.*

Schmitt's argument in *Der Hüter der Verfassung* places the economy at the center of the modern state but draws inconsistent consequences from that. On the one hand, pluralism and polyarchy demonstrate the irrelevance of liberal theory, especially the legality concept based on parliamentarism, but Schmitt also wants to retrieve a classically liberal notion of the strong state reshaped for the twentieth century, authoritative with respect to the economy and civil rights. Such a state would not be indifferent or neutral to interests and power in society but would govern these authoritatively for the sake of political unity. The pillars of such a state are the German professional civil service, an independent, unpolitical judiciary and legal or economic "experts" outside the state.[126]

In Schmitt's broader vision of the constitution as it *might* be developed, the distinction of "negative" from "positive" neutrality leads him toward the office of president as the "defender of the constitution." The special powers of the executive branch, Schmitt argued, were needed to govern "the economic and financial state of emergency."[127] Neither the courts nor the legislature, in which the predicaments of the polycratic and pluralist state were manifest, could serve this function. It was an argument that would come to fruition the following year, in the deepest crisis—"the case on which everything depends"—of the Republic.

6 Constitutional Failure

One must take every intellectual movement metaphysically and morally seriously not as an example of abstract principle, but as a concrete historical reality in the context of historical processes.—CARL SCHMITT, *Politische Romantik*

The crisis that began on Black Friday deepened into a general crisis of the state. With the appointment of Heinrich Brüning as chancellor on March 3, 1930, the evacuation of parliamentary democratic elements in the constitution began. That summer a presidential decree for "The Security of the Economy and Finances" was issued; there would be no return to parliamentary government in Germany until 1949. After the September elections, Brüning could govern only by decree issued through the president's authority in Article 48. The Social Democrats "tolerated" this situation because a vote of no confidence would have given power to the Nazis and Communists. What had been conceived as exceptional became the rule between 1930 and 1932. During the discussion of constitutional reform, many had been aware of the possibility of such a situation. "From the beginning," Dieter Grimm writes,

> The Weimar constitution lacked a broad consensus. Recurrent crises hindered stabilization of the constitutional state. Long before [the state crisis of 1932] a number of possibilities had been considered under the title "Reich reform" including the reorganization of relations between the Reich and Länder, dissolution of the dualism of the Reich and Prussia as well as new territorial divisions. With the col-

lapse of the parliamentary system the question of governability came to the fore. Strengthening the government was particularly important, and that appeared possible only through increased independence from the parliament.[1]

When the constitution failed in 1933, it was a failure at every level. Constitutionalism as the political theory of liberalism had failed. The constitutional order, as a political system, had failed. And the constitution as the foundation of law, as the referent of legal and political discourse, and as the framework of political action had failed.[2]

Political Power in the Constitution

In the beginning was the end: the state crisis of 1932 was prefigured in the turbulence of the first years, and neither the practice of emergency government nor the interpretation of its constitutional foundation in Article 48 can be understood from the last year alone. Between 1921 and 1924 the Republic was shaken by political violence and the complete collapse of its currency, and the doctrine of presidential power developed in response to those events. These years saw an increase in the powers of central government, too, that shifted the political balance among the Länder that became part of the final crisis in the conflict between Prussia and the Reich. After the assassination of Matthias Erzberger in 1921, an executive order mandated the minister of the interior to prohibit publication of newspapers and magazines and public assemblies should these tend toward "anticonstitutional agitation." That order was rescinded at the demand of the Reichstag. When Walther Rathenau was murdered the following year, the legislature passed a "Law for the Protection of the Republic" that incorporated the provisions of the previous executive order, and expanded the authority of the central government over internal security questions. This law created the Staatsgerichtshof as a court of the Reich to adjudicate federal conflicts and whose authority extended to the ministries of *Land* governments. It also empowered the minister of the interior to demand that Länder governments enforce the suspension of certain rights (assembly, press, speech) when "necessary" for the security of the Republic. A law created a federal criminal police with authority within an area usually reserved to the Länder and not only worked to coordinate information on criminal activity but could order the Länder to carry out specific police functions.

In the summer of 1922, Bavaria issued its own order containing much of the substance of the Reich law, but reserving these powers to itself. In this action, the Bavarians claimed to protect "individual rights and the principles of true democracy." For the first time since the foundation of the Reich, a state had refused to obey a Reich law.[3] In the face of this resistance, the central government declined to enforce it. The new police legislation was abandoned, and the Bavarian government retracted its own order. Federal-state conflicts the following year were more serious. A communist government in Saxony defied the Reich government in 1923 but quickly submitted. That conflict became an occasion for further defiance by Bavaria. In the context of the Ruhr crisis and the complete collapse of the German currency in the Great Inflation, the Bavarian government asserted its right to make policy independent of Berlin. In response, a state of emergency was declared throughout Germany, and a commissioner for Bavaria was appointed. The Reichswehr minister was given executive power for the entire Reich to enforce whatever measures were necessary to end the emergency and hold the central state together. The two commissioners came into conflict over measures in Bavaria, and the Reichswehr minister ordered General Otto von Lossow, commander of the army regiment in Bavaria, to carry out the order. Von Lossow too refused and was promptly dismissed from his post. The Bavarian government attempted to replace him with a general of its choice and also placed the army stationed in Bavaria under special obligation to the Land. Behind these maneuvers against the central government and the Reich as such were the political forces that allied with the Nazis and attempted to overthrow the government in the Hitler-putsch a few days later.[4]

Parliament and Government: Divided and Conflicted

Schmitt wanted a "strong state" that could govern Weimar's polyarchy and end the system of "pluralistic parties," but he did not want an "economic constitution" such as that foreseen in Article 165.[5] Schmitt's interpretation of the direct democratic elements of the constitution removed "financial questions" from the people, and he also wanted to remove them from the legislature, as well, and placed such decisions in the hands of the civil service headed by the "positive" neutral power of the president.[6]

Law, in the formal sense, is "that which is undertaken by an office charged with legislation."[7] In no area of the law are the resulting "abbreviations and fictions" more important than in constitutional law, where the identity of governed and governing in a democracy has removed the original meaning of the phrase "on the basis of a law." Representation of the people before a monarch required the consent of parliament (the popular assembly) to all significant legislation—taxation, the budget, declarations of a state of siege or of war, appointments, pardons—and it has become, Schmitt asserts, "nothing more than an artificial expression when such things are done 'on the basis of a law.' " Form loses its meaning here; nothing substantial is given a form. Rather, such usage is "an abbreviated description of the extraordinarily extended competence of a particular instance."[8]

The Reichstag was to be elected in "universal, equal, direct and secret ballot by all men and women twenty years of age, according to the principles of proportional representation" (Article 22). Elected representatives were "representatives of the whole German people," subject only to "their conscience" and "not bound by directions" (Article 21). Electoral law gave the parties—not an institution of the text—power to select representatives, however, and the people voted only for "lists" chosen by parties. These intervened between the people (as electorate) and the parliament (as their representative), reproducing the contradiction of elites and masses already present before the revolution, a contradiction that theorists such as Robert Michels thought to be an inescapable part of government in the modern state.[9] The primary function of the elector's vote, Joseph Schumpeter remarked, "is to produce government," but only in one case—the United States—does this occur directly; in all others, "the electorate's vote . . . produces an intermediate organ, henceforth called parliament, upon which the government-producing function devolves."[10] Weimar's electoral laws prescribed a version of proportional representation that maximized representation of minorities, encouraging splinter parties and discouraging stable coalitions. Governments could be and frequently were brought down without another being in place, a situation that seemed to confirm Max Weber's pessimistic prognosis in summer 1917 for parliamentary government in Germany.[11] Although a more normal pattern of government returned between 1924 and 1928, parliament remained a source of "negative" politics, and the Weimar coalition of parties committed to the new constitution (SPD, DDP, and Center) governed for only four and a half of the Republic's fourteen years. For the rest there were weak coalitions and minority governments in which "more or less antirepublican parties were represented," or "bureaucratic governments" were appointed by the president without an effective parliamentary base in office.[12]

Hugo Preuß and Max Weber knew the Reichstag would play a crucial role in the transition to democracy and the creation of a less authoritarian state. But Preuß—the father of the Weimar constitution and author of its first part—was more optimistic than Weber. Weber advocated a presidential office as a second executive next to the chancellor, should parliament prove unable to build a government. Preuß's hopes were disappointed within a few years:

> The profusion of old and new oppositions, political, religious, economic and social, that ran through [the German] people in combination with proportional representation prevented the building of majorities. Multi-party coalitions, at odds on many important issues, were the only way to form a government and it was often not even possible to form a majority capable of governing, and minority governments stayed in power only because there was not an explicit vote of no confidence.[13]

Under those circumstances, the president's power to appoint a cabinet became something quite different from that envisaged by parliamentary law. Writing in early 1930, Richard Thoma described German parliamentarism as "lame" and hobbled administratively and legislatively. Unable to form a consensus, fragmented and splintered, the Reichstag could not be certain that should the upper house (the Reichsrat) overrule its laws, they could be passed on return, because a two-thirds majority could not be found. Moreover, the Reich president could refuse to sign a bill into law and could dissolve the parliament and call new elections. It was, Thoma wrote, "a suffocating dualism" within the constitution.[14]

Thoma's argument lays out the positive law of German parliamentary government as it had developed, with a glance backward to Preuß's intentions and understanding of parliamentary government. It was not, Preuß argued, government by the fractions in parliament but the formation of a government of "responsible persons with standing at home and abroad, representatives of those parties in the Reichstag [that] represent the consensus of public opinion."[15] This ideal, Thoma conceded, was far from reality; there was no consensus of public opinion on the major issues of the times, on foreign, economic, or cultural policy, and this fact drove parliamentary politics ever further into the politics of the cloakroom, intrigues, and schemes.

The law of parliamentary government devolved, as a result of the "free renunciation of its own constitutional tasks,"[16] onto the law of presidential powers and prerogatives in the constitution. The offices of the president and the Reich government were specified in Articles 41–59. Alone of all central offices, the president was elected directly by the German people (Article 41) and swore to serve "the good of the German people" and do his duty to the laws and constitution. The term of seven years could be shortened by the Reichstag with a two-thirds majority and if supported by a popular referendum (Article 43). He could not be a member of the parliament (Article 44), and he was head of state, representing Germany in international law. Declarations of war required passage of a law by the Reichstag (Article 45), but the president was commander in chief of the armed forces (Article 47). Had parliamentary politics in Weimar not been so fragmented—had there been more consensus or had the cleavages of the electorate not been deepened further by the electoral system—one is tempted to say that the president's role in Weimar could have developed much as that of the *Bundespresident* after 1949: symbolic head of state, a moral leader on occasion, but not the office that determined policy.[17] Instead, the office of president took on the tasks that should have been those of a parliamentary government.

The government of the Reich consisted of the chancellor and ministers (Article 52). They were appointed by the president (Article 53) and "required for the execution of their offices the confidence of the Reichstag," which could remove the government through a vote of no confidence (Article 54). The directive to appoint persons who would enjoy the confidence of the Reichstag was, like the problem of representing public opinion, difficult given the composition of the legislative body. It meant by 1930 that the president should not appoint governments that would be "forced to resign immediately by a vote of no confidence." But that is not the same thing as building a cabinet capable of governing. The trust expected by this appointments process came to mean that the government would enjoy the confidence of the president: "there have been, and will continue to be for the foreseeable future, circumstances in which faced with the choice of appointing persons who will carry out his policies in line with his views and exponents of party political positions," the Reich president will choose the former. Nevertheless, Thoma asserted, there could under no circumstances be a "responsibility of the government to the president."[18]

Presidential Power

Next to the normal role of the president in forming governments with a parliamentary basis were his emergency powers of Article 48, paragraph 2. These allowed the president to take "the necessary measures when public security and order are disturbed" and specifically authorized him to mobilize the military and to temporarily suspend certain individual rights.[19] Such powers belonged to the law of the constitution before 1919 as "classic measures of emergency demanding the use of military force."[20] In 1922 their character changed from a provision for "immediate response to danger when Parliament was not assembled" to a means of governing without regard for parliament.[21] More than half the decrees issued by President Ebert between October 1922 and 1925 concerned economic, fiscal, and social problems, and "in that way Article 48 had become an instrument of emergency legislation for the executive."[22]

The first provision of Article 48 allowed the central Reich government to take over the governmental powers of any Land unable to fulfill its responsibilities under the provincial or Reich constitution. The president was required to inform the Reichstag of any measures taken under this provision, and "to lift them upon the demand of the Reichstag." The extent of presidential power was immediately at issue, and a statute determining it was never passed. The usual interpretation limited presidential power to the suspension of only those seven articles. Based on its practice under Ebert, Schmitt argued for a broad interpretation of Article 48. "From the beginning," he argued in April 1924 at the annual meeting of the Association of German State Lawyers, "the Reich government made use of executive prerogatives in a state of exception, sometimes suspending those (enumerated) articles (first in the Executive Orders of January 11, 1920, and January 13, 1920) and sometimes without doing so (Executive Order of March 22, 1920)." Schmitt's argument tended to expand the powers of Article 48 allowing the president and Reich government broad discretion in their extent. Of particular importance in the last crisis of the Republic was Schmitt's claim that "even intervention in the institutional structure of the constitution" is permitted.[23]

Schmitt's reading of the constitutional law of Article 48 was based on a larger political theory of dictatorship developed before the first crisis of the Republic. *Die Diktatur* (1921) drew on the Roman practice of an "exceptional magistrate" in times of danger for the *imperium*.[24] Appointed by the Senate, this magistrate was charged with putting an end to danger either through war against an external enemy or the suppression of civil war, and later with supervising elections. In the later history of Rome under the dictatorships of Sulla and Caesar, the republican office of magistrate was transformed into a sovereign power.[25] Schmitt's concepts of "commissarial" and "sovereign" dictatorship were based on that history of legal practice and its political transformation. His theory of "constitutional defense" sharpened the distinction by incorporating elements of early modern political thought, including Bodin's argument in *Six livres de la republique* (1583) that the commissar is a public official bound to discharge a specific function specified by edict. The distinction between a commissar and a magistrate was developed by Bodin, according to Schmitt's reading, not as a specification of positive law but as a factor in the realization of law "bound to the idea of justice."[26] Schmitt presented this interpretation to the first conference of the

Association of German Constitutional Lawyers (April 14–15, 1924) at Jena against the criticisms of Gerhard Anschütz and Richard Thoma, Hans Nawiasky, and Fritz Stier-Somlo, who stressed its possible abuse. The issue was, of course, how far a president could go under Article 48. The text entitled him to suspend seven articles of the constitution; Schmitt's interpretation gave the president wider latitude. "He could not permanently alter the constitution," Clinton Rossiter writes, "but he could temporarily prevent the operation of a large part of it."[27] Schmitt thought an "organizational minimum" was required (president, cabinet, Reichstag), who jointly executed the functions foreseen by Article 48 in a specific manner (signatures, countersignatures, and other procedures). "Any temporary abridgement of other articles was not a serious and unconstitutional matter . . . but a necessary method of action permitted by Article 48, employed to save those articles for future operation."[28] The question of a "defender of the constitution" is not, as Kelsen would have it, a question about constitutional jurisdiction but the existential question of when circumstances justify suspension or violation of specific provisions in order to save the constitution itself.

Such exercise of state power is only legitimate when the constitutional power (the subject of sovereignty) remains the same, and Schmitt distinguished between it and the institution of a constitutional defender.[29] He also offered a practical criterion for the limitation of judicial review. The division of powers between legislative, executive, and judiciary in the liberal state makes sense because each of these performs specific functions in the constitution. The legitimacy of law rests on these distinctions being preserved, and one of the most striking features of political life in Weimar (and in other liberal-democratic states since World War I) was their erosion. What Kelsen wanted to give to the judiciary in Weimar belonged, according to the constitutional theory of the liberal state as Carl Schmitt saw it, to the executive branch or to the legislative (the "political" branches of the state) or, as an *ultima ratio* of constitutional life, to the constitution-giving power of the people.

Der Hüter der Verfassung concluded by advancing the office of president to fulfill that role in the German constitution. Only the presidential office could act as a positively neutral power, an institution Schmitt thought of in explicitly monarchical terms: one who reigns but does not govern.[30] In the Weimar democracy, only this office is directly chosen by the people, moreover, and could provide the legitimacy of a personal leader. It was the central element in a strong state as Schmitt understood it that "democracy creates a competent government . . . a government that rests on a democratic foundation, that enjoys the approval and acclamation of the people, is stronger and more intense than any other kind of government."[31]

Liberal political theory assumed the separation of politics and law, and the special position of the judiciary in the liberal constitution is based on that assumption. Kelsen and Schmitt both accepted this theory but interpreted it differently. Kelsen thought that by giving political decisions over to the judicial branch once normative procedures for constitutional jurisdiction were in place, these political conflicts could be solved by a neutral power. Schmitt's theory too assumes that a "neutral power" is both possible and necessary in the state, but he also distinguishes between "negative" neutralities (those not leading to a decision) and "positive" ones (those that produce a binding decision).[32] The function of a positive neutral power could not be filled by the judiciary in Kelsen's legal-technical sense of it, nor could a "political judiciary" act as "defender of the constitution." The result would be either indecision or a radical politicization that destroys the liberal element of the constitution completely. The liberal system of neutralities—the rule of law as a process, the division of powers as checks and balances, the ideal of *Justizförmigkeit* in politics, which is the intellectual basis of these—had not neutralized public life under mass democratic political circumstances. The reverse is true:

> Ten years ago experienced authors and leaders of all sorts assured us that one only needed to do away with the political and politicians, and all our difficult problems would be solved. A radical "depoliticization" would mean that technical, economic, judicial and other experts would decide all hitherto political questions according to purely juridical, in short according to purely "objective" criteria. . . . This kind of "depoliticization" has now revealed itself to be a useful political means to postpone unpleasant problems and necessary reforms and thus preserve an absurd status quo in which every decisive will for change runs out of steam. After such experiences with a "non-politics" *(Nichtpolitik),* it must be obvious that all problems are potentially political problems.[33]

The primacy of the political means, if we look at the relationship between the state and politics in Schmitt's work, that an "order" is never established once and for all beyond its dynamic. Schmitt leaves us in no doubt about the importance of this fact; the political is a relationship of intensity (friendship or enmity) that includes war as its most extreme possibility. Political conflicts "can neither be decided through an existing general norm nor through the decision of an 'impartial' and therefore nonpartisan third."[34]

Presidential authority to dissolve the parliament in the circumstances of gridlock characteristic of Weimar shifted power away from that body to the executive branch. With the appointment of Brüning as chancellor and the Nazis' electoral success in September 1930, the flow became a flood that effectively replaced the constitution of parliamentary government with the "reserve constitution" contained in Article 48. Thoma had noted that the text of Articles 53 and 54 and the system of appointment as a whole conflicted with Article 25, which allowed the president to dissolve the Reichstag.[35] A government "needs the confidence of the Reichstag" (Article 54) but could be dismissed by the Reich president (Article 25). That article further specified that the president must give his reason for dismissing a government, which could only be used "once"—although the actual grounds for the six presidential dissolutions from March 1924 until September 12, 1932, were the same: parliamentary incapacity. The authors of the constitutional text designed its organization on the assumption that "the parliamentary system would function normally" with clearly recognizable majorities. It did not. Presidential dissolutions did not resolve policy differences about which there was a clear public opinion. They did not put an either/or question to the electorate. Instead, dissolution of the Reichstag was "an attempt to create a parliament that could form a government and have an opinion."[36]

In 1930 the interests that had formed around the president and within the Große Koalition were determined to replace parliament with a presidential regime. The Reichstag, Heinrich Winkler writes, had functioned badly, but its existence still gave the masses of German voters participation in the choice of government. Presidentialism would necessarily exclude them and provoke mass protest: the only question was which elements in the state would benefit from that protest.[37]

The appointment of Heinrich Brüning as chancellor began "the moderate phase" of presidential government.[38] In Schmitt's terms this was a period of "commissarial dictatorship," but not of effective government. After the appointment of Franz von Papen, the circle around General Kurt von Schleicher, advised by Schmitt and others, began to advance specific constitutional changes, but still with "commissarial" intent: to reform but preserve the existing constitution of the Republic.[39] Events and the intentions of some in the clique around Papen and Hindenburg shifted the presidential regime toward "sovereign dictatorship" in mid-1932. Throughout both phases, the rule of law remained intact, despite the exclusion of the Reichstag from government.[40] No new elections were necessary until September 1934, and Hindenburg might have retained Brüning until then, and the economic depression might have lifted, leading to a reorganization of the political center. It is an attractive view in hindsight.

Instead Hindenburg appointed the "unpolitical" Franz von Papen, an archconservative with ties to those around Hitler, and there were already signs of the Nazis' increasing power. The appointment of von Papen's "Cabinet of Barons" on June 1, 1932, followed Hindenburg's two-round victory over Hitler in the presidential election that spring. The candidate of the NSDAP had taken 37 percent of the votes—an indication of whom the protest against Brüning's policies benefited. In Prussia, where the violence was worst, the Social Democratic government had banned the party-political military formations of the National Socialists and Communist Parties in an atmosphere of civil war. The German army was outnumbered four to one by the combined military formations of the Sturmabteilung (SA) and Schutzstaffel (SS). Schleicher's office was directly concerned with the strategic response of the military should a full-scale conflict erupt.

In that context, Papen made two strategically disastrous choices. At his request, Hindenburg dissolved the Reichstag, and new elections were called for July 31. Less than a fortnight before election day, the Reich government, acting on the powers in Article 48, appointed a Reich commissioner for Prussia and removed the elected government.

During this period, Schmitt advised the group of men in the Wehrmachtsabteilung of the War Ministry, the personal staff of General Kurt von Schleicher, on questions of the constitutional law and the law of emergency. We do not know exactly what advice he gave them, but *Legalität und Legitimität* was written simultaneously and published that summer with the remark that it was completed on July 10, 1932.[41] Parts of the text appeared in newspaper articles before the election, warning against a vote for the anticonstitutional parties.[42] It was an angry and polemical text, in which Schmitt set legality against legitimacy and forcefully rejected a "thin" concept of the latter, even turning "legality" into the opposite of "legitimacy." Only two types in the Weberian paradigm of legitimacy remained, "traditional" and "charismatic." Drawing on his earlier analysis of parliament and the substance of democratic homogeneity, Schmitt asserted that the legislative branch no longer functioned to produce law because the real composition of the Reichstag prevented the formulation of common will in norms, because the division of power presumed in the Rechtsstaat had been broken, and its laws were the mere products of power.[43] The source of authority that established a congruence of "justice" and "legislation" and was the origin of genuine law had been evacuated from contemporary parliament.[44]

The centerpiece of Schmitt's argument warns against adherence to an "equal chance" for all parties to compete for votes in the forthcoming election, and against the procedural, formal notion of democracy.[45] It is more important, he argues, that certain parties not participate, even if they do express the opinion of the people. This text also develops Schmitt's concept of the "political premiums" of power that can destroy the state: "The governing party controls the overwhelming power that inheres in *possession of the legal means of power.* . . . The majority is no longer just a party, it is the state itself."[46]

In the circumstances of parliamentary incapacity, the Weimar constitution provides three "extraordinary" legislators, Schmitt argues: the material laws in part 2, "The Rights and Duties of Germans"; the plebiscitary power of the people; and the provisions of Article 48. He urges appeal to all these as the only exit from the emergency and, in a famous conclusion, divided the constitution in two: must one choose between them, and the choice must fall to the "extraordinary" constitution. Clinging to the "dilatory formal compromises" of Weimar, insistence on thin legality and its forms will open the doors of the state to a party that will close those behind it in the worst outcome of antagonistic pluralism. Should that happen, "there will be a quick end to the fictions of the value and truth of neutral majority functionalism. Then the truth will avenge itself."[47]

The elections went ahead and produced an outcome that only weakened the presidential cabinet further. There was a large increase in the Nazi vote. Although the NSDAP did not have a majority, in combination with the Communist Party, the two could call a vote for a vote of no confidence in the presidential cabinet and win it. Overtures to Hitler offered him a cabinet post, but not the chancellorship. The time was not ripe for inclusion of the radical Right; Hitler would settle for nothing less than chancellor, and before the autumn, at least, he was unwilling to submit to Hindenburg's stipulations.[48] After the July elections, Papen's "Cabinet of Barons" and the military used the time before the Reichstag would reconvene for maneuver that some hoped would avoid the inclusion of Hitler.

At the first cabinet meeting after the July elections, the "state of emergency plan" was on the agenda. The Preußenschlag on July 20 had been an opening salvo in a complete reform of the constitution that was laid out by interior minister Gayl in a speech on August 13. Its major points advocated (1) electoral law reform (abolition of proportional representation, additional votes for heads of families, limits on splinter parties); (2) an upper body of "notables" appointed by the president; and (3) an end to the "dualism" of Prussia in the Reich. Gayl did not indicate how these reforms were to be effected, but they could not come about via Article 76, the only constitutionally prescribed route, given the composition of the Reichstag.[49] Papen seemed to support these measures in public but continued to work privately for the appointment of NSDAP members to the cabinet. At a meeting between Hindenburg and Hitler in late August, the Nazi leader insisted on the chancellorship as the "price" for participation. Hindenburg declined, and the meeting ended on a sour note. Civil war seemed to come closer. A week later, in preparation for reconvening the Reichstag, Hindenburg prepared an order dissolving it.[50]

Over the summer, Oberstleutnant Ott, a member of Schleicher's staff with close ties to Schmitt, had conducted a war game between the army and the SA and SS forces of the Nazis. In late summer and early autumn, the military became increasingly skeptical about a direct clash with the Nazi forces. Ernst Rudolf Huber described Schmitt's involvement with the planning of a state of emergency and his relationship with Ott and others in Schleicher's office.[51] On the night of August 28, 1932, Huber (Schmitt's student and colleague) attended a meeting at Schmitt's Berlin apartment to discuss the constitutional-legal aspects of the "state of emergency," specifically the plan to postpone elections. Schmitt and Huber advised Ott that the elections could be postponed, and based their argument on the presidential oath to defend and protect the constitution. The necessity of pacifying radical paramilitary forces and the overall condition of the nation made for "a genuine state of emergency."[52] Article 48 and the presidential oath trumped Article 25: the substance of the constitution could only be defended if its electoral provision was sacrificed.

Meeting at Hindenburg's East Prussian estate, Neudeck, Papen and Gayl urged the president to implement the emergency plan. He agreed and signed the Reichstag dissolution paper; the men discussed further constitutional reforms that would be implemented while there was no sitting parliament. On September 12, the new parliament met under the chair of Hermann Göring for its first session. Papen held the dissolution order in his hand and looked up at Göring from the government bench. Göring looked resolutely away and recognized a Communist Party member, who called for a vote of no confidence.[53] As Papen fumed—the chancellor was, by the rules of the house, entitled to speak first—the vote proceeded. At the end, 512 were for, and 42 against, dissolution. New elections were scheduled for November 6. The government had suffered a terrible blow in the vote of no confidence, which undermined its credibility among the public and encouraged the intransigence of anticonstitutional parties.

The Communists and National Socialists called a transit strike in the capital on election day, November 6, 1932. Huber was once again in Berlin

The Reichstag vote of no confidence, September 12, 1932. Göring recognizes the KPD member as Papen stands waiting with the dissolution order. Reprinted from Franz von Papen, *Memoirs* (London: A. Deutsch, 1952).

at Schmitt's request and walked through the desolate streets of the city with him and Otto Kirchheimer, Schmitt's doctoral student.[54] "In Kirchheimer's presence," Huber recalled in 1986, "we did not speak of the emergency plan. . . . but it was clear that Schmitt now regarded it as hopeless."[55] Schleicher and his group began to build a crosscutting alliance based on the military and civil service but appealing to the left wing of the NSDAP under Gregor Strasser, the SPD trade unions, and others. He was emerging as "the social general." On December 3, 1932, Hindenburg dismissed Papen and appointed Schleicher to the chancellorship. Over the next six weeks, he made frantic efforts to consolidate the social and political basis of his presidential cabinet. The Reichstag would be dissolved on January 31, 1933, at its first meeting, and Schleicher tried to convince Hindenburg to postpone new elections past the legal deadline until autumn 1932 and allow him to use that time "to crush the radical movements."[56]

He failed. Schleicher was ultimately brought down by a combination of democratic parties, especially the Catholic Center, weary of the political stalemate, and the president's refusal to break the law requiring elections as specified in Article 25. In the meantime, the coup against Prussia had been the subject of the greatest constitutional case in the Republic,[57] in which all the major constitutional lawyers participated. The case turned on Schmitt's constitutional theory and the arguments of *Legalität und Legitimität*. Both sides, the Reich and Prussia, claimed to have acted legitimately to defend the constitution earlier that year, Prussia in forbidding the radical parties, the Reich in removing the Prussian government. The case tested, so to speak, both constitutional methods, statute positivism and the pure theory of law and the political science of the constitution, but the advocates were aligned on both sides of the case. Schmitt led the defense of the Reich; Heller was on the Prussian legal team, and Kelsen supported the Prussian case with written briefs. The court's decision was a compromise. It ruled in favor of both parties, reinstating the elected government but removing its powers to the Reich commissar, Johannes Popitz.

In the definitive study of Schmitt's role in the emergency of summer and autumn 1932, Lutz Berthold considers Schmitt's denial that he instigated the plan for an emergency or was directly involved with its implementation.[58] Documents now available in the Schmitt Nachlaß point to a paper drafted by Horst Michael in mid-1932 in answer to the question "How can an effective presidential government be protected from an incompetent and obstructionist Reichstag, with the goal of defending the constitution?"[59] On the basis of Schmitt's diary for this period, now in preparation for publication, Berthold concludes that there is no doubt that the document was written under Schmitt's influence and with his constitutional advice.

Schmitt's interpretation of Article 25 (parliamentary dissolution), Article 48 (presidential powers), and Article 76 (constitutional reform) would have allowed constitutional reforms despite the incapacity of the Reichstag based on Schmitt's political theory of legitimacy and constitutional sovereignty, and on equity principles and the supralegal quality of emergency.[60] This empirical evidence only demonstrates what careful reading of Schmitt's published work has long made obvious. The last opportunity for a commissarial solution was the final meeting of the Schleicher cabinet on January 16, 1933. Schleicher began by saying it was now a question of whether the Nazis would participate in government or fight, and he argued that when the Reichstag assembled on January 30, 1933, it should immediately be dissolved and elections postponed.[61] In the next two weeks, however, the democratic parties voiced their opposition, and Ludwig Kaas, chair of the Catholic Center, wrote to Schleicher warning him against "unconstitutional plans" devised from within the circle around Carl Schmitt.[62] The plan was never implemented.

When Hindenburg appointed Hitler chancellor on January 30, 1933, the emergency of parliamentary government was over in Germany. A government with a majority in the Reichstag was in office for the first time since 1928. The moment of constitutional defense had passed, but the Weimar constitution remained in effect formally until the German defeat in May 1945.

Constitutional Failure

With Hitler's appointment, liberal constitutionalism ceased in Germany. It was dead as legal theory, and its forms too would soon cease.[63] The foundation of law, as Schmitt recognized, was no longer *ratio* but *voluntas,* now conceived as "the will of the führer." What remained of the constitution was "mere text" successively reshaped by Enabling Laws (the first on March 24, 1933), presidential decrees, and constitutional reform laws. Less than a year after becoming chancellor, Adolf Hitler presided over a Germany legally and constitutionally unrecognizable from that a few years earlier. Most of the changes that Schmitt and others around Schleicher favored were realized—but with substantively different meaning: there was a state of emergency,[64] the Länder were "coordinated" with the Reich in accordance with a law drafted in part by Carl Schmitt and Johannes Popitz,[65] the parties were abolished, and the NSDAP was the only legal organization.[66]

Schmitt's role in these events and this transition has remained a source of fascination and controversy. No constitution has failed with such terrible consequences as that of Weimar, and reflection on its causes, on the moments at which it might yet have succeeded, is always a work of grief.[67] Whether Schmitt's political theory is useful or not depends less on the misuse to which critiques of liberalism can be put than on its power to explain the dysfunctional effects of liberal-democratic constitutions today. To the question of Carl Schmitt in Weimar, the question of his role under Hitler must present itself as one about his political theory as a connection between Weimar and the Third Reich. Immediately after World War II, many wanted to draw a simple line between political critique and consequences. According to that view, Schmitt's work "more or less covertly aimed at the destruction of the Weimar Republic, because he opted for the National Socialists long before 1933."[68] In popular-intellectual culture Schmitt, like Martin Heidegger, became a *Sündenbock* for the Federal Republic, but such views have few proponents today. Addressing the relation between Schmitt's critique of law and the political system of the Republic and his later advocacy of fascism, Ingeborg Maus offers a subtle and persuasive reading of the texts.[69] Schmitt was not a traditional

"The Red Peril." Hindenburg gives Hitler emergency powers as the Reichstag burns. Originally published in the *Montreal*, March 23, 1933. Reprinted from Ernst Hanfstaengl, *Hitler in der Karikatur der Welt* (Berlin: Braune Bücher Carl Rentsch, 1933).

"Whither?" Originally published in the *Daily Express* (London), June 29, 1933. Reprinted from Ernst Hanfstaengl, *Hitler in der Karikatur der Welt* (Berlin: Braune Bücher Carl Rentsch, 1933).

"Legal." Originally published in *Der Wahre Jacob* (Berlin), February 23, 1932. Reprinted from Ernst Hanfstaengl, *Hitler in der Karikatur der Welt* (Berlin: Braune Bücher Carl Rentsch, 1933).

conservative and rightly saw the political problems of "organized capitalism" and the necessity of a new kind of political authority after the end of the monarchy, she argued. The vision of the state Schmitt advanced, its critique of the "regulative" and "welfare" states of the twentieth century, has much in common with the current ideology of "privatization": a strong state, but a neutral state that allows maximum room for the economy was Schmitt's and Popitz's goal. Neoliberals today have found his argument against the welfare state and "big government" appealing, and F. A. Hayek defines such developments as a "failure of the constitution."[70] Finally, some have argued that Schmitt's support for the presidential system intended "to support the Weimar Republic in difficult times and defend it against its totalitarian enemies." Advocates of that interpretation see a radical break between Schmitt's pre- and post-1933 work.[71] The recent wave of English-language scholarship on Schmitt has tended toward readings that are less captive to the German context, but they too still struggle with the contagion of fascism that might lurk in his critique of liberalism.[72]

What is living and what is dead, then, in the political theory of Carl Schmitt? In one dimension, Schmitt is the premier theorist of "interim regimes" and "transitional states":[73] his work is a constant warning against the presumption that having a "written constitution" is being a constituted political unity; and the lessons one might draw from the example of Weimar on the justification of political authority direct us toward other, nonempirical concerns. By the time Schmitt wrote the *Verfassungslehre,* he saw the reform question as a problem less of specific elements than of the whole constitution, a reading that necessarily construed its "metajuristic" elements to impose institutional coherence on a document that created a competition of executive and legislative powers alongside provisions for direct democratic initiatives in part 1 (Articles 73 and 76) and irreconcilable political values and perspectives in part 2 (Articles 109ff.).[74] In the emergency of 1932, Schmitt decided for the substantial elements in the "extraordinary legislators" of the text: the material laws in part 2, "The Rights and Duties of Germans"; the plebiscitary power of the people; and the provisions of Article 48.

Schmitt had further derived the notion of the constitution as "inviolable."[75] The result was a conservative reading of the Weimar constitution that denied that it could be changed essentially except through the intervention of a constitution-giving power.[76] In the emergency, the president was the only institution that could act as the people's "commissar": the courts could not; the Reichstag was the source, institutionally, of the crisis.

An appeal to higher values was part of Schmitt's larger political theory from the start: but what higher values? One set was political. The Weimar constitution was more than statute law and more than norms: it was the concrete political decisions defining the political existence of the German people and "the basis for all further norms including the constitutional laws. . . . They make up the substance of the constitution."[77] This distinction separated constitutional provisions from "the" constitution. Schmitt's theory had sought to limit revision within the normal legislative procedure (which might reform certain laws of the constitution) but recognized it through a sovereign act. To abolish, reform, or otherwise change the makeup of the Weimar constitution as *substantive decisions* for democracy, liberal representation, federalism, and the basic rights of the bürgerliche Rechtsstaat would be not reform but revolution, he argued in the *Verfassungslehre.* But the emergency of 1932 brought the exception into the constitution itself, offering both roads to its political resolution: commissarial or sovereign change.

Even though several definitions and distinctions are intended to limit the prospect of constitutional violation,[78] these pale in comparison to brute political fact: no constitution can be "defended" from its sovereign. The second part of the constitutional text incorporated the results of debate in the National Assembly, where the entire spectrum of political opinion in revolutionary Germany was represented, and which generated what Schmitt called its "compromise character." Some of these compromises contributed to the decisive core of the text; others did not. Of the former, the most important was the question of a socialist or liberal republic, of a *bürgerlich* or a socialist organization of the economy and thus of German society. In the politics of the Assembly, those alternatives became objects of compromise among the interested parties that found a certain "middle station" between the two perspectives. Despite that, Schmitt asserts, "the basic decision was for a liberal Rechtsstaat and constitutional democracy."[79] The aim of these compromises was to avoid a principled decision, even though the decision between liberal Rechtsstaat and proletarian class-state fell to the first type of constitution. These were genuine decisions, Schmitt writes, and the second part of the constitution contained a range of genuine compromises on issues of principle. It also contained "inauthentic compromises" that were only superficial. The political issues behind them ranged the entire field of friend/enemy relations from simple conflicts of interest to class warfare, and these were neither decided nor really compromised at Weimar. Instead they sat within the text as specters, Schmitt seems to have felt, of the popular revolutionary potential.[80]

In the political circumstances of the Republic, Schmitt's argument worked to check the power of political parties and limit the authority of the parliament. It conceived the dynamic of constitutional events in the political system from its boundaries—from the "outside" *(Extremfall)* inward. The most radical of these was destruction of a constitution, but the set included change, violation, suspension, conflicts, and treason.[81] The distinctions Schmitt draws between constitutional change in the form of amendment and constitutional violation (a norm is not changed, but in a particular case "violated") and constitutional suspension (a temporary caesura in the norms of constitutional practice) are the most important for our concerns here, because they form the basis of Schmitt's identification of constitutional laws. Since including all positive-legal provisions of the constitutional document in the definition of the constitution itself would make nonsense of its unity, there must be some basis on which to distinguish one kind of law from another. Schmitt replaces the abstract hierarchy of laws (Kelsen) with real distinctions. While the "fundamental decision" of the sovereign people cannot be ignored in times of emergency, specific provisions can be:

> The constitution in its true sense, i.e., the fundamental political decision about the existential form of a nation, cannot of course be temporarily suspended, but general constitutional-legislative norms promulgated in its realization surely can be—and precisely in the interest of maintaining these decisions. In particular, the typical liberal democratic Rechtsstaat guarantees of individual freedom can come under a temporary suspension.[82]

To critics, Schmitt's otherwise constructive reading of Weimar's text moves toward concepts that empty out the notion of normal democratic sovereignty. Most unsettling, and in retrospect ominous, is the argument that rights as legal institutions can remain even when these are not secured to the individuals or groups who bear them.[83] As commissarial dictatorship gave way to sovereign dictatorship in 1933, the dualism of Schmitt's theory of rights haunted his attempt to theorize plebiscitary democracy and divided again the notion of sovereignty from that of constitutional power in the triad of *Staat, Bewegung, Volk.*

Beyond the higher political values of democracy, however, Schmitt's theory appealed to "ultimate values"—God, Mankind, and the World—which he had warned against inserting into the "scuffles of daily politics."[84] But a theory so referentially bound to revelation as his would necessarily engage precisely those values when it entered the realm of actual politics. In "the people" of Schmitt's *Verfassungslehre* and those of

Staat, Bewegung, Volk, many have seen an argument that led Schmitt—and the German people—ineluctably into the Third Reich. Hans Kelsen, and following him H. L. A. Hart, defined the constitution through the "rule of recognition."[85] Schmitt too emphasizes "recognition," but not the recognition of a norm. The recognition that matters—the case on which everything depends—is the people's own recognition of themselves as actors and agents in the larger horizon of the ultimate value of "a politically substantive decision": "In general one can say that [this] concept is relativized and pluralized as soon as the consciousness of political existence begins to dissipate, and the idea of unity increases when this consciousness comes to life again."[86] Accordingly, the precondition and foundation of the constitution is political will, the will of an existing people whose constitutional power is not exhausted in giving itself a constitution.[87] Such values are part and parcel of the successful democracies Schmitt referred to as "strong states," England and the United States, where their reference does not intensify other political conflicts only because, and only so long as, they enjoy general acceptance. Detached from the formal restraints of legality and the ethos of a positive constitution, however, appeals to God, Mankind, and the World radicalize political struggle to the point of total enmity. Political theology reveals, Schmitt argued, the radical conceptual connections between law, the state, and theology, and only such a political theory, "followed to its final consequences in metaphysics and theology," is capable of truth. The line visible in Schmitt's work takes that argument from theological monism and the unitary state through dualism and constitutional democracy into the pragmatic pluralism of a disenchanted world and its "weak total state." Schmitt saw himself as a "poor unworthy Christian Epimetheus" who struggled to recover meaning in those moments of the political when the exceptional reveals itself.[88]

Fascism has been described as the metapolitical phenomenon of "resistance to transcendence," a "revolution of nihilism" that denied any meaning beyond that immanent in race and racial belonging.[89] Its annihilating drive to reduce the individual to his mere nature, his finite being, made fascism seem to many contemporaries, and others since, a form of Antichrist, or ultimately explicable only in religious terms.[90] Fascism's irrational, mass-hysterical content has often been described as a revolt against modernity, and an attack on reason. It has also been understood as a "secular religion" in which the state and führer replace God.[91] This approach has been revived recently by Michael Burleigh: an extraordinary rape of the soul, in which "sections of the German elites and masses of ordinary people chose to abdicate their individual critical faculties in favor of a politics based on faith, hope, hatred and sentimental collective self-regard for their own race and nation." The Nazis offered "redemption from a national ontological crisis," Burleigh writes, and can only be understood as "totalitarianism," as "secular religion."[92]

At first glance, Carl Schmitt's political theory would seem to offer little support for such historiography. It is often explicitly Christian and Catholic, and Schmitt himself could accurately be described as a latter-day counterrevolutionary who wished that Rome and its church could return a world based on the values of European Christendom. In *Römischer Katholizismus und Politische Form* (1923), Schmitt presented the church as the only institution able to overcome the trap of romanticism that encapsulated the modern individual because the church alone represents the highest truth, a God who is substantial, personal in and above time.[93] Only such limits, Schmitt argues, safeguard against the destructive powers of technology and economy. It was a text to rehabilitate the Catholic ethic against Weber's Puritan ethic that found its way into Schmitt's constitutional theory in his insistence on the personal and the direct, and on the immanence of the people. Yet Schmitt's constitution included *and* excluded; not all were called to be members of "the people."

This theory of constitutional power builds, as so much of Schmitt's work, on the history of revolution in Europe from the English Civil War and the wars of religion through the French Revolution and its aftermath. It is, for Schmitt, "the transformation of the divine into the civic."[94] As Patrick Riley has shown, the idea of the general will was an established part of theology, a theory for reconciling God's will with the fate of individual men to salvation or damnation. In that context, "the general will referred to the *kind* of will that God (supposedly) had in deciding who would be granted grace sufficient for salvation and who would be damned." At stake was the question posed by Paul: If God wills all men to be saved, does that mean he has a general will to that effect, and if so, why are some particular men not saved?[95] The distinction between general and particular will that Rousseau made famous, Riley argues, was "parts of a larger question about the justice of God; they were always 'political' questions, in the largest sense of the word 'political'—in the sense that even theology is part of what Leibniz called 'universal jurisprudence.' "[96]

The theodicy problem became in Schmitt's work the complex of questions about modern constitutions that issue from political theology. As God created the world, so the people create a constitution. Their power to do so is explicitly compared in the eighteenth century, and again by Schmitt at the beginning of the twentieth, to the power of God. Both have "will" that creates an existence, and the "power" and "authority" of that will are not, he asserts, questions for a constitutional theory but questions for political or state theory in its largest horizon. That placement links Schmitt's argument, however, back to "universal jurisprudence" and the metalegal questions it contained. The distinction of *potestas* and *auctoritas* is made here in temporal terms; power ("necessarily real") is the referent of terms such as "sovereignty" or "majesty," while authority signifies "an appearance that rests within the moment of continuity and refers to tradition and permanence."[97] Its classic locus was Roman law, with the original distinction between the Senate (auctoritas) and the people (potestas and imperium). With the end of the Roman Empire and the rise of Christianity, these two are broken apart. The letter of Pope Gelasius I to Emperor Anastasius claimed authority for the church, an assertion of power that would become the center of political controversy in the later Middle Ages. The "two swords" controversy and the question of justification persisted into the modern world, Schmitt argues, where its agent and the substance of creation are transformed. This is the deeper meaning of "secularization" and also the origin of the problem of "higher values" in modern political theory.

In *Politische Romantik,* Malebranche and Rousseau are the decisive figures in the transformation of the divine into the civic, Malebranche because his philosophy introduces the oppositions of thought and being that make the real "irrational," and Rousseau for his insertion of the romantic will into the general will of the social contract. Both men drew the comparison between a well-governed earthly kingdom and Creation, explicitly politicizing the general will. The dynamic of that will, secularized and released from its theological and institutional context, appears in Schmitt's political theory in two remarkably dissimilar forms: the romantic subject and the constitutional power. While the former seems capable only of Dionysian self-obsession and is a source of chaos, the constitutional power is ordering and creative without, however, Apollonian restraint. Both are products of *occasio;* one leads toward "the political" confrontation of wills and existences, the other toward the order of "a concrete political existence."

The *Verfassungslehre* draws on concepts of popular power analogous to God's power. The nation is "formless Former" capable of changing its form and "the original source of all political life" (81). It follows from this that the constitutional power does not rest on a norm and cannot be justified; it "is." Schmitt explicitly rejects the older questions of "good" and "right" associated with theodicy: "it does not matter whether the law in general is essentially command or *ratio*" because the concrete instance of constitutional power need not even address that dispute. Its will is the substance of "the constitution," which particular laws execute. The constitution does not exhaust, consume, or absorb the power of its creator: "this will remains next to and above the constitution," and every genuine political conflict could be resolved by the constitutional power. It is "unitary and indivisible" (75–81). During the French Revolution, Sieyes, following Spinoza, distinguished between "pouvoir constituant" and "pouvoirs constitues" in a metaphysical analogy to *natura naturans* and *natura naturata.* The "positive concept of the constitutional power," Schmitt remarks, must not be considered part of "the pantheistic metaphysics," although such arguments are part of political theology (80). Schmitt's theory deliberately leads the reader away from such problems, toward a practical political science of the state in a democratic age. The construct can be laid out thus:

State Form	*Political/Constitutional Subject*
nation	the people
monarchy	the king
oligarchy	a minority

The last is to be determined not "mathematically" by counting votes, or percentages, but by reference to a "definite organization," and there are two contemporary examples: the communist and fascist regimes.

The failure of Weimar was, for Schmitt, ultimately the failure of that substance informing the constitution of political unity; the institutions of the text did not cease to function in a technical fashion—they were evacuated of all meaning and significance. They became objects, at the end, of popular *disbelief,* "a mortal god" that had failed and with him failed all his rituals and forms.[98]

Political Theology: An Epilogue

The Nazi state combined oligarchy and nationalism in a deadly mixture of modernity and reaction.[99] Between 1928 and 1938, Carl Schmitt returned over and over again to the problem of the modern state, and in his conversations with Johannes Popitz as the regime became ever more total, the grounds of obedience and political authority were a continual topic. But the Nazi state had erased all the navigation points of political philosophy, most importantly the security created by "the real will of them all" in sovereignty. Embedded in Hobbes's *Leviathan* was a silent and fatal flaw, Schmitt concluded, that permitted the historical emergence of "a providential enemy."[100]

Liberal political thought and the practice of its constitutions remove the possibility of substantial values by separating public affairs from the private satisfactions and thoughts of individuals. These have often been conceived as "interests," and as such liberal theory implies a necessary connection between the personal and the public. Schmitt denied the possibility of that connection on the most radical grounds. Interiority constructed in this way not only insulated the individual from the practices of state authority; "privacy" would ultimately destroy public authority. *Leviathan* presented a purely decisionist theory: "nothing here is true, everything is command," Schmitt comments.[101] Sovereign power over subjects is essentially material: "Liberty, or Freedome, signifieth (properly) the absence of Opposition; (by Opposition, I mean external Impediments of motion)."[102] Sovereign command extended theoretically to every motion by every creature rational or irrational, and the sovereign authority to define included those theological questions that rent early modern Europe: "a miracle," Schmitt writes, "is what the sovereign state authority commands its subjects to believe to be a miracle." But the reverse is also true: "Miracles cease when the state forbids them."[103] Religious dispute after 1517 centered on one miracle in particular, the transubstantiation of bread and wine into the body and blood of Christ. This miracle defined the political unity of Christendom—and marked its schism. When Hobbes, as the founder of the modern theory of the state, gave to sovereign state authority the power to establish and disestablish the church, it was an instance of "the public reason in contrast to the private reason of subjects" (85). At this point, the rupture of the "overpowering unity" of the modern state occurs:

> Hobbes declares the question of wonder and miracle to be a matter of "public" in contrast to "private" reason; but on the basis of universal freedom of thought—*quia cogitatio omnis libera est*—he leaves to the individual's private reason whether to believe or not to believe and to preserve his own *judicium* in his heart, *intra pectus suum.* But as soon as it comes to public confessions of faith, private judgment ceases and the sovereign decides about the true and the false. (85)

Cromwell defined "natural" enemies as those created by God, and whoever thought these accidental does not know "the Scripture" and the "things of God." In Carl Schmitt's theologico-philosophical history, the Jew bears this central concept of liberalism, freedom of thought. As a historical actor, the Jewish people thus occupy center stage in the drama of Revelation and are more important for Schmitt than any other nation. As liberty of thought enlarges its sphere—as the boundaries of private and public shift—the former grows at the expense of the latter, but also at the expense of *truth* and the highest value to which the political can be referred: "Jesus is the Christ." Hobbes subtitled *Leviathan* "The Matter, Forme and Power of a Common-wealth Ecclesiasticall and Civill."[104] Schmitt returns Hobbes's contemporary context to his reading of *Leviathan* and of the political in relation to it as the questions "Who construes and gives legal effect to a truth requiring constant interpretation? Who decides what is true Christianity?"[105] Hobbes's answer, "Auctoritas, non veritas, facit legem," assumed that truth could not realize itself and that command issued from the direct power of the sovereign. From the "truth" in this sense of a public cult there follows the whole construct of modern state theory, including its legitimate claim to the obedience of individuals. Schmitt's radical reading of Hobbes turns that theory, literally, on its head for the sake of understanding the "decisive question of political anthropology," human nature. This is not whether man is good or evil but whether he is a *dangerous* species.[106] What matters are not the "natural needs" of human beings but their openness to transcendence, a relationship Schmitt sketches in the figure below.

In this figure the modern state finds its beginning and its end. Schmitt's sketch was "the fruit of lifelong work on the great theme [of political anthropology] in general and the work of Thomas Hobbes in particular" (121); it appears in the 1963 edition of *Der Begriff des Politischen* in explanatory remarks on constructions of human nature and the state of nature in modern political theory. Hobbes (not Hegel) is the first theorist of the state as "the realm of reason," Schmitt argues, but the Hobbesian theory of nature is not merely material. It "leaves the gate of transcendence open."

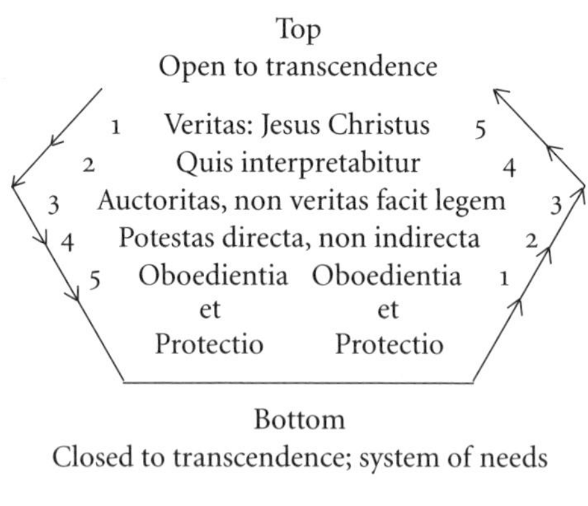

Source: *Der Begriff des Politischen* (Berlin: Duncker und Humblot, 1979), 121–22. This edition is a reprint of the 1963 edition; it includes the 1932 edition with a new foreword, three corollaries, and the "Hinweise"—a section of remarks, references, and replies ("Hinweise") to the literature on *Der Begriff des Politischen* that had appeared since 1959.

That "Jesus is the Christ" is not a private question of belief, but "the truth of a public faith." Hobbes posits this public faith *not* as "a mere tactical preventative, a useful or necessary lie that would protect him from torture and censorship," but as a political structure in which theological truth is realized. The terrors of the religious war immediately present the question, "who decides what is true Christianity?" (122). For both theorists this is simultaneously "who interprets?" and "who judges?," questions referred in the "Hobbes Crystal" to its central axis, a phrase that is the key to Hobbes's theory of the state and the ecclesiastical polity: *Auctoritas, non veritas, facit legem*. From this (number 3 in the figure) the construction of human nature can be read up to transcendence and down to material needs.

The highest truth for Hobbes is "Jesus is the Christ" (number 1 and 5 at the top of the figure). Could another "highest truth" be substituted for this one—a truth, Schmitt remarks, such as "Allah is great," "liberty, equality, fraternity," "man is good," "from each according to his means, etc.," or any of those other contentious truths—another truth "whose realization and execution are causes of conflict and war"? In Schmitt's view, such principles neutralize the central truth of Hobbes's philosophy, the truth of a public Christian faith. As the ground of Hobbes's political philosophy, it is unaffected by questions about his personal commitment to Christianity. Schmitt's silence on the implication of a public truth that must be established within a diversity of opinion should not be read as ignorance of its potential complications. Here and more clearly in his 1938 book on Hobbes's *Leviathan,* Schmitt shows himself painfully aware of the inherent conflict between private conscience and public truth. The liberty of subjects carried the seed of private religion, an interiority that destroys "public reason" and with it the relation of security and protection offered by the rule of law in concrete efficacy. The public then becomes the destroyer of the private, a realm of potential violence that manifests the political as civil war, the end of sovereignty.

In the work of many contemporary political theorists, "the public" of our secular world is more, not less, free and comfortable. This view has even been projected back to the Greek polis and the birth of political philosophy by Hannah Arendt; in her account, the polis is "the most talkative of all bodies politic," a view that deliberately excluded the Greek discovery of the political in precisely Schmitt's sense.[107] That politics in the ancient world took a variety of forms (as they do for us today) should be obvious. But in precisely that phase usually referred to explicitly or assumed to be the referent when Arendt (and Leo Strauss) writes of "the Greeks"—the fifth century B.C.—the Athenian state had begun to crumble, and "the word *political* breaks off from the state," entering into the social with consequences familiar to the twentieth century. The "public" or "general" interest is not obvious; the private is determinate.[108]

Heinrich Meier concludes that the central meaning of Carl Schmitt's work is that "divine revelation is the highest authority and ultimate ground" of the political.[109] "Intensity" allows Schmitt to refer the political to an ultimate, "Providential" source in the Fall from the Garden of Eden and original sin: "enmity," according to this reading, finally refers to God's declaration to Adam, "I will put enmity between thee and the woman, and between thy seed and her seed" (Gen. 2:15).[110] Why does Schmitt conceal this central purpose from all but the most careful readers? Because in liberalism, Schmitt sees an opponent that "would like to dissolve even metaphysical truth into discussion," and because "the things of revelation are unsuited for discussion with unbelievers."[111]

Meier's interpretation has been one of the most influential readings of Schmitt in recent years. His view, like that of Jacob Taubes, revives the mystical reading of Schmitt among some Catholics in the early 1920s, a perspective obvious in Hugo Ball's famous review of *Political Theology.* While Meier ends with harsh criticism of Schmitt, Taubes wants to reassert the "spiritual condition of our time as a conflict between Enlightenment and Orthodoxy." Schmitt is "the twentieth-century Hobbes" for Taubes in a profoundly Christian way: the center of their political thought is Christological.[112] That Schmitt remained a devout believer throughout his life is indisputable; so too are the many explicit (and hidden) Catholic and Christian references in his work. His interest in, and commitment to, Roman Catholicism is obvious in many of the early works,[113] and Schmitt's long note on Hobbes in the 1963 reprint of *Der Begriff des Politischen,* with its "Hobbes-Crystal," indicates a persistent interest in questions of belief and political theory.[114] In a commentary that is also a justification that he "as a Jew" should honor Schmitt, Taubes grasped the difficulty of a *purely* theological reading of Schmitt's political work. He "was a jurist, not a theologian, but a jurist who set foot on the dangerous place that had been vacated by the theologians."[115] In so doing, Schmitt, as Bodin and Hobbes before him, tried to construct juridical forms to contain the dangers of the political, which for him, as for his predecessors, were never simply empirical.

This theological reading of Schmitt, however, risks missing his *political* intentions and the meaning of his constitutional jurisprudence. Schmitt's was never merely a positivist understanding of law and the state—but it was always a profoundly temporal perspective. Hobbes allowed "natural freedom" in the private, the secret place of thought, which not even the almighty sovereign could penetrate. What was done and said in public was part of the state, but here the individual remained free. In the very structure of *Leviathan*—and thus of the modern state and its society—Hobbes placed its destruction. The people in public could be constituted; the private individual could not. This is the womb of liberalism. The ultimate referent of his work is that "divine revelation is the highest authority and ultimate ground" of the political.[116] Original sin is the beginning of politics (the "enmity" of Genesis 2:14, Meier argues, is the inescapably political condition of man's existence), and the fortunes of world history are the workings of salvation—sin, conflict, suffering are the concrete form that time takes and *must* take until the Last Judgment. Only then will the political cease. For Christian political thought, "the decisive concept of its continuity is that of a *Kat-echon,*" and the historical power of Christendom delays the Antichrist. After World War II, Schmitt wrote, "no other image of history than that of the *Kat-echon* is possible for an originally Christian belief."[117] The necessity of politics is founded in theology, and "the political by its essence has a theological destination."[118]

In the end, however, Carl Schmitt's singular achievement was to challenge more radically and effectively than any other thinker the tendency to abstraction in liberal political thought about the state. In their very temporality, as existent in time, the state and the rule of law reveal the political as the gateway into the substantive concerns that constitute the seriousness of human life and are at times its affliction and at others the source of its grandeur. Neither possibility comes from the deeper recesses of the individual any more than "history" itself has been the result of private persons and their private thoughts. To risk the public, in Schmitt's terms, is to confront the ever-present contingency of the political as a mortal being in time. Whether that engagement is meaningful or the source of darkest nihilism will depend on precisely those elements of the political beyond the system of needs. That in Carl Schmitt's time this venture ended in horror does not negate its necessity if we are to lead human lives.

Afterword

The appeal of Carl Schmitt's political theory in the 1920s and since comes from its radical critique of liberal institutions and liberal constitutionalism. That is also what provokes hostility to it, hostility made more profound by the political distemper of twentieth-century Germany. My purpose here has been to excavate the first-order questions that structure Schmitt's political theory by situating Schmitt and Weimar in a longer tradition of political thought about the state and its law.

Schmitt is the end point and the negative of that tradition. Jean Bodin's argument for a sociological concept of sovereignty developed in response to the religious turmoil and violence of his time. Bodin and philosophical deism grounded the secular basis of the modern state after the Protestant Reformation and made possible a political order that bracketed out the original questions of political thought: the relation of political life to morals, metaphysics, and the jurisprudential forms of theism. In Schmitt's terms, the modern state and its constitution necessarily assume the constancy of "the normal." As natural science defined miracles as transgressions of the laws of nature, so the political theory of the modern state banishes "the sovereign's direct intervention in a valid legal order."[1] The result, Schmitt argued, is that the "normal" can only be defined as the formal and procedural; all the concepts of modern jurisprudence circle around "a formula, a sign, a symbol," ignoring the task of conceptualization as "an adequate expression of reality."[2]

If Bodin's intention had been to remove sovereignty from dependence on scriptural interpretation and give it a pragmatic criterion, Schmitt's was to challenge the pragmatic basis of political institutions in an age no less violent than Bodin's and whose legitimacy was just as unsettled. Every political institution, Schmitt argued, is specifically intended, and each has a particular principle on which it rests, which must be the criterion of institutional legitimacy—these justify every institution in its own terms and by reference to a more inclusive theory, such as divine right or popular sovereignty.[3] While those might be justified pragmatically—Weber's substitution of "leadership selection" for the liberal principles of discussion and the public sphere is one example—they do not and could never justify them in terms other than the tolerably functional, that this institution is better than some other alternative. In the 1920s, Weimar's new constitution appeared to Schmitt justifiable in precisely those pragmatic terms, and his interpretation of it often aimed at its stabilization, at preserving the state from imminent civil war and securing a peaceful society.

But not always. Schmitt's political theory reached to overcome modernity—its deontology, the dualism of inner and outer, spirit and matter—and the peculiar loneliness of the modern individual in a disenchanted world. The romantics rebelled against the rationalism of the Enlightenment through feeling, a revolt that failed in Schmitt's account because its creative impulse left the individual to live his life as if it were a novel.[4] A fantastic possibility opened up through this assertion of romantic will and the political culture of liberalism. If one denied the political as the existential (as Hegel and Kierkegaard understood it), politics and political institutions became entertainment. This is consistent with the deontology of liberalism as a political doctrine and with its formal rationality. If, after Kant, knowledge is only knowledge of appearances and, after Weber, constrained to be "value free," then its political theory must lead to a neutral, objective logic such as that offered by Rawls and Kelsen. In this way, the technical replaces the political, and the purpose of a political life is detached from questions of meaning. Liberal politics erases the Other; in place of fundamental difference, it sets "humanity," an unproblematic freedom, and material satisfaction.

Leo Strauss commented on Schmitt's political theory that "liberalism, sheltered by and engrossed in a world of culture, forgets the foundations of culture, the state of nature, that is, human nature in its dangerousness and endangeredness."[5] This is why, for Schmitt, "the political is not only possible" as a negation of liberalism "but also real; not only real but also necessary" (95). The compartmentalization of life spheres possible in the modern world fragments the rule of law into specialties and drives forward the neutralization of cultural questions as a whole. Agreement and peace are possible on this basis. The seriousness exemplified by Plato in the *Euthyphro* and *Phaedrus* is not possible in the liberal world: "Agreement and peace here mean agreement at all costs" (102). If the end is already fixed, as Strauss reading Schmitt reading liberalism assumes, the discussion concerns only the means, not the end (102).

As Germany became a republic, Schmitt commented that the new constitution represented *self-evident* truths about the state and political, beliefs about liberal and representative democracy that need not be justified because they were part of the identity of the times. No political theory can survive without some such assumptions; but when those assumptions cease to be so obvious, when the self-evident appears as contentious or foolish, or when its ideal structure seems to reflect only partial truths that must themselves be established, as they were for much of the Weimar Republic, theory alone cannot hold together the polity. All constitutions come under stress at some time. Whether those periods are genuine crises depends on the relation of a constitution's political ideas and their realities. Constitutions are supposed to mediate between those, and their success depends on doing so effectively. The failure of the Weimar constitution is not singular, and other failed constitutions come quickly to mind: the Articles of Confederation, the various constitutions of 1848, or the French Republic in 1958.

Is Schmitt a realist? His political vision insists on the real possibility of enmity and understands the life of an individual and the purpose of the modern state in those terms. The political assumes that there may be discussion, and disagreement, over ends, not only means, and that those ends include life-and-death questions. A deeper reading of Schmitt's political theory, however, directs one toward other matters: the meaning of history, the providential quality of human existence, the fragile constitution of the normal in the face of the exceptional. Sovereignty after 1789 is not represented in the figure of a king, and its transformation into legal technique does not, Schmitt argues, remove the basis of the political in the nature of man's condition. Democracy makes that basis, when it emerges, even more volatile. Like Weber, Schmitt saw the limits of legality and sought its solution in charismatic legitimacy. Like the elite theorists, Schmitt thought "the masses" capable of acclamation, but not decision, and hoped at times that would suffice to preserve the constitution. The alienation of voters, the widespread assumption that a power elite matters more than the people in contemporary democracy, is evidence that these remain problems for liberal democracy nearly a century later. Thucydides presented the dilemma of Athenian democracy in the course of the Peloponnesian War as a conflict between the *logos* of democratic rule and its *ergon,* the ruler and ruling classes. As long as the latter remained conscious of their public duty, the logic of democracy remained; when rule fell to self-interested men, the balance was destroyed, and Athens went down to defeat. Schmitt understood the crisis of liberal democracy in similar terms. The weakness of its constitution came from the primacy of individual freedom and private interest, which worked against democratic unity. As externalities or inherent conflict, sovereignty—the specifically political agency—is revealed in exceptional moments.

Much of Weimar was exceptional. Fascism and national socialism, and before them communism, rejected both the hegemonic claims of the old imperial nation-states and those of the United States. Indeed, they can all be read as political religions or a "revolt of the masses" against the disenchanted but disciplined world of liberal capitalism. Michael Burleigh recently described the messianic national regimes of this period as keeping their subjects "in a permanent state of emotional fervor. . . . This was a children's politics for grown-ups, bored and frustrated with the prosaic tenor of post-war liberal democracy, and hence receptive to heroic gestures and politics as a form of theatrical stunt, even at the expense of their freedom. . . . Europe's demagogues were archly aware of the manipulative techniques they needed to generate mass faith, knowing the impact of masses, flags, songs, symbols and colors. These men were artist-politicians."[6]

The confrontation between "Islamic fundamentalism" and liberal democracy parallels the political ruptures that characterized Europe between the world wars. The fault lines of Weimar's failure are those of all contemporary liberal democracies, fissures traced and sometimes exacerbated by Carl Schmitt. At the beginning of *The Politics,* Aristotle compares the work of political theory to that of the pathologist. Constitutions are cadavers, whose tissues reveal the history of their diseases. Like Aristotle, Schmitt saw stability and the preservation of constitutional rule as the central question of political theory, a theme woven back into his legal theory and jurisprudence.

As a figure in the history of political thought, he shared the personal fate of many men who have sought political influence and access to the powerful. In late June 1945, Eduard Spranger, a Mittwochsgesellschaft member who survived retaliation after the July 20 plot failed, demanded of Carl Schmitt, "Who are you?" in his denazification proceeding: "It was a terrible accusation that said, 'What you think and say may be interesting and clear; but what you are, your Self, your Being, is murky and unclear.' "[7] Today we might say that the text of liberal constitutions is clear and interesting, but their being is murky and unclear, and the future open. It is a narrative of incoherence about the Weimar Republic, and of the incoherence of liberalism as an element in the Weimar constitution. Seen through Carl Schmitt's lens, the constitutional failure of the Weimar Republic questions us as aggressively as Spranger did Schmitt that day in June 1945.

Notes

Citations and translations: Unless otherwise noted, all translations from the German are my own. When I make a series of references to the same source, the page number is given in parentheses in the text.

Introduction

1 Bauakademie der DDR, Institut für Städebau und Architekur, *Karl Friedrich Schinkel: Eine Austellung aus der Deutschen Demokartischen Republik* (Berlin: Henschelverg, 1982).

2 Georg Friedrich Wilhelm Hegel, *Die Verfassung Deutschlands* (1800–1802; Frankfurt: Suhrkamp, 1971), 451–610.

3 Fritz Stern, "The Political Consequences of the Unpolitical German," in *The Failure of Illiberalism* (New York: Knopf, 1972), 3–25.

4 Anthony Nicholls and Erich Matthias, eds., *German Democracy and the Triumph of Hitler* (London: Allen and Unwin, 1971).

5 "Article 48 of the Weimar Constitution, Its Historical and Political Implications," Hans Boldt's account of emergency powers, refers to several authorities on Article 48, including Carl Schmitt, but the extensive literature on presidential powers and emergency situations in Weimar is ignored in favor of simpler institutional descriptions.

6 M. R. Lepsius, "From Fragmented Party Democracy to Government by Emergency Decree and National Socialist Takeover: Germany," in *The Breakdown of Democratic Regimes: Europe*, ed. Juan J. Linz and Alfred Stepan (Baltimore: Johns Hopkins University Press, 1978); Yossi Shain and Juan J. Linz, "The Role of Interim Governments," *Journal of Democracy* (1991): 73–87; Juan J. Linz and Alfred Stepan, eds., *The Breakdown of Democratic Regimes: Europe*. Numerous studies appeared in the 1920s and 1930s as Germany became a foreign policy issue, but concern for the "totalitarian" phase overshadowed inquiry into the republican failure. Studies that

focused on the totalitarian phase suited American interests in the Cold War, when West Germany was a major example of Western economic and political success.

7 Carl Schmitt, *The Concept of the Political*, translation, introduction, and notes by George Schwab, with comments on Schmitt's essay by Leo Strauss, new foreword by Tracy Strong (1932; Chicago: University of Chicago Press, 1996). Schwab's monograph, based on a dissertation presented to the political science faculty at Columbia, found no American publisher and appeared in English through a German publisher as *The Challenge of the Exception: An Introduction to the Political Ideas of Carl Schmitt between 1921 and 1936* (Berlin: Duncker und Humblot, 1970). A partial translation of *Römischer Katholizimus und politischer Form* appeared as *The Necessity of Politics: An Essay on the Representative Idea in the Church and Modern Europe* (London: Sheed and Ward, 1931) in a series that included works by Jacques Maritain, Christopher Dawson, and Nicholas Berdyaev.

8 Joseph Bendersky, *Carl Schmitt: Theorist for the Reich* (Princeton: Princeton University Press, 1983).

9 The first two appeared in 1985 as *The Crisis of Parliamentary Democracy*, translated with notes and introduction by Ellen Kennedy, and *Political Theology*, translated by George Schwab. The following year, MIT published *Political Romanticism* in a translation by Guy Oakes and with a brilliant introduction.

10 John McCormick, *Carl Schmitt's Critique of Liberalism* (Chicago: University of Chicago Press, 1995); Peter Caldwell, *Popular Sovereignty and the Crisis of German Constitutional Law* (Durham, N.C.: Duke University Press, 1997); David Dyzenhaus, *Legality and Legitimacy* (New York: Oxford University Press, 1997); William Schuermann, *Carl Schmitt: The End of Law* (Lanham, Md.: Rowman and Littlefield, 1999); Chantel Mouffe, ed., *The Challenge of Carl Schmitt* (London: Verso, 1999); David Dyzenhaus, ed., *Law as Politics* (Durham, N.C.: Duke University Press, 1998).

11 Articles on Schmitt (and his contemporaries in German public law) have appeared in leading journals, including *Political Theory, Telos, American Political Science Review*, and *The History of Political Thought*. Law reviews in America, too, have discovered Schmitt: The *Canadian Journal of Law and Jurisprudence* recently devoted a whole issue to him; the *Texas Law Review* carried a special section on Schmitt; and another special issue on Schmitt is forthcoming in the *Cardoza Law Review*.

12 John Rawls, *A Theory of Justice* (Cambridge: Harvard University Press, 1972).

13 Michael Sandel, *Liberalism and the Limits of Justice* (New York: Cambridge University Press, 1982).

14 Rawls, *Political Liberalism* (New York: Columbia University Press, 1993), xvi–xvii.

15 Ibid.

16 David Dyzenhaus, *Legality and Legitimacy* (Oxford: Clarendon, 1999), 231.

17 Carl Schmitt, *Der Begriff des Politischen* (Berlin: Duncker und Humblot, 1979).

18 Detlev Peukert, *Die Weimarer Republik* (Frankfurt: Suhrkamp, 1987), 11.

19 Hasso Hofmann, *Legalität gegen Legitimität* (Munich: Luchterhand, 1964), 9, quoting Hermann Heller, *Die Souveranität* (1927), 65ff., esp. 67.

20 Margaret Kraft-Fuchs, "Prinzipielle Bemerkungen zu Carl Schmitts Verfassungslehre," *Zeitschrift für öffentliches Recht* 9 (1930): 511–41.

21 Hans Kelsen, *Hauptprobleme der Staatsrechtslehre entwickelt aus der Lehre vom Rechtssatze* (Tübingen: J. C. B. Mohr, 1911); Eric Kaufmann, *Das Wesen des Völkerrechts und die clausula rebus sic stantibus* (1911; Aalen: Scientia, 1964).

22 Carl Schorske, *Fin-de-Siècle Vienna: Politics and Culture* (New York: Vintage Books, 1981), xix, quoting Arnold Schoenberg.

23 Carl Schmitt, *Verfassungslehre* (1928; Berlin: Duncker und Humblot, 1970), xi.

24 Ernst Vollrath, "Politik und Existenz," in *Politisches Denken: Jahrbuch 1991* (Stuttgart: Metzlersche, 1991), 157.

25 Heinrich Meier, *Die Lehre Carl Schmitts: Vier Kapitel zur Unterscheidung Politischer Theologie und Politischer Philosophie* (Stuttgart: J. B. Metzler, 1994).

1 In the Dark Years

1 Elizabeth Wiskemann, *The Europe of the Dictators, 1919–1945* (London: Fontana, 1966).

2 Carl Schmitt, "Die Lage der europäischen Rechtswissenschaft," in *Verfassungsrechtliche Aufsätze aus den Jahren 1924–1954: Materialien zu einer Verfassungslehre* (Berlin: Duncker und Humblot, 1973), 386–429; translated by G. L. Ulmen as "The Plight of European Jurisprudence," *Telos*, no. 83 (spring 1990): 35–71. All citations here are to Schmitt's original text.

3 Schmitt, "Die Lage der europäischen Rechtswissenschaft," 397.

4 Michael Stolleis, *The Law under the Swastika* (Chicago: University of Chicago Press, 1998), 44.

5 Ibid. An inheritance from idealist philosophy, Stolleis contends, that made National Socialism appear attractive to the Germanists.

6 Even where Roman law was not incorporated into common law, its features entered into their jurisprudence via concepts such as natural law, rational law, jus gentium, and general legal theory: "In so doing they created an inventory of firm legal concepts, which was translated into all European languages. Through the work of European jurists, Roman law became a *lingua franca*—the language of a jurisprudential community, a recognized model of juridical thinking, and thereby a spiritual and intellectual 'common law' of Europe" (Schmitt, *Verfassungsrechtliche Aufsätze*, 396).

7 Schmitt, "Die Lage der europäischen Rechtswissenschaft," 426.

8 Carl Schmitt, "Der Hüter der Verfassung," *Archiv für öffentliches Recht*, no. 16 (March 1929): 161–237.

9 Schmitt criticized Germany's position under the Versailles treaty, an opinion shared across political boundaries that otherwise divided Germans. Gerhard Anschütz's lecture at Heidelberg on November 22, 1922, the day that President Ebert named businessman Wilhelm Cuno to lead a minority cabinet (DDP, Centrum, BVP, DVP) with moderately Right tendencies, took note of the political chaos surrounding Walter Rathenau's assassination in the previous June. Anschütz located the source of the republican instability in the Treaty of Versailles, which he called a "peace *diktat*" that allowed the French both to encourage "domestic opponents of the state . . . to exercise the power of the streets" and "to encircle Germany." Anschütz was nonetheless a staunch defender of the Weimar constitution, whose weaknesses he thought the result "not of democracy but of the reparations and peace treaty" (Anschütz, *Drei Leitgedanken der Weimarer Reichsverfassung* [1923]). Bendersky views Schmitt as a *Vernuftrepublikaner* (a supporter of Weimar out of reason rather than belief) and writes that "like all German nationalists, Schmitt was appalled by the unjust and oppressive nature of a treaty that infringed upon the very sovereignty

of his country. . . . He hoped that the new constitution would provide the basis for the future security and stability of the state." See Bendersky, *Carl Schmitt: Theorist for the Reich* (Princeton: Princeton University Press, 1983), 29. Throughout the interwar period, Schmitt was a relentless critic of Versailles and of every element in internationalism and humanitarianism.

10 Max Weber, "The President of the Reich," in *Political Writings* (Cambridge: Cambridge University Press, 1994), 307.

11 Weber distinguished between "token" and strong parliamentary institutions, and in the article entitled "Parliament and Government in a Reconstructed Germany," he associated "weak" parliaments with "negative" politics. When parliaments were responsible for forming governments, and accountable to the electorate for their policies, Weber believed they would serve as recruitment sites for leadership and as protectors of liberty. See David Beetham, *Max Weber and the Theory of Modern Politics* (Cambridge: Polity Press, 1985), 95ff. Weber's position is more complex than this comparison suggests, and his political theory conveys a profound pessimism about the institutions of electoral democracy under modern conditions. See Wolfgang Mommsen, *Max Weber and German Politics, 1890–1920,* trans. Michael S. Steinberg (Chicago: University of Chicago Press, 1984); Wilhelm Hennis, *Max Weber: Essays in Reconstruction* (London: Allen and Unwin, 1988); earlier, Karl Jaspers, *Max Weber: Politiker, Forscher, Philosoph* (Munich, 1958); and Karl Loewenstein, *Max Weber's Political Ideas in the Perspective of Our Time* (Amherst: University of Massachusetts Press, 1966). Loewenstein's comment that although Weber considered a strong presidency indispensable to counterbalance a party-dominated parliament "with wise foresight [he] also recommended a safeguard against any abuse of the presidential powers" is an oversimplification of Weimar's constitutional circumstances (*Max Weber's Political Ideas,* 16).

12 The Basic Law of the Federal Republic commits it to "unity of living standards" among the Länder, a constitutional provision that has led to complex financial relations between them and the federal government. The principal techniques are federal payments to poorer Länder, sharing of common tax revenues, payments by richer Länder to poorer ones, and various intergovernmental grants. See David P. Conradt, *The German Polity* (London: Longman, 1989), 209–10.

13 Popitz's years in this position are known as the "Era of Popitz" in German financial history. See Lutz-Arwed Bentin, *Johannes Popitz und Carl Schmitt: Zur wirtschaftlichen Theorie des totalen Staates in Deutschland* (Munich: Beck, 1972), 10–14. Were there any German Keynesians? Knut Borchardt and others have argued recently that there were and that even Brüning's deflationary fiscal policies may have been more inflationary than we have thought. Popitz was one of those invited to take part in a "secret conference" at the Reichsbank, September 16–17, 1930, to discuss the question "how to finance economic stimulus for production that is economically and socially necessary." See "Wirtschaftliche Sachzwänge oder Primat der Politik? Die Ära Brüning im Widerstreit der historischen Forschung," in *Die Deutsche Staatskrise, 1930–32,* ed. Heinrich August Winkler (Munich: Oldenburg, 1992), 109–32. Popitz and others, including the former SPD finance minister Rudolf Hilferding, were skeptical about deficit financing of job creation (120).

14 Bentin, *Johannes Popitz und Carl Schmitt,* 36.

15 Ludwig Kaas, chair of the Center Party, wrote to Schleicher on January 26, 1933, warning him against "Carl Schmitt and his cohorts" and their constitutional relativ-

ism. See "Kaas an Reichskanzler Kurt von Schleicher," in *Das Ende der Parteien 1933*, ed. Erich Matthias and Rudolf Morsey (Frankfurt: Athenäum, 1973), 428–29.

16 The definitive study of the ensuing constitutional case (*Preußen v. Reich*, 1932) is David Dyzenhaus, *Legality and Legitimacy: Carl Schmitt, Hans Kelsen, and Hermann Heller in Weimar* (Oxford: Clarendon, 1998).

17 Schleicher reversed Papen's policies toward the working class in an attempt to forge a crosscutting coalition that would effectively remove Hitler's political base. He announced a program of job creation and fiscal stimulus and a variety of social assistance programs, including "winter help" through coal subsidies and "aid to the east" in the form of debt forgiveness for east Elbian landowners. German industrialists would not cooperate and began to reach out to Hitler. See Tom Childers's analysis of electoral politics in the last year of the republic, "Proletarianization and Collapse: The Elections of 1932," in *The Nazi Voter: The Social Foundations of Fascism in Germany, 1919–1933* (Chapel Hill: University of North Carolina Press, 1983), 192–261.

18 Childers, commenting on the "tenuous" position of the NSDAP at the polls, concludes that "it remains one of history's most tragic ironies that at precisely the moment when the party's electoral support had begun to falter, Hitler was installed as chancellor by representatives of those traditional elites who had done so much to undermine the parliamentary system and who still believed that the National Socialist movement could be safely harnessed for their reactionary purposes ("Proletarianization and Collapse," 268–69). See also Heinrich August Winkler, *Mittelstand, Demokratie, und Nationalsozialismus: Die politische Entwicklung von Handwerk und Kleinhandel in der Weimarer Republik* (Cologne: Kiepenheuer und Witsch, 1972); David Abraham, *The Collapse of the Weimar Republic: Political Economy in Crisis* (Princeton: Princeton University Press, 1981); Henry A. Turner, *German Big Business and the Rise of Hitler* (New York: Oxford University Press, 1985).

19 Bentin, *Johannes Popitz und Carl Schmitt*, 124–25.

20 Besides Popitz, other members involved in the July 20, 1944, plot were Ludwig Beck, Ulrich von Hassell, and Jens Jessen. After a show trial by the Volksgerichtshof, Popitz, Jessen, and von Hassell were tortured and finally executed at Plötzensee near Berlin. Ludwig Beck committed suicide on July 20. Von Hassell's diary records, from the perspective of a high-ranking diplomat, domestic and international events from the Munich settlement until a week before the assassination attempt (*Vom andern Deutschland* [Zurich: Atlantis, 1946]). See Hans Mommsen, "The German Resistance against Hitler and the Restoration of Politics," *Journal of Modern History* 64 (1992): 112–27.

21 Schmitt is mentioned in three presentations by Johannes Popitz ("Recent Developments in Germany," meeting 895, 26 April 1933; "On the Concept of a Reich and Whether It Is Useful for the Reconstruction of Europe," meeting 1005, 11 December 1940; "Is There a General Theory of the State?" meeting 1054, 28 June 1944), and in a presentation by the philosopher Eduard Spranger, "Is There a 'Liberal' Science?" meeting 924, 17 April 1935. See Klaus Scholder, *Die Mittwochsgesellschaft: Protokolle aus dem geistigen Deutschland, 1932–1944* (Berlin: Severin und Siedler, 1982).

22 Schmitt's biographer reports: "The aftermath of the July 20 plot caused Schmitt much more anxiety than he had felt in 1936. Popitz had broken the Hobbesean

covenant of protection and obedience. . . . The failure of the plot and the consequences suffered by the conspirators confirmed Schmitt in his belief that resistance to the modern state was futile" (Bendersky, *Carl Schmitt*, 263–64). Bendersky comments that head of SS security Ernst Kaltenbrunner's report to Hitler on the conspiracy mentions Schmitt's name, but Bendersky accepts George Schwab's view that Schmitt was never really in danger (Schwab, *The Challenge of the Exception*, 142).

23 Schmitt's polemic of the preceding summer, *Legalität und Legitimität*, had warned against just that possibility. Rejecting the principle of an "equal chance" for anticonstitutional parties to compete in elections for access to state power, Schmitt asserted that a party in legal possession of the instruments of power can determine for itself what the terms "legal" and "legitimate" mean. Schmitt, *Legalität und Legitimität*, in *Verfassungsrechtliche Aufsätze* (Berlin: Duncker und Humblot, 1973), 289–91.

24 Johannes Popitz, meeting 895 of the Mittwochsgesellschaft, 26 April 1933, at Popitz's house; cited in Scholder, *Die Mittwochsgesellschaft*, 66–69.

25 Ibid.

26 See the reactions of middle-class Germans who were not involved directly in political affairs as was Popitz in Jeremy Noakes and Geoffrey Pridham, *Documents on Nazism, 1919–1945* (New York: Viking Press, 1974), 160–62, 165–66.

27 Harry Graf Kessler, *Tagebücher, 1918–1937: Politik, Kunst und Gesellschaft der zwanziger Jahre* (Frankfurt: Insel, 1979), 703.

28 Quoted in Ian Kershaw, *Hitler, 1889–1936: Hubris* (New York: Norton, 1998), 427. This is not to say that Ludendorff supported the Republic or that he did not bear a significant responsibility for the German disaster.

29 Quoted in Helmut Quaritsch, *Positionen und Begriffe Carl Schmitts* (Berlin: Duncker und Humblot, 1986), 91.

30 Ferdinand Hermens, *Zwischen Politik und Vernunft: Gesammelte Aufsätze aus drei Welten* (Berlin: Duncker und Humblot, 1969), 158. See also Bendersky, *Carl Schmitt*, 195ff.; Paul Noack, *Carl Schmitt* (Frankfurt: Propyläen, 1993), 166–67.

31 Noakes and Pridham, *Documents on Nazism*, 163–64. Wilhelm had said, "I no longer recognize parties; I recognize only Germans" (Gordon A. Craig, *Germany, 1866–1945* [Oxford: Clarendon, 1978], 341).

32 Noakes and Pridham, *Documents on Nazism*, 168. The audience on February 20 included members of the board of I. G. Farben, the president of the Reich Association of German Industry, the chief of the United Steelworks, mine owners, and Dr. Hajmar Schacht, former head of the Reichsbank, who would take that position again under the Nazis.

33 *Gesetz zur Behebung der Not von Volk und Reich*, 28 February 1933.

34 "Die Deutsche Geisteswelt für Liste 1," *Völkischer Beobachter*, no. 62 (3 March 1933).

35 His diary entry for April 4 records a visit to the Deutschen Gesellschaft, where he met Erich Kaufmann and Popitz. "Poor Popitz sat between us, just like the child Jesus in the Temple. No one sees the problem. Everybody just hopes to get through this. It's good that I'm going to Cologne [to take up a university chair]. The situation is dreadful." Schmitt's record of Hitler's speech to civil servants and military officers on the occasion of the promulgation of the Reichsstatthaltergesetz also suggests, Helmut Quaritsch writes, "distant observation" of the surroundings rather than support (*Positionen und Begriffe Carl Schmitts*, 91, 96).

36 Hermens comments, "Those three months [January–March 1933] created a completely new attitude in Schmitt. Apparently he was one of those who had to be part of things in whatever way possible, even when it meant a reversal of their previous positions" (*Zwischen Politik und Vernunft*, 339).

37 Carl Schmitt, "Gesetz zur Behebung der Not von Volk und Reich: Vom 24 März 1933," *Reichsgesetzblatt*, 24 March 1933, 141.

38 Bendersky, *Carl Schmitt*, 199. His commentary on the law "co-coordinating" Reich and local functions (Das Reichsstatthaltergesetz), which destroyed Federalism, one of Schmitt's "core institutions of the constitution," indicates how far he had moved toward the new regime. In the foreword, Schmitt contrasts "the German revolution" of 1933 with "November 1918," a phrase that would immediately suggest to his readers the "November criminals" and complex of political flash points surrounding the origins of the Republic: the "treason" of politicians against the German military, the "diktat" of Versailles, and the series of crises that beset the new Republic. The new law allowed the president to appoint commissioners in all the Länder, supplanting elected governments. The effect of the text suggests that unity, the preservation of the German nation as a political entity, not merely a cultural or geographic expression, and electoral democracy are inimical. Further, what could not be accomplished in half a millennium had now been done in a few days: "Reform plans of every sort have accompanied the destruction of the Reich helplessly. . . . In the last decade the old fate seemed to repeat itself. Now in one blow the German revolution has already created the foundation for building the Reich, and taken the most important step in the Reichsstatthaltergesetz of April 7, 1933, toward a new state order of Reich and Länder." It has the character, Schmitt concludes, of a "fundamental law." *Das Reichsstatthaltergesetz* was Schmitt's *laudatio* to the new regime, a blend of political interpretation and constitutional law that legitimated Hitler's destruction of federalism and the separation of powers in the republican constitution by reference to the long historical problem of German unification. See Schmitt, *Das Reichsstatthaltergesetz* (Berlin: Carl Heymann, 1933), 3, 21, quoting from the May 5, 1993, edition published a few days after Schmitt joined the NSDAP.

39 Carl Schmitt, *Die Diktatur: Von den Anfängen des modernen Souveränitätsgedankens bis zum proletarischen Klassenkampf* (Berlin: Duncker und Humblot, 1978), 6ff.

40 "Law does not come from the state . . . the state is not the creator of law, rather law is the creator of the state." Carl Schmitt, *Der Wert des Staates und die Bedeutung des Einzelnen* (1914; Hellerau: Jakob Hegner Verlang, 1917), 46, 20. The text was written between January and May 1913. The argument parallels central features of Hans Kelsen's philosophy of law that were later the target of Schmitt's critique. Hasso Hofmann, *Legitimität gegen Legalität: Der Weg der politischen Philosophie Carl Schmitts* (Neuweid: Luchterhand, 1964), esp. 44ff.

41 The distinction appears on the first page of *The Prince* (Cambridge: Cambridge University Press, 1997).

42 These spheres are aesthetic, moral, and economic. *Der Begriff des Politischen* (Berlin: Duncker und Humblot, 1979), 25–26.

43 "We read Machiavelli today," Schmitt said in 1927, "because of 'machiavellianism.'" Schmitt, "Machiavelli: Zum 22 Juni 1927," *Kölnische Volkszeitung*, 21 June 1927, 1. Schmitt gave the lectures on "the concept of the political" at the Deutsche Hochschule für Politik in Berlin that summer; he developed the argument in the context of foreign policy questions and questions about modern democracy.

44 "Men should either be caressed or crushed . . . any injury done to a man must be such that there is no need to fear his revenge." Machiavelli, *The Prince,* chap. 3, 9.

45 Schmitt, *Legalität und Legitimität* (Berlin: Duncker und Humblot, 1932), 37, 61. Earlier, *Verfassungslehre* (Berlin: Duncker und Humblot, 1928), 20, 103, 104; *Der Hüter der Verfassung* (Tübingen: Mohr, 1931).

46 These core institutions were democracy, republic, federalism, parliamentary and representative government, and a liberal Rechtsstaat (Schmitt, *Verfassungslehre,* 23–24).

47 For the positivist position, see Gerhard Anschütz and Richard Thoma, eds., *Handbuch des Deutschen Staatsrechts,* 2 vols. (Tübingen: Mohr, 1930, 1932), vol. 1, 182ff., 193ff.; vol. 2, 153ff.

48 Gerhard Anschütz, *Die Verfassung des Deutschen Reichs* (Berlin: Georg Stilke, 1933), 405.

49 Georg Jellinek, *Allgemeine Staatslehre,* 3d ed. (Berlin: O. Häring, 1921), 332, 340. Earlier Georg Meyer asserted, "The right to use state power does not come out of legal considerations, but from the actual possession of it. . . . Legitimacy is not an essential moment of state power" (*Lehrbuch des deutschen Staatsrechts,* 4th ed. [Leipzig, 1895]). On the history of this idea and its effect on the Weimar constitution, see E. R. Huber, *Deutsche Verfassungsgeschichte seit 1789: Die Weimarer Reichsverfassung* (1981).

50 Carl Schmitt, *Ex captivitatae Salus* (Cologne: Graeven, 1950), 75. Cereno was a "situation-symbol" for Schmitt, as he told Ernst Jünger, to whom Schmitt sent a copy in late February 1941. The correspondence indicates how closely he identified with the story: "11/12.3.43 at 2:30 am. A fantastic situation: the St. Dominik in a maelstrom. B.C. says to himself, better to die *through* it than *for* it. Such Tacitus-like developments go far beyond such phrases as 'existential' " (*Ernst Jünger–Carl Schmitt: Briefe, 1930–1983,* edited with a commentary by Helmuth Kiesel [Stuttgart: Klett-Cotta, 1999], 129, 159). See also Sava Klickovic, "Benito Cereno: Ein moderne Mythos," in *Epirrhosis: Festgabe für Carl Schmitt,* vol. 1 (Berlin: Duncker und Humblot, 1968), 265–73, who credits Schmitt's essay with introducing Benito Cereno as "a European myth . . . a symbol for the situation of intellectuals in mass society" (268). Klickovic's comment that Schmitt had attempted a continuation of the Cereno story has since been confirmed by the publication of Schmitt's diary for 1947–1951. Schmitt, *Glossarium: Aufzeichnungen aus der Jahre 1947–1951,* ed. Eberhard Freiherr von Medem (Berlin: Duncker und Humblot, 1991), 54.

51 Michael Stolleis, "Community and National Community: Reflections on Legal Terminology under National Socialism," in *The Law under the Swastika,* 64–83; and "In the Belly of the Beast: Constitutional Legal Theory under National Socialism," ibid., 87–101.

52 Ibid., 64.

53 Anonymous review, *Deutsche Verwaltung,* 20 February 1934, 75. Karl Dietrich Bracher called this "the mystical trinity of the new system," in *Die Deutsche Diktatur: Entstehung, Struktur, Folgen des Nationalsozialismus* (Cologne: Kiepenhauer und Witsch, 1969), 255. In the English translation the phrase is secularized: "tripartition of political unity." Karl Dietrich Bracher, *The German Dictatorship: The Origins, Structure and Consequences of National Socialism,* trans. Jean Steinberg (London: Penguin, 1973).

54 Reinhard Mehring comments of the connection between fascism and Hegel's philos-

ophy, a relationship apparent to contemporaries. Mehring, *Pathetisches Denken: Carl Schmitts Denkweg am Leitfaden Hegels—Katholische Grundstellung und antimarxistische Hegelstrategie* (Berlin: Duncker und Humblot, 1989), 153. Mehring's work leaves little doubt about Schmitt's intellectual debt to Hegel.

55 Schmitt, *Verfassungslehre*, pt. 1, 20, 11. See also Schmitt, "Ein Jahr nationalsozialistischer Verfassungsstaat," *Deutsches Recht* 4 (1934): 27–30.

56 The term "absolute" describes elements of Germany's real constitution, or historic actuality, and refers to the meaning of a constitution as (1) "the concrete totality of political unity and social order in a particular state"; (2) "a particular type of political and social order . . . such as monarchy, aristocracy or democracy. Constitution here [equals] the state form"; and (3) "constitution as the principle of dynamic becoming of political unity . . . strength and energy," such as the notion of "integration" that Rudolf Smend suggests (Schmitt, *Verfassungslehre*, 4–5).

57 Carl Schmitt, *Staat, Bewegung, Volk: Die Dreigliederung der politischen Einheit* (Hamburg: Hanseatische Verlagsanstalt, 1933), 5.

58 Ibid., 41. J. P. Stern's brilliant and systematic analysis of Hitler's messianic impulse and the pseudoreligious quality of the movement reveals the mystical aspects of National Socialism. See, for example, his description of the 1936 party rally at Nuremberg in which Hitler's speech "centered on a sustained identification with Christ the Redeemer": "The man with the spontaneous speech habits of the Austrian lower classes is addressing 140,000 political functionaries in a solemn declamatory style superimposed on the intimately personal language of Luther's New Testament. What is enacted here is a situation of total immanence, where nobody believes in anything; or rather, where few if any believe in the man before them but all, including Hitler himself, fully believe in the image they have created." Stern, *Hitler: The Führer and the People* (London: Fontana, 1975), 88–89.

59 Leo Strauss, "Notes on *The Concept of the Political*," in *The Concept of the Political*, by Carl Schmitt, trans. George Schwab (Chicago: University of Chicago Press, 1996), 83, 84, 101.

60 Carl Schmitt, *Die Drei Arten des Rechtswissenschaftlichen Denkens* (Hamburg: Hanseatische Verlagsanstalt, 1934).

61 Bracher, *The German Dictatorship*, 301–6.

62 Quaritsch, *Positionen und Begriffe Carl Schmitts*, 80ff.

63 Carl Schmitt, "Der Führer schützt das Recht: Zur Reichstagsrede Adolf Hitlers vom 13 Juli 1934," in *Positionen und Begriffe im Kampf mit Weimar, Genf, Versailles* (Hamburg: Hanseatische Verlangsanstalt, 1939). The article originally appeared on the first page of the *Deutsche Juristen Zeitung*.

64 Koellreutter was an early supporter of National Socialism. The others were Paul Rittersbusch and Gustav Adolf Walz. Stolleis, *Geschichte des öffentlichen Rechts in Deutschland*, vol. 3: *Staats- und Verwaltungsrechtswissenschaft in Republik und Diktatur, 1914–1945* (Munich: Beck, 1999), 251.

65 Schmitt's prominence in the legal profession was a source of envy among Nazi jurists and law professors who had joined the party before 1933. Not only did Schmitt hold the chair of public and constitutional law in Berlin, he was also editor of the *Deutsche Juristen Zeitung*, the leading journal for his profession, and head of the association of university teachers in the Nazi organization for lawyers, the Reichsfachgruppe Hochschullehrer des Bundes Nationalsozialistischer Deutscher Juristen. The attacks on Schmitt culminated in an article in the *Schwarze Korps*, the

magazine of the ss, condemning his "political Catholicism" and his association with General Kurt von Schleicher; the opposition of Heinrich Himmler and others within the regime made his public position untenable, and at the end of 1936, Schmitt resigned all those posts. "Koellreutter engaged in a private campaign to rally other party members against Schmitt" from 1934 onward. Schmitt believed that Popitz's intervention with Hermann Göring saved him from much worse. On his friend's advice, he resigned from all public posts except that of Prussian state counselor, by then a purely honorific title. See Bendersky, *Carl Schmitt,* 222–42.

66 "All the great religions have stolen gods from their opponents and put them in their own pantheons; many intellectual conquests announced themselves by taking over the rituals, hymns and formulae of their opponents, and in political struggles that are always total and therefore to the greatest extent spiritual, one even takes over the songs and marches of the opponent and gives them a new text." Schmitt, "Was bedeutet der Streit um den Rechtsstaat?" *Zeitschrift für die gesamte Staatswissenschaft* 2, no. 95 (1935): 197. Schmitt notes that in the Republic, the Wehrmacht was forbidden (August 2, 1922) to sing or play "party-political" melodies and marches.

67 Schmitt, "Nationalsozialismus und Rechtsstaat," *Juristische Wochenschrift* 63, nos. 12–13 (24 and 31 March 1934): 715.

68 Herman Finer notes that the idea of civil service is to German political culture what "parliament" is to the English. Caplan, *Government without Administration: State and Civil Service in Weimar and Nazi Germany* (Oxford: Oxford University Press, 1989), 1.

69 Schmitt, "Was bedeutet der Streit um den Rechtsstaat," 191–92.

70 Ibid., 195.

71 Ibid., 199. Elsewhere Schmitt follows Reich justice minister Hans Frank, "Der deutsche Rechtsstaat Adolf Hitlers," *Deutsches Recht* (1932). See Schmitt, "Der Rechtsstaat," in *Nationalsozialistisches Handbuch für Recht und Gesetzgebung,* 2d ed., ed. Hans Frank (Munich, 1935).

72 Schmitt, "Was bedeutet der Streit um den Rechtsstaat," 201.

73 See Schmitt, "Der Rechtsstaat," 715, where Anschütz is cited as a "classical thinker" of the Rechtsstaat theory: "the constitutional state wants, above all else, to be a Rechtsstaat." Anschütz continues with an argument supporting the division of powers. Schmitt quotes Anschütz, "Deutsches Staatsrecht," in *Enzyklopädie,* vol. 2 (Berlin: Holßendorff-Köhler, 1903), 593.

74 Milton, "The Tenure of Kings and Magistrates," in *Political Writings* (Cambridge: Cambridge University Press, 1991), 33.

75 Smend, who was pushed out of his chair at Berlin by the ambitious political scientist and ss man Reinhard Höhn in 1933, retreated to Göttingen; Kaufmann was retired by the Nazi administration in 1934; Heller fled to Spain, where he died in 1933. Stolleis, *Geschichte des öffentlichen Rechts in Deutschland,* vol. 3, 256–61.

76 Friedrich Balke, *Der Staat nach seinem Ende: Die Versuchung Carl Schmitts* (Bonn: Wilhelm Fink, 1996).

77 Carl Schmitt, "Großraum gegen Universalismus: Der Völkerrechtliche Kampf um die Monroedoktrine," *Zeitschrift der Akademie für Deutsches Recht* 4, no. 7 (May 1939): 333–37.

78 The "secret" chancellor of the German nation; Johannes Popitz, "Dem heimlichen Kanzler deutscher Nation zum Gedächnis," *DJZ* 36 (1931): 789–94. Schmitt also referred frequently to von Stein, especially his studies of the social movements in

France from the Revolution to 1830 *(Soziale Geschichte der französischen Revolution bis zum Jahre 1830)*; Schmitt, "Die Stellung Lorenz von Stein in der Geschichte des 19. Jahrhunderts," *Schmollers Jahrbuch* 64 (1940): 641–46. Von Stein was a professor of economics at the University of Vienna and the author of numerous works on public finance and administration including the *Lehrbuch der Finanzwirtschaft* (1860) and *Verwaltungslehre* (1865–68). For Popitz's classical tendencies see also "Ansprache zur Eröffnung der ersten öffentlichen Tagung der Gesellschaft für antike Kultur," *Die Antike: Zeitschrift für antike Kultur,* ed. W. Jäger, vol. 3, no. 3 (1927): 161–66; "Das Ideale im Recht und das Steuerrecht," AÖR 40 (1921): 129–55.

79 Bentin comments that the "glorious height" of the unitary state in Germany and "the misery of German liberty" that led to particularism were the constant poles of Popitz (*Johannes Popitz und Carl Schmitt,* 31–32).

80 That its state ethic is not the exclusively conservative property is obvious in Hermann Heller's development of its core concepts into a political theory of social democracy and the "social Rechtsstaat." Ellen Kennedy, "The Politics of Toleration in Late Weimar: Hermann Heller's Analysis of Fascism and Political Culture," *History of Political Thought* 5 (1985): 109–27; I. Staff and C. Müller, eds., *Der soziale Rechtsstaat: Gedächtnisschrift für Hermann Heller* (Baden-Baden: Nomos, 1984), especially the contributions on Heller's reading of Marx and Hegel in part G, "Hermann Hellers Auseinandersetzung mit Marx und dem Marxismus"; and, most recently, David Dyzenhaus, *Legality and Legitimacy.*

81 Popitz's attachment to German classicism was a constant theme, even when references to it were risky. At a conference held during the war, his lecture honored Schinkel as a repository of values beyond "the empty militarism of the present" (*Festrede zur Schinkel-Gedenkfeier vom 13 März 1941, Eigendruck des veranstaltened Architeckten- und Ingenieur-Vereins zu Berlin,* 6, quoted in Bentin, *Johannes Popitz und Carl Schmitt,* 41). During his last days in prison, Popitz occupied himself by writing a study of Goethe and Fontane, which was dedicated to his children. Reprinted as "Meine beiden Freunde: Goethe und Fontane," in *Antidoron–Edgar Salin zum 70. Geburtstag,* ed. Erwin von Beckerath et al. (Tübingen: Mohr, 1962), 31–51.

82 Meeting 1005 of the Mittwochsgesellschaft, in Scholder, *Die Mittwochsgesellschaft,* 260–61.

83 Ibid., 262.

84 Popitz mentions the appellation "Holy Roman Empire of the German Nation" with the implicit claim of German kaisers to be the successors of the Roman emperors (ibid., 262–63).

85 Popitz does not mention Heinrich Triepel, *Die Hegemonie: Ein Buch für führende Staaten* (1938). Written in the year that Germany invaded Czechoslovakia and when Austria "came home to the Reich," Triepel's book offered the National Socialists numerous concepts for an expansionist foreign policy and provided the view that "hegemonic impulses were typical of the great powers at all times in history." See Stolleis, *Geschichte des öffentlichen Rechts in Deutschland,* vol. 3, 388–89. Popitz's silence can be read as disagreement with the regime.

86 Bentin, commenting on his use of the phrase "nationally homogeneous people" in this presentation, sees it as "a rejection of the National Socialist metaphysic of race" (*Johannes Popitz und Carl Schmitt,* 59).

87 Schmitt, "Staat als konkreter, an eine geschichtliche Epoche gebundener Begriff," in

Verfassungsrechtliche Aufsätze, 375–85. This article grew from a paper for the Historiker-Tag (February 8, 1941), "Staatliche Souveränität und freies Meer—über den Gegensatz von Land und See im Völkerrecht der Neuzeit." After the war he developed aspects of it in *Der Nomos der Erde* (1950) and in a commentary on the Atlantic partnership in the Cold War, "Zwischen Freiheit und Diktatur—das atlantische System im permanenter Ausnahmezustand" (*Universitas,* 1950–53).

88 Brunner, *Land und Herrschaft: Grundfragen der territorialen Verfassungsgeschichte Südostdeutschlands im Mittelalter* (Baden and Vienna: Veröffentlichtungen des Instituts für Geschichtsforschung und Archivwissenschaft, 1939). Brunner's work is now available in an English translation with a brilliant introduction by Howard Kaminsky and James Van Dorn Melton, *Land and Lordship: Structures of Governance in Medieval Austria,* Middle Ages series (Philadelphia: University of Pennsylvania Press, 1992); all quotations are from the English translation.

89 Ibid., 81, 91–96.

90 Brunner's sources are Austrian and lower Bavarian.

91 Where "legitimate" is not, obviously, solely related to the "state" but can describe the actions of persons entitled to feud, clans, and the nobility (Brunner, *Land and Lordship,* 94).

92 Ibid., 31 (on friend/foe relations), 95 (on the constitution as defined in Schmitt's *Verfassungslehre*).

93 Brunner follows Schmitt's conceptual framework within the concrete conditions of medieval Austria, and Schmitt later regarded Brunner's work as evidence for his own approach to constitutional theory. See Schmitt's 1958 comment on Brunner's "clarification" of historians' and jurists' confused use of nineteenth-century political theory, whose "state concept was generalized and absolutized into a something silently self-evident" (Schmitt, *Verfassungsrechtliche Aufsätze,* 384, commenting on his 1941 essay "Staat als konkreter, an eine geschichtliche Epoche gebundener Begriff").

94 Jean Bodin, *On Sovereignty* (Cambridge: Cambridge University Press: 1996), 49.

95 Ibid., 51.

96 Carl Schmitt, *Der Begriff des Politischen* (1927).

97 Scholder, *Die Mittwochsgesellschaft,* 347–50.

98 Ibid., 348.

99 Ibid.

100 This was a substantive break with the theory of the racial state expounded by Carl Schmitt from 1933 until 1937 and 1938, when his attention turned toward other justifications for Hitler's rule. Hasso Hofmann, *Legitimität gegen Legalität* (Neuwied: Luchterhand: 1964), 199ff.

101 Popitz specifically excludes Rudolf Smend's constitutional theory of "integration." Smend, *Verfassung und Verfassungsrecht* (1928).

102 Popitz, in Scholder, *Die Mittwochsgesellschaft,* 350.

103 *Plötzensee: Stätten der Verfolgung und des Widerstandes in Berlin, 1933–1945,* 20.

104 Von Hassell, *Vom andern Deutschland,* 355–56.

105 J. L Austin, *The Province of Jurisprudence Defined* (1832); F. H. Hinsley, *On Sovereignty* (Cambridge: Cambridge University Press: 1986).

106 This did not, however, prevent Popitz from suggesting "a general power of dismissal" for the government in 1933 specifically aimed at the tenure rights of the professional civil service. See Caplan, *Government without Administration,* 147.

107 Bentin, *Johannes Popitz und Carl Schmitt,* 135–36. Popitz's concept of the state, Bentin remarks, remained "conservative, he was himself trapped in the old concepts of Lorenz von Stein and could not free himself from a concept of the state as the opposite of society." By contrast, Schmitt was "incomparably more flexible and creative" and just ahead of the political trends, while Popitz's idea of the state was "an idealized relict of the German past."

108 Scholder, *Die Mittwochsgesellschaft,* 43.

109 Ibid., 354.

110 Fechtner, *Menschen und Zeiten,* cited in Scholder, *Die Mittwochsgesellschaft,* 355.

111 Schmitt, *Verfassungsrechtliche Aufsätze,* 421, where he refers to Savigny's call for a "jurisprudence that is the protector of a law that is not just statute."

112 Leo Strauss, *Persecution and the Art of Writing* (Glencoe: Free Press, 1952).

113 Carl Schmitt, "Die Lage der europäischen Rechtswissenschaft," 427.

114 In a note written for the text's later publication (1958), Schmitt comments: "Hegel's state was a legislation-state and his jurists no longer an independent estate [*Stand*] but civil servants." The mutation of appearance and reality, image and substance—his example here is that "legality" ceased to be connected to legitimacy in the "bourgeois revolution" of 1830—can be grasped "very well with Hegel's categories" (ibid., 429 n. 4).

115 Ibid., 418, 408.

116 These are 1848 (the liberal revolution), 1871 (German unification), and 1890 (the dismissal of Bismarck by Wilhelm and the beginning the "Kaiserreich").

117 Carl Schmitt, *Hugo Preuß—sein Staatsbegriff und seine Stellung in der deutschen Staatslehre* (Tübingen: J. C. B. Mohr, 1930), 20. In this text, Schmitt seems, in part at least, to accept the liberal alternative to Prussian authoritarianism and Marxism, which appeared in the German constitutional discussions of 1918 and 1919 as "monarchy" or the socialist forms of "council democracy." Elsewhere, he excoriates liberal compromises as the agents of constitutional failure.

118 Carl Schmitt, "Staat als ein konkreter, an eine geschichtliche Epoche gebundener Begriff" (1941), in *Verfassungsrechtliche Aufsätze,* 375–85.

119 Schmitt, *Der Begriff des Politischen,* 10. Further, "The churches in particular become either means to maintain public order or instruments of state welfare or the private affair of pious individuals" (ibid.).

120 Schmitt, *Verfassungsrechtliche Aufsätze,* 427.

121 "The positivism that has dominated the theory and practice of European law for a century regards the exclusive object of jurisprudence as an effectively valid norm, and for positivism that is simply whatever laws of the state are currently in effect, or a rule backed by force and the will to carry it out" (ibid., 386).

122 See the entry in von Hassell's diary, *Vom Andern Deutschland,* for July 7, 1944, describing the atmosphere at the last meetings of the Mittwochsgesellschaft and indicating that the conspirators were aware of being watched by German intelligence.

123 Schmitt, *Verfassungsrechtliche Aufsätze,* 426.

124 When the lecture was finally published in 1950, Walter Lewald suggested that Schmitt's account of the Festschrift was fabricated. See "Carl Schmitt redividus?" *Neue Juristische Wochenschrift* 3 (1950): 377. Werner Weber, Schmitt's student at the time, replied in a letter to the *Neue Juristische Wochenschrift* that "Carl

Schmitt and his wife were close friends for more than a decade and that they continued to help him even during his imprisonment" (Bentin, *Johannes Popitz und Carl Schmitt*, 128; also, Bendersky, *Carl Schmitt*, 275–76).

125 Popitz was closely involved in the Resistance until August 1943, when his attempt to persuade Himmler to overthrow Hitler was discovered by German counterintelligence. Popitz was under surveillance from then on, and Bentin argues that he was probably not directly involved in the July 20 attempt (Bentin, *Johannes Popitz und Carl Schmitt*, 72).

126 His pension was restored in 1950 through a West German amnesty act for former civil servants, a class that included German professors.

127 Among those to visit were A. Kojeve, R. Koselleck, R. Aron, and E. Jünger (Noakes and Pridham, *Documents on Nazism*, 276ff).

128 Bendersky, *Carl Schmitt*, 273.

129 Stolleis, *Geschichte des öffentlichen Rechts in Deutschland*, vol. 3, 246–28.

130 Hans Mommsen, "The German Resistance to Hitler and the Restoration of Politics," *Journal of Modern History* 64, supp. (December 1992): 112–27, 115.

131 Igebourg Maus, "Zur 'Zäsur' von 1933 in der Theorie Carl Schmitts," *Kritische Justiz* 1 (1971), reprinted in *Rechtstheorie und politische Theorie im Industriekapitalismus* (Munich: Wilhelm Fink, 1986). Walter Struve, *Elites against Democracy: Leadership Ideals in Bourgeois Political Thought in Germany, 1890–1933* (Princeton: Princeton University Press, 1973).

132 Jane Caplan, "Civil Service Support for National Socialism: An Evaluation," in *Der "Führerstaat": Mythos und Realität*, ed. G. Hirschfeld and L. Kettenacker, publications of the German Historical Institute London (Stuttgart: Klett-Cotta, 1981), 167–93. Caplan's argument about this traditional affinity of the professional civil service for National Socialism is pursued from a Marxist theoretical perspective in "The Imaginary Universality of Particular Interests: The 'Tradition' of the Civil Service in German History," *Social History* 4 (1979): 299–317, where Hegel's philosophy of the state is reduced to an ideology.

133 Both men knew the question of the state was not simply a matter of ideology, and they knew the risks involved. This is not to say that by 1943, an academic argument could have altered the German course or that, even in hindsight, the debates of lawyers or economists could have shifted the Third Reich from its irrational and destructive path. After "the second revolution" (1934), the Nazis dispensed with men such as Schmitt. "Just as the old state will not return, the old constitutional theory will cease to have any meaning. It is equally useless, however, to write learned treatises about the nature of the new state—here too the pens are scribbling in vain. Today only one person knows what the new structure of the state will look like after ten years, the Führer, and he won't allow himself to be influenced by any writers, no matter how learned" (W. Sommer, "Die NSDAP als Verwaltungsträger," quoted in Stolleis, *The Law under the Swastika*, 218).

2 The Sovereign Moment

1 Christian von Krachow, *Die Entscheidung: Eine Untersuchung über Ernst Jünger, Carl Schmitt, Martin Heidegger* (Stuttgart: Göttinger Abhandlungen zur Soziologie unter Einschluß ihrer Grenzgebiete, 1985), 25.

2 "The Weimar ideal was both old and new. The striking mixture of cynicism and

confidence, the search for novelty and for roots—the solemn irreverence—of the twenties, were a child of war, revolution, and democracy, but the elements that made it up came from both the distant and the recent past, recalled and revived by a new generation. Goethe and Schopenhauer, historic dates like 1848 and 1871, were living realities for the new Weimar, while the immediate ancestry of the Weimar style, still passionately debated, went back to the turn of the century and the 1890s." Peter Gay, *Weimar Culture: The Outsider as Insider* (London: Secker and Warburg, 1968), 2.

3 Keith Wittington, "On the Relative Absence of Constitutional Crises in the United States," paper presented at the Georgetown/PEGS Discussion Group on Constitutionalism, 2001.

4 Jürgen Habermas, *Legitimationsprobleme im Spätkapitalismus* (Frankfurt: Suhrkamp, 1973), 113.

5 Gottfried Benn, "Der Expressionismus," in *Das Hauptwerk*, vol. 2, *Essays, Reden, Vorträge* (Wiesbaden: Limes Verlag, 1980), 125.

6 Schmitt's comments in the preface to the second edition of his *Parlamentarismus* (1926) are representative: "A calm and factual debate that distances itself from all party political exploitation, and serves as propaganda for no one, might appear impractical, naive, and anachronistic today" (*Die geistesgeschichtliche Lage des heutigen Parlamentarismus* [Berlin: Duncker und Humblot, 1979]).

7 Nor did the precursors of Nazi race politics, Chamberlain and Spengler, matter to Schmitt.

8 Wassily Kandinsky, "The Problem of Form," in *Voices of Expressionism*, ed. Victor H. Meisel (Englewood Cliffs, N.J.: Prentice-Hall, 1970), 48.

9 Schmitt, *Politische Theologie: Vier Kapitel zur Lehre von der Souveränität* (Berlin: Duncker und Humblot, 1985), 59.

10 Martin Buber, *Du und Ich* (1920), was just one example.

11 On the proximity of political radicalism to expressionism see the memoirs of Kasimir Edschmid, *Lebendiger Expressionismus: Auseinandersetzungen, Gestalten, Erinnerungen* (Munich: Welt im Buch, 1961), 257ff. Peter Gay comments, referring to Emile Nolde's fate as a "degenerate artist" after 1933, that "while not all Expressionists loved Weimar, the enemies of Weimar hated all Expressionists" (Gay, *Weimar Culture*, 108). It is certainly true of the Nazis but oversimplifies the political constellations of the Republic.

12 Quoted in Wolfgang Rothe, *Der Expressionismus: Theologische, soziologische, und anthropologische Aspekte einer Literatur* (Frankfurt: V. Klostermann, 1977).

13 Henri Bergson, *Les deux sources de la morale et de la religion* (1932).

14 A leading expressionist publicist and editor of *Tribüne der Kunst und Zeit*, which published Gottfried Benn's "Das Moderne Ich"; Beckmann, Klee, Pechstein, and Marc on art; Kurt Hiller's activist manifesto, "Geist werde Herr"; and Carlo Mierendorff's influential essay on the cinema as a new art form, "Hätte ich das Kino!"

15 Franz Marc, "Die 'Wilden' Deutschlands," in *Der blaue Reiter* (Munich: Piper, 1984), 28.

16 Gottfried Benn, "Das moderne Ich," in *Essays, Rede, Vorträge*, 17.

17 Wolfgang Rothe, *Der Expressionismus*, 14.

18 Carl Schmitt, *Jugendbriefe: Briefschaften on seine Schwester Auguste 1905 bis 1913*, ed. Ernst Husmert (Berlin: Akademic Verlag, 2000), letter of 3 March 1913, 134–36.

19 Ellen Kennedy, "Politischer Expressionismus: Die kulturkritischen und metaphysischen Ursprünge des Begriffs des Politischen von Carl Schmitt," in Helmut Quaritsch, ed., *Complexio Oppositorum: Über Carl Schmitt* (Berlin: Duncker und Humblot, 1988), 233–68; Ellen Kennedy, "Carl Schmitt und Hugo Ball: Ein Beitrag zum Thema, politischer Expressionmus," *Zeitschrift für Politik* (1988): 143–62. Schmitt's diary from this period appeared too late to be considered here. Carl Schmitt, *Tagebücher vom Oktober 1912 bis Februar 1915* (Berlin: Akademie Verlag, 2003).

20 These focus on legal philosophy or technical questions in the law, such as medical malpractice; Carl Schmitt, "Über Tatbestandsmäßigkeit und Rechtswidrigkeit des kunstgerechten operativen Eingriffs," *Zeitschrift für die gesamte Straftrechtswissenschaft* 31 (1910): 467–78.

21 "Drei Tischgespräche," *Die Rheinlande* (1911).

22 "Der Spiegel," *Die Rheinlande* (1912): 62.

23 Ibid.

24 "Don Quijote und das Publikum," *Die Rheinlande* (1912): 348–50.

25 "Kritik der Zeit," *Die Rheinlande* (1912): 324.

26 *Schattenrisse* was published under the pseudonym "Johannes Negelius, Mox Doctor." Reprinted in Ingeborg Villinger, *Carl Schmitts Kulturkritik der Moderne* (Akademie Verlag, 1995), with a detailed and brilliant commentary on the figures and their place in contemporary German history.

27 Schmitt, *Schattenrisse,* 18–20.

28 Villinger, *Carl Schmitts Kulturkritik der Moderne,* 191.

29 Schmitt, "Die Buribunken," *Summa* (1919).

30 Schmitt, *Theodor Däublers 'Nordlicht': Drei Studien über die Elemente, den Geist und die Aktualituat des Werkes* (Munich: Georg Müller, 1916), 68.

31 Schmitt, *Jugendbriefe,* 26 August 1912, 159.

32 Schmidt-Rotluff, Pechstein, Kirchner, Heckel, Nolde, and others; he despised the representational work of Böcklin and Klinger, favorites of the kaiser. Däubler wrote "Im Kampf um die moderne Kunst" (1919) for *Tribüne der Kunst und Zeit.*

33 Däubler, "Im Kampf um die moderne Kunst," 45, 34. A figure Benn conveniently omits in 1933 from the list of Aryan expressionists in "Der Expressionismus," 124.

34 Schmitt, *Ex captivitate Salus* (Cologne: Greven Verlag, 1950), 45.

35 "The German language first became through Däubler the wonderful instrument of a new tonality. What impressionism was for the nineteenth century, what futurism, cubism and expressionism began in many chaotic attempts, found unexpected fulfillment in the German language" (ibid., 46).

36 Ibid., 49.

37 Schmitt, *Der Wert des Staates,* 3.

38 Däubler, *Nordlicht,* 31.

39 Schmitt, *Theodor Däublers 'Nordlicht,'* 70.

40 Ibid., 70, 65, 71.

41 Ibid., 77.

42 Schmitt, *Aus meinem Leben: Aufzeichnungen des Deutschen Pietisten Johann Arnold Kanne* (Berlin: Furche, 1919).

43 It is not implausible that Kierkegaard's "Schattenrisse: Psychologischer Zeitvertreib," part of *Entweder/Oder,* was the model for Schmitt's and Eisler's satire of the same name.

44 Kierkegaard, *Begriff des Auserwählten,* trans. Th. Heckel (Hellerau: Jacob Hegner Verlag, 1917). Also in the Schmitt Nachlaß are *Angriff auf die Christenheit* (1896) and *Der Einzelne und die Kirche* (1934), Stadtarchiv Düsseldorf, carton 159.

45 See Guy Oakes's brilliant introduction to the English translation comparing the antiwar activities of Normal Mailer in the 1960s to the romantic politics of Schmitt's time. Max Weber referred to them as a "revolutionary carnival." Max Weber, "Das neue Deutschland," in *Gesammelte Politische Schriften,* ed. Johannes Winckelmann (1920; Tübingen: Mohr, 1971), 483–87.

46 Schmitt, "Die Sichtbarkeit der Kirche: Eine scholastische Erwägung," *Summa* 2, no. 1 (1917–18): 75.

47 Schmitt, *Politische Romantik,* 27.

48 Sören Kierkegaard, "Das Gleichgewicht zwischen dem Aesthetischen und dem Ethischen in der Herausarbeitung der Persönlichkeit," in *Entweder/Oder,* vol. 2 (Gütersloh: Gütersloher Verlagshaus Mohn, 1980).

49 Schmitt's copy of *Begriff des Auserwählten* is heavily marked. He seems to have been especially interested in Kierkegaard's analysis of the newspaper readers of the time, which Kierkegaard regarded as a culture of the trivial, destructive of "geist" and seriousness. "Our time shouts constantly" Kierkegaard wrote, and that is "a political, a religious problem" (10).

50 Representatives were chosen in a national election on January 19, 1919, and first gathered in Weimar on February 6. The assembly met twenty-eight times in Weimar between February 6 and April 15, 1919, and from May 12 until June 22 in Berlin; the final forty-seven sittings were held in Weimar, and the Reichstag sat in Berlin beginning on September 30, 1919. The parties represented (and their seats) were the Deutschnationale Volkspartei (44), Deutsche Volkspartei (19), Zentrum (91), Deutsche Demokratische Volkspartei (75), Sozialdemokratische Partei (163), Unabhängige Sozialdemokratische Partei (22), and seven others from splinter parties.

51 Walter Jellinek, "Die Nationalversammlung von Weimar und ihr Werk," in *Handbuch des Deutschen Staatsrechts,* vol. 1 (Tübingen: J. C. B. Mohr, 1930), 122–23. Also, Hans Beyersdorff, "Die Staatstheorien in der Verfassungsgebenden Deutschen Nationalversammlung von 1919" (Ph.D. diss., Kiel, 1928).

52 Friedrich Meinecke, *Weltbürgertum und Nationalstaat: Studien zur Genesis des deutschen Nationalstaats* (Munich: Duncker und Humblot, 1922), 63, 69.

53 Quoted in Meinecke, *Weltbürgertum und Nationalstaat,* 73. Isaiah Berlin has described the romantic tradition as opposed to "universality, objectivity, rationality, and the capacity to provide permanent solutions to all genuine problems of life or thought and (no less important) accessibility of rational methods to any thinker armed with adequate powers of observation and logical thinking." Isaiah Berlin, *Four Essays on Liberty* (Oxford: Oxford University Press, 1969).

54 Schmitt, *Politische Romantik,* 39.

55 Habermas, *Legitimationsprobleme im Spätkapitalismus.*

56 There were many examples of the romantic persuasion in German politics as Schmitt wrote: in Bavaria, Eric Muhsam, Ernst Toller, and others led the Socialist Republic, and many artists signed the manifesto of the November Group, which began with the slogan of the French Revolution, "Liberty, Fraternity, and Equality!" and ended with a call to "Cubists, Futurists, and Expressionists—Join Us!" Meisel, *Voices of German Expressionism,* 169–70.

57 Schmitt, *Politische Romantik*, 77.

58 He had begun a love affair with the wife of a friend, which made their communal living arrangements awkward, so the departure served this purpose as well.

59 Schmitt, *Politische Romantik*, 67.

60 Ibid., 72. He was, Schmitt concludes, only an "ambitious servant of various systems, someone always prepared to throw away part of his ideas that might stand in the way of his unhindered functioning, or assimilate new ones to himself" (74).

61 Ibid., 121.

62 "The contradiction of the sexes is resolved in 'humanity,' the contradiction of individuals in a higher organism, the 'state' or people, the division of states through a higher organization, the church" (ibid., 126–27).

3 Norm and Exception

1 Carl Schmitt, *Politische Romantik* (Berlin: Duncker und Humblot, 1982), 16, 25.

2 In the late 1930s Schmitt defined the "two great dualisms" of contemporary legal systems in terms of the subfields within jurisprudence, international and national law, and within the latter, public and private law. Schmitt, "Über die zwei großen 'Dualismen' des heutigen Rechtssytems" (1939), *Positionen und Begriffe im Kampf mit Weimar, Genf, Versailles* (Hamburg: Hanseatische Verlagsanstalt, 1939). The larger perspective of this aspect of Schmitt's thought on the relationship of philosophical dualism and the law became more visible through the war years and after in Schmitt's work on international law.

3 Still definitive is Hasso Hofmann, *Legitimität gegen Legalitat: Der Weg der politischen Philosophie Carl Schmitts* (Neuwied: Luchterhand, 1964); but see also David Dyzenhaus, *Legality and Legitimacy* (Oxford: Clarendon Press, 1998); and W. Scheuerman, *Carl Schmitt: The End of Law* (Lanham, Md.: Rowman and Littlefield, 1999). Most of the jurisprudential literature on Schmitt deals with his opposition to positivism and the resources of his work for an alternative theory of law.

4 Carl Schmitt, *Gesetz und Urteil: Eine Untersuchung zum Problem der Rechtspraxis* (Berlin: Liebmann, 1912), vi.

5 Carl Schmitt, *Der Wert des Staates und die Bedeutung des Einzelnen* (Tübingen: Mohr, 1914), 1.

6 Carl Schmitt, *Die Diktatur: Von den Anfängen des modernen Souveränitätsgedanken bis zum proletarischen Klassenkampf* (Berlin: Duncker und Humblot, 1978), xi.

7 Carl Schmitt, *Verfassungsrechtliche Aufsätze aus den Jahren 1924–1954: Materialien zu einer Verfassungslehre* (Berlin: Duncker und Humblot, 1973), 427.

8 No attempt to recount in detail the schools of German jurisprudence during the century preceding the Great War will be made here, but the definitive history is now Michael Stolleis, *Geschichte des öffentlichen Rechts in Deutschland*, vol. 2: *Staatsrechtslehre und Verwaltungswissenschaft, 1800–1914* (Munich: C. H. Beck, 1992). This volume is now available in English as *Public Law in Germany, 1800–1914* (New York: Berghahn Books, 2001).

9 One must know this to understand Hegel's angry assertion in the *Philosophy of Right* that "Jurisprudence is a branch of philosophy."

10 G. F. Puchta, *Cursus der Institutionen* (1800). Puchta was the intellectual father of the *Pandektenwissenschaft*, or scientific study of the Roman law, in the nineteenth century. Puchta was a student of Savigny and came under Hegel's influence while

still at the *Gymnasium*. His influence extended throughout Europe and can be seen in W. W. Buckland's *Roman Law from Augustus to Justinian* (Cambridge: Cambridge University Press, 1921).

11 Leo Strauss, *Natural Right and History* (Chicago: University of Chicago Press, 1953).

12 Hegel, like many early supporters of the French Revolution, turned against it after the Terror and called its "abstraction" the source of fanaticism and anarchy: "Universal freedom can . . . produce neither a positive achievement nor a deed; there is left for it only negative action; it is merely the rage and fury of destruction." Freedom in this sense is pure negation, incapable of mediation, "the negation of the individual as a factor existing within the universal. The sole and only work and deed accompanied by universal freedom is therefore death—a death that achieves nothing, embraces nothing within its grasp . . . the most cold blooded and meaningless death of all, with no more significance than cleaving a head of cabbage or swallowing a draught of water." That anarchy is contrasted to government, "a power to will and perform . . . a determinate order and action." Hegel, "Absolute Freedom and Terror," in *Phenomenology of Mind*, trans. J. B. Baillie (London: George Allen and Unwin, 1971), 604–5. Joachim Ritter demonstrates that a simply reactionary reading of Hegel is unsatisfactory; the Revolution was *necessary*, and the break with tradition and metaphysics that it achieved was the central problem of modernity. Ritter, *Hegel und die französische Revolution* (Frankfurt: Suhrkamp, 1965).

13 Immanuel Kant, "On the Common Saying: That May Be Correct in Theory but It Is of No Use in Practice" (1793), in *Immanuel Kant: Practical Philosophy*, trans. and ed. Mary J. Gregor (Cambridge: Cambridge University Press, 1996), 276–309.

14 Wolfgang Kersting, "Politics, Freedom, and Order: Kant's Political Philosophy," in *The Cambridge Companion to Kant*, ed. Paul Guyer (Cambridge: Cambridge University Press, 1992), 342.

15 Ibid.

16 Ibid., 344.

17 Kant, *The Metaphysics of Morals*, trans. Mary Gregor (Cambridge: Cambridge University Press, 1991), 6:230.

18 Natural science too is phenomenological, not knowledge of things in themselves but knowledge of their appearances.

19 Kant, *The Metaphysics of Morals*, 7–9.

20 Kersting, "Politics, Freedom, and Order," 345. Law, in this sense, is to be judged not in terms of its content but on the basis of its formal properties and has been criticized by many as "empty," including, of course, Schmitt. But see also Hermann Cohen, *Kants Begründung der Ethik nebst ihren Anwendung auf Recht, Religion, und Geschichte* (Berlin: Cassirer, 1910); and Erich Kaufmann, *Kritik der neukantischen Rechtstheorie* (Tübingen: J. C. B. Mohr, 1921).

21 "A statute book can no more be derived from [it] than a specific canon of duties can be derived from the categorical imperative" (Kersting, "Politics, Freedom, and Order," 346).

22 Ibid., 347.

23 Ritter, *Hegel and the French Revolution*, trans. Richard D. Winfield (Cambridge: MIT Press, 1982), 40. Ritter quotes *The Philosophy of Right*.

24 "Hegel takes up the problem of historical discontinuity; it raises the question of what signifies, underlies and brings forth the interpretation of the present as the end

of history, an interpretation decisive for the Revolution itself in the same way as for its opponents" (ibid., 61).

25 Charles Taylor, *Hegel* (Cambridge: Cambridge University Press, 1975).

26 Ritter, *Hegel and the French Revolution*, 62.

27 George Kelly comments that "the Enlightenment had furnished a sense of momentum; it had not restored the conviction of harmony. Both the mind and social order were implicated. If society was in process, then the mind could not be explored statically as the rationalists had taught. Hegel attempts to mediate these elements, by recognizing that mind has a history of its own, a sequence of pitfalls and half-truths which, however, constitute its necessary *Bildung*." Kelly, *Idealism, Politics, and History* (Cambridge: Cambridge University Press, 1969), 336.

28 Although Puchta still referred to the life of legal principles within the nation, this is no more than a rhetorical repetition of Savigny's authentic starting point. In the Pandektenwissenschaft, and later in the legal positivism of Gerber and Jhering, the substance of law, still seen by Savigny, was replaced with a purely logical system. See Puchta, "Geneologie der Begriffe," in *Cursus der Institutionen* (1800).

29 *The Metaphysics of Morals* (1787) is cited.

30 The phase is Hans Kiefner's, from "Der Einfluß Kants auf die Theorie und Praxis des Zivilrechts im 19. Jarhundert," in *Philosophie und Rechtswissenschaft: Zum Problem ihrer Beziehung im 19. Jahrhundert*, ed. J. Blühdorn and J. Ritter (Frankfurt: V. Klostermann, 1969), 4.

31 Kant, *What Is Enlightenment?* (1784). James Sheehan remarks on the material culture of this idea as not just a cluster of genius but a "dramatic quantitative increase in cultural consumption," primarily magazines and newspapers, but also clubs, societies, and lodges, in the later eighteenth century. Sheehan, *German Liberalism in the Nineteenth Century* (Chicago: University of Chicago Press, 1978), 7.

32 Ibid., 27.

33 Leonard Krieger, *The German Idea of Freedom: History of a Tradition* (Boston, 1957). Sheehan remarks in agreement that this was almost entirely the creation of civil servants (*German Liberalism in the Nineteenth Century*, 43).

34 There was no unitary liberal view of which institutions would best serve the substantial purposes of progressive politics, and considerable disagreement on the role of the legislature in a republican constitution. See Sheehan's discussion (*German Liberalism in the Nineteenth Century*, 44).

35 Quoted in Sheehan, *German Liberalism in the Nineteenth Century*, 45.

36 Puchta's *Cursus der Institutionen* (1841–47) aimed at a "genealogy of concepts," but it was neither a genealogy nor a study of institutions.

37 Paul Laband, *Das Staatsrecht des Deutschen Reichs*, 3 vols. (Tübingen: J. C. B. Mohr, 1876–82), 13.

38 Franz Wieacker, *Privatrechtsgeschichte der Neuzeit* (Göttingen: Vandenhoeck und Ruprecht, 1967), 401–2.

39 Hofmann, *Legitimität gegen Legalität*, 29.

40 The greatest contributions were Max Weber's, but even his epochal study of the three types of legitimacy was not published until after the war. "Die drei reinen Typen der legitiminen Herrschaft," *Preußischer Jahrbücher* 187 (1922): 1–12; reprinted in *Gesammelte Aufsätze zur Wissenschaftslehre*, ed. J. Winckelmann (Tübingen: J. C. B. Mohr, 1988). Others were Heinrich von Treitschke, Ernst Trolsch, Friedrich Meinicke, and the founders of modern sociology, Werner Sombart and

Georg Simmel. Stolleis comments about law at the turn of the century, "real innovation came from outside, from the geographically and academically marginal area of constitutional law" (*Public Law in Germany, 1800–1914*, 435).

41 Carl Schmitt, *Über Schuld und Schuldarten* (Breslau: Schletter'sche Buchhandlung, 1910). His adviser Fritz van Calker was an expert on the criminal law, but his work extended to questions of morality and punishment, and in 1899 he published a book on the science of politics, *Politik als Wissenschaft.* Van Calker was elected to the Reichstag in 1912. *Schattenrisse* (Berlin: Skimachten Verlag, 1913); *Gesetz und Urteil: Eine Untersuchung zum Problem der Rechtspraxis* (Berlin: Liebmann, 1912); *Der Wert des Staates* (Tübingen: J. C. B. Mohr, 1914). *Gesetz und Urteil* was dedicated to van Calker; *Schattenrisse* was published under the pseudonym "Johannes Negelinus" and was written together with Fritz Eisler.

42 Schmitt published on medical malpractice: "Tatbestandsmäßigkeit und Rechtswidrigkeit des kunstgerechten operativen Eingriffs," *Zeitschrift für die gesamte Staatsrechtswissenschaft* 31 (1910): 467–78.

43 On January 22, 1911, he wrote to his sister describing a wedding party at the Lamberts, "There were eleven different wines. I was very moderate. My waitress wore edelweiss in her hair. The wine was good. There was some theatre. The burgundy was too heavy for me. Four people gave speeches. That's OK. Oh and the pommery was very good. Also the orchestra. There were some very pretty ladies. I also had some pineapple sorbet. Two ladies played Chopin waltzes. Fine. And the coffee was not of bad parentage. Caviar on an ice block is nonsense. Schiller is still the greatest poet." Carl Schmitt, *Jugendbriefe: Briefschaften an seine Schwester Auguste 1905 bis 1913* (Berlin: Akademie, 2001), 93.

44 In *Pathetisches Denken,* Reinhard Mehring comments that its terminological purpose leads Schmitt to a kind of nominalism based on Husserl's revisions of Kant's psychology (28).

45 Carl Schmitt, *Schuld und Schuldarten: Eine terminologische Untersuchung* (Breslau: Schletter'sche Buchhandlung, 1910), 15.

46 One of the leading positivists, Walter Jellinek, reviewing *Gesetz und Urteil,* praised Schmitt's emphasis on "methodological clarity and attention to reality" but remained skeptical about "the new criterion Schmitt proposed." He wanted to demonstrate the inadequacy of "legality" (Gesetzmäßigkeit) as the criterion of determining a right legal decision. The appeal to have decided "on the basis of the law" begs the question of what the law *is* and requires. Into that interpretative quandary Schmitt brings not a literary or textual solution but one that must refer to the reality of legal practice. Jellinek agreed that the problem Schmitt addressed was important but rejected the solution as replacing one hypothetical subject (the legislator) with another (the other judge). Jellinek, "Besprechung der Schrift 'Gesetz und Urteil' von Carl Schmitt,"*Archiv für öffentliches Recht* 33 (1914): 296–99.

47 Felix Halldack, "Besprechung der Schrift 'Gesetz und Urteil' von Carl Schmitt," *Kant-Studien* 17 (1912): 464–67.

48 Hans Vaihinger, *Die Philosophie des Als-ob: System der theoretischen, praktischen, und religiösen Fiktionen der Menschheit auf Grund eines idealistischen Positivismus, mit einem Anhang über Kant und Nietzsche* (Berlin: Reuter und Reichard, 1911), and Hegel, *Philosophie des Rechts,* both appear in the first chapter, as does Aristotle's *Logic;* these structure Schmitt's extensive review and critique of the contemporary literature, including Stammler, Zitelman, Simmel, and Kantorowicz.

49 Schmitt, *Gesetz und Urteil,* 1. His emphasis on something beyond the methodological principle distinguishes Schmitt's project from the logical constructions of formal jurisprudence that Puchta, for example, assessed by reference to their "productive constructions," "economy" and "beauty." Wieacker, *Privatrechtsgeschichte der Neuzeit,* 451 n. 60. There is a striking similarity to social science and rational choice language today.

50 Schmitt, *Gesetz und Urteil,* 15.

51 Stolleis, *Geschichte des öffentlichen Rechts in Deutschland,* vol. 3: *Staats- und Verwaltungsrechtswissenschaft in Republik und Diktatur, 1914–1945* (Munich: C. H. Beck, 1999), 165.

52 Stolleis, *Public Law in Germany, 1800–1914,* 446. The major figures were Jellinek, Triepel, Anschütz, Kaufmann, Schmitt, Kelsen, Smend, Thoma.

53 Hans Kelsen, *Das Problem der Souveränität und die Theorie des Völkerrechts* (Tübingen: J. C. B. Mohr, 1920), applied the argument to international law.

54 Stolleis, *Public Law in Germany, 1800–1914,* 445–49.

55 Rudolf Stammler, *Die Lehre vom richtigen Rechte* (Berlin: J. Guttentag, 1902), 429–30. Stammler called the question of "right law" unavoidable, and this extremely influential work proposed its "methodological" solution in formal terms beginning with the assumption that there is "a unity of all imaginable human desires" that can be harmonized "absolutely" (ibid., 140–43). This was Stammler's ideal, not as a utopian scheme but as a method of reconciling all possible individual desires with "right law." That such a method is, however, loaded with normative content and could never be otherwise was noted by many critics. Karl Larenz, *Richtiges Recht: Grundzuge einer Rechtsethik* (Munich: Beck, 1979). Larenz reads Stammler as addressing the central problem of law and political theory; the "inner right" of law is in fact the question of its legitimacy and obligatoriness. See Schmitt's discussion of Stammler's "old hermeneutic" in *Gesetz und Urteil,* 34.

56 Schmitt, *Gesetz und Urteil,* 43–44.

57 Ibid., 69.

58 Schmitt, *Die geistesgeschichtliche Lage des heutigen Parlamentarismus* (Berlin: Duncker und Humblot, 1923).

59 Jürgen Habermas, *Strukturwandel der Öffentlichkeit: Untersuchungen zu einer Kategorie der bürgerlichen Gesellschaft* (Darmstadt und Neuwied: Luchterhand, 1962).

60 "What is the normative principle at the basis of modern legal practice?" (Schmitt, *Gesetz und Urteil,* 1).

61 Carl Schmitt, "Juristische Fiktionen," *Deutsche Juristen-Zeitung* 12 (1913): 804–5. Schmitt takes the title of his article from "Juristische fiktionen," chap. 5 of Vaihinger's *Die Philosophie des Als-ob* (Berlin: Reuter und Richard, 1911). Vaihinger notes that legal fictions are a special kind of analogical fiction and distinguishes them from "presumptions" and compares juristic fictions to epistemological fictions. There is a relationship "in principle" between law and logic even though the material of law is taken from real life. Jurisprudence and mathematics have developed the purest forms of fiction (Vaihinger, *Die Philosophie des Als-ob,* 46–47). The year before publishing this text, Schmitt had argued with reference to Vaihinger that "fictions" are practical and also that "intuitive knowledge" makes the connection between art and philosophy. Schmitt, "Der Adressat," *Rheinland* 21 (1911): 429–30.

62 Schmitt to Auguste Schmitt, 7 July 1913, in *Jugendbriefe,* 175; other quotations are on pp. 88, 98, 108, 130.

63 Vaihinger, *Die Philosophie des Als-ob,* 771. This brief chapter entitled "Nietzsche and the Will to Appearances" brilliantly demonstrates the connection between him and Kant, and Nietzsche's fascination with the human determination to lie and deceive oneself. The madness of Don Quixote testifies to a dedication to truth beyond public opinion.

64 Schmitt, "Der Adressat," 430; he is quoting Richard Wagner.

65 Schmitt, "Richard Wagner und eine neue 'Lehre vom Wahn,' " *Bayreuthische Blätter* 35 (1912): 239–41.

66 Fritz Mauthner, *Wörterbuch der Philosophie: Neue Beiträge zu einer Kritik der Sprache* (Munich: Georg Müller, 1910).

67 Ibid., vol. 1, xiv.

68 Ibid., xix.

69 In the 1980s Schmitt was likely to refer to Mandeville's *Fable of the Bees* or Aesop's *Fables* in conversation and was fascinated by various problems of translation.

70 Carl Schmitt, "Die Philosophie und ihre Resultate," *Der Rheinland* 23 (1913): 34–36. The article is a review of Mauthner's *Wörtertbuch der Philosophie.*

71 Ibid., 36.

72 Theodor Däubler, *Das Nordlicht,*vol. 2, 542.

73 Stolleis, *Public Law in Germany, 1800–1914,* 440.

74 Schmitt, *Der Wert des Staates,* 10.

75 Ibid., 2.

76 Hermann Cohen, *Ethik des reinen Willen* (1910). Schmitt remarks that Cohen's psychology wanted to create a jurisprudential science on the model of natural science, with mathematical certainty (*Der Wert des Staates,* 12–13).

77 Schmitt, *Der Wert des Staates,* 72, 53–54.

78 Ibid., 55.

79 Ibid., 78.

80 "For Schmitt both paths—that of decisionism and that of normativism—were open" (Stolleis, *Public Law in Germany 1800–1914,* 440).

81 Schmitt's concern with fictions in the law and merely hypothetical reasoning is evident through this period (1911–1914); see also "Die Philosophie und ihre Resultate," 34–36.

82 Ibid., 98; 78–79.

83 "Legal rules cannot be a 'form' of social life because they are thought of as valid, therefore not a form of the real: the empirical legal rules are however a component of the real, not its form" (ibid., 54). See also Weber, "Rudolf Stammlers 'Überwindung' der materialistischen Geschichtsauffassung," in *Gesammelte Aufsätze zur Wissenschaftslehre,* 142.

84 Schmitt, *Gesetz und Urteil,* 98. Schmitt refers to Weber's critique of Stammler in Weber's "Kritische Studien auf dem Gebiet der kulturwissenschaftlichen Logik," in *Gesammelte Aufsätze zur Wissenschaftslehre,* 215–90.

85 Procedural rules all have this character to some extent.

86 Schmitt, *Gesetz und Urteil.*

87 Among these were Theodor Haecker, Max Scheler, and the publisher A. P. Gütersloh. It has been suggested that Blei's contacts with Hugo Ball brought Schmitt's work to his attention. Manfred Dahlheimer, *Carl Schmitt und der deutsche Katholizismus, 1888–1936* (Paderborn: Schöningh, 1998), 545. On the Catholic intellectual milieu around Blei, see Dietrich Harth, ed., *Franz Blei: Mittler der Litera-*

turen (Hamburg: Europäische Verlagsanstalt, 1997). The collection of Blei's letters to Schmitt contains a useful commentary on the various figures and events referred to in the correspondence. Franz Blei, *Briefe an Carl Schmitt 1917–1933*, ed. Angela Reinthal, with Wilhelm Kuhlmann (Heidelberg: Manutius Verlag, 1995).

88 Schmitt wrote the piece on Karl Kraus, "Der Fackel-kraus," a reference to Kraus's journal *Die Fackel.*

89 Blei, "Ein deutsches Gespräch," *NSR* 24 (1931): 518–33.

90 Ibid., quoted in Dahlheimer, *Carl Schmitt und der deutsche Katholizismus,* 547.

91 Schmitt "Franz Blei," *Frankfurter Zeitung* (Literaturblatt), 22 March 1931, 1.

92 Schmitt, "Recht und Macht," *Summa* 1 (1917): 37–52, 52.

93 Ibid., 40.

94 Ibid., 40–41.

95 Ludwig Waldacker's review, *KVGR* 17 (1916): 326–45. See also Otto Tesar (1916), and later Heinrich Wohlgemuth (1932), Hans Krupa (1937).

96 See Dahlheimer's excellent discussion in *Carl Schmitt und der deutsche Katholizismus,* 27ff.

97 Rudolf Sohm, *Wesen und Ursprung des Katholizismus* (1912); see Dahlheimer, *Carl Schmitt und der deutsche Katholizismus,* 90.

98 Dahlheimer, *Carl Schmitt und der deutsche Katholizismus;* Schmitt, "Die Sichtbarkeit der Kirche: Eine scholastische Erwägung," *Summa* 2 (1917–18): 71–80.

99 Schmitt calls Christ's submission to earthly power "the only real revolution in human history." Jesus obeyed God, not the emperor, and thus created a new basis for political authority and obligation to the law ("Die Sichtbarkeit der Kirche," 74).

100 Schmitt, "Die Sichtbarkeit der Kirche," 71.

101 Stolleis, *Geschichte des öffentlichen Rechts in Deutschland,* vol. 2, 351.

102 On the earlier generation and its legacy for the jurists of Weimar, see Peter Caldwell, *Popular Sovereignty and the Crisis of German Constitutional Law* (Durham, N.C.: Duke University Press, 1997).

103 Carl Schmitt, *Der Hüter der Verfassung* (Tübingen: J. C. B. Mohr, 1931), 1.

104 Richard Thoma, "On the Ideology of Parliamentarism," in Carl Schmitt, *The Crisis of Parliamentary Democracy*, trans. Ellen Kennedy (Cambridge: MIT, 1985), 82.

105 Carl Schmitt, *Römischer Katholizismus und politische Form* (Hellerau: Jacob Hegner, 1923), 13. *Der Begriff des Politischen* retains this, but revised as the question of whether man is "dangerous" by nature.

106 Schmitt, *Politische Theologie,* 28.

107 Max Weber, "Die drei reinen Typen der legitimen Herrschaft," in *Gesammelte Aufsätze zur Wissenschaftslehre,* ed. J. Winckelmann (Tübingen: J. C. B. Mohr, 1988), 475.

108 Max Weber, "The Profession and Vocation of Politics," in *Political Writings* (Cambridge: Cambridge University Press, 1994), 311.

109 Weber, "Die drei reinen Typen der legitimen Herrschaft," 476; italics mine.

110 Ibid., 477.

111 Joseph Bendersky, *Carl Schmitt: Theorist for the Reich* (Princeton: Princeton University Press, 1983), 35. He may have been present when Weber gave two of his most famous lectures, "Wissenschaft als Beruf" and "Politik als Beruf." Paul Noack, *Carl Schmitt: Eine Biographie* (Berlin: Propyläen, 1993), 21–22. Weber (1864–1920) and Schmitt (1888–1985) were contemporaries, but separated by a

generation. The Schmitt Nachlaß contains no correspondence from Weber. The diaries from this period have not yet been made available.

112 Carl Schmitt, "Soziologie des Souveränitätsbegriffes und politische Theologie," in *Erinnerungsgabe für Max Weber,* ed. Melchior Palyi (Munich: Duncker und Humblot, 1923), vol. 2, 3–36. Schmitt's foreword to the second (1933) edition of *Politische Theologie* notes that this version appeared in March. As the title indicates, *Politische Theologie: Vier Kapitel zur Lehre von der Souveränität* contained a fourth chapter ("The State Philosophy of the Counter-revolution—de Maistre, Bonald Donoso Cortes). The second edition (November 1933) added a new and triumphal foreword reflecting Schmitt's engagement with the Nazi state.

113 Richard Thoma, "Zum Begriff der modernen Demokratie in seinem Verhältnis zum Staatsbegriff"; Carl Brinkmann, "Soziologie und Staatswissenschaft"; Karl Lowenstein, "Zur Soziologie der parlamentarischen Repräsentation in England vor der ersten Reformbill," all in Palyi, *Erinnerungsgabe für Max Weber.*

114 Brinkmann, "Soziologie und Staatswissenschaft," 71, 67. "The science of the state as a unitary field of knowledge as constructed by the Enlightenment and the great European legal systems into the mid–19th century . . . has since fallen into internal conflicts or atrophy [*Schwund*]."

115 Weber, "Die 'Objektivität' sozialwissenschaftlicher und sozialpolitscher Erkenntnis," *Archiv für Sozialwissenschaft und Sozialpolitik* 19 (1905); reprinted in *Gesammelte Aufsätze zur Wissenschaftslehre,* 146–214.

116 Brinkmann, "Soziologie und Staatswissenschaft," 75; quoting Weber's *Körperschaftslehre.*

117 Schmitt, *Politische Theologie,* 13, 25, 26.

118 Ibid., 26, 46.

119 At the conclusion of his preface to the second edition of *Politische Theologie* Schmitt quotes one of the most famous dicta in contemporary German jurisprudence: Georg Meyer, *Lehrbuch des deutschen Staatsrechts* (Leipzig, 1878). Ibid., 8

120 Schmitt, *Die Diktatur,* 24. On Pufendorf, see Schmitt, *Politische Theologie,* 19.

121 Schmitt, *Politische Theologie,* 12.

122 Ibid., 12–13.

123 Ibid., 18.

124 Schmitt refers to Robert von Mohl, *Mongraphien,* 626.

125 Schmitt, *Politische Theologie,* 13.

126 Schmitt, "Die Einwirkung des Kriegszustandes auf das ordentliche strafprozessuale Verfahren," *Zeitschrift für Strafrechtswissenschaft* 38 (1917): 786–87. Schmitt was directly involved with the administration of this law in Bavaria while assigned to the military command in Munich for most of the war and throughout the revolution.

127 Ibid., 794.

128 Schmitt, *Politische Theologie,* 13–14.

129 "In political reality there is no irresistible highest or greatest power that operates according to the certainty of natural law" (Schmitt, *Politische Theologie,* 26). Empirical political science today would call this the problem of many variables, few cases.

130 Schmitt, *Politische Theologie,* 27.

131 Ibid., 29.

132 Ibid., 30–31.
133 Such as: "However one wants to approach it, the doctrine of the sovereignty of law is either a record of what is real or a postulate that ought to be realized" (Schmitt, *Politische Theologie*, 31; quoting Krabbe, *Die moderne Staatsidee* [1919], 39).
134 Schmitt, *Politische Theologie*, 33.
135 Ibid., 35–36.
136 Weber, "Die 'Objektivität' sozialwissenschaftlicher und sozialpolitscher Erkenntnis." The passage continues: "Our aim is understanding of the characteristic uniqueness of the lived reality in which we find ourselves. We wish to understand" (141).
137 Schmitt, *Politische Theologie*, 40.
138 As the subtitle of William Scheuerman's *Carl Schmitt: The End of Law* indicates.
139 Schmitt, *Politische Theologie*, 42.
140 Ibid., 42.
141 Ibid., 29.
142 Carl Schmitt, *Der Leviathan in der Staatslehre des Thomas Hobbes: Sinn und Fehlschlag eines politischen Symbols* (Cologne: Hohenheim, 1982), 25–26. In *Politische Theologie II: Die Legende von der Erledigung jeder politischen Theologie* (Berlin: Duncker und Humblot, 1984), Schmitt expands the analysis of this illustration and its relation to the "complicated vertical and horizontal connections between political reality and religious ideas. . . . The great leviathan, the state of Thomas Hobbes, is a tetramorph: he is the great, but mortal god as well as an animal, and he is also a gigantic man and a machine" (40–41).
143 Schmitt, *Politische Theologie*, 44–45.
144 Hermann Kantorowicz, *The King's Two Bodies: A Study in Medieval Political Theology* (Princeton: Princeton University Press, 1981), 193.
145 Ibid., 223; quoting *Parliamentary History of England* (1806).
146 Schmitt, *Politische Theologie*, 51.
147 Ibid., 54. "This pattern of thinking is characteristic of the natural sciences. It is based on the rejection of all 'arbitrariness,' and attempts to banish from the realm of the human mind every exception."
148 Ibid., 55.
149 Schmitt, *Gesetz und Urteil*, 71.
150 Jellinek, "Besprechung der Schrift 'Gesetz und Urteil' von Carl Schmitt," 296–99.
151 Schmitt, *Politische Theologie*, 59–60.
152 Peter Gay, "The Hunger for Wholeness: Trials of Modernity," in *Weimar Culture: The Insider as Outsider* (London: Secker and Warburg, 1968), 70.
153 Otto Dix, "*Kriegsbehinderten*" (1920), "*Großstadt*" (1927–28); Beckmann, *Tanzbar in Baden-Baden* (1923).
154 Rathenau, *Zur Kritik der Zeit* (Berlin: Fischer, 1919), 15.
155 Schmitt, "Recht und Macht," *Summa* 1 (1917): 44–47.
156 Schmitt, *Der Leviathan in der Staatslehre des Thomas Hobbes*, 42.
157 Hannah Arendt, *The Origins of Totalitarianism* (New York: Harcourt Brace, 1973), chap. 12.

4 The Political and Its Theory

1 Heinrich August Winkler, *Der Schein der Normalität: Arbeiter und Arbeiterbewegung in der Weimarer Republik, 1924 bis 1930* (Berlin: Dietz, 1985), 13ff., 177.

Winkler's history brilliantly follows the development of German politics and institutions through the Weimar period via the role, struggles, and ultimate failure of the workers' movement and the Social Democratic Party.

2 The term "ideological" is not intended to convey any derogatory connotation but is employed as an unsatisfactory substitute for the German *geistesgeschichtlich,* which means, literally, "intellectual-historical."

3 M. R. Lepsius, "From Fragmented Party Democracy to Government by Emergency Decree and National Socialist Takeover," in *The Breakdown of Democratic Regimes,* ed. Juan Linz and Alfred Stephan (Baltimore: Johns Hopkins University Press, 1978); Hans Mommsen, *The Rise and Fall of Weimar Democracy* (Chapel Hill: University of North Carolina Press, 1966), esp. chap. 10, "Government in Crisis," dealing with the political position of the Brüning government after the September 1930 elections.

4 In 1871 Germany and Great Britain each had approximately 21,000 kilometers of railroads. By 1913, the German figure was 63,378, the British 32,623. Michael Stürmer, *Das ruhelose Reich: Deutschland, 1866–1918* (Berlin: Siedler, 1998), 76. Germany had also overtaken British production in the critical industries for military production.

5 Hemut Plessner, *Die verspätete Nation: Über die politische Verfürbarkeit bürgerlichen Geistes* (Stuttgart: Kohlhammer, 1959); Geoff Ely and David Blackbourn, *The Peculiarities of German history: Bourgeois Society and Politics in Nineteenth-Century Germany* (Oxford: Oxford University Press, 1984).

6 Carl Schmitt, *Staatsgefüge und Zusammenbruch des Zweiten Reiches: Der Sieg des Bürgers über den Soldaten* (Hamburg: Hanseatische, 1934); Stürmer, *Das ruhelose Reich,* 95–199; Walter Struve, *Elites against Democracy: Leadership Ideals in Bourgeois Political Thought in Germany, 1890–1933* (Princeton: Princeton University Press, 1973).

7 Stürmer, *Das ruhelose Reich,* 102.

8 Max Weber, "Der Nationalstaat und die Volkswirtschaftspolitik," in *Gesammelte Politische Schriften,* ed. Johannes Winckelmann (1920; Tübingen: J. C. B. Mohr, 1971), 22–27.

9 Stürmer, *Das ruhelose Reich,* 117.

10 Weber, "Der Nationalstaat und die Volkswirtschaftspolitik."

11 Paul Laband, *Das Staatsrecht des Deutschen Reiches,* vol. 1 (Tübingen: Laupp, 1876–82), 150–51, quoted in Peter Caldwell, *Popular Sovereignty and the Crisis of German Constitutional Law* (Durham, N.C.: Duke University Press, 1997), 29–30.

12 Schmitt, *Der Begriff des Politischen* (Berlin: Duncker und Humblot, 1979), 20.

13 Contemporary law defined the state as "the political status of a people."

14 Schmitt, *Der Begriff des Politischen,* 46.

15 Schmitt, *Verfassungslehre* (Berlin: Duncker und Humblot, 1970) and *Der Begriff des Politischen.*

16 Ellen Kennedy, "Carl Schmitt and the Frankfurt School: A Rejoinder," *Telos* 73 (1987): 107.

17 Carl Schmitt, "Der Begriff des Politischen," *Archiv für Sozialwissenschaft* 58 (1927): 4. In the foreword to the American edition of Heinrich Meier, *Carl Schmitt and Leo Strauss: The Hidden Dialogue* (Chicago: University of Chicago Press, 1995), Joseph Cropsey calls Schmitt's argument "provocative to the point of appearing perverse" (ix).

18 Carl Schmitt, *Verfassungsrechtliche Aufsätze aus den Jahren 1924–1954: Materialen zu einer Verfassungslehre* (Berlin: Duncker und Humblot, 1973).

19 David Dyzenhaus, *Legality and Legitimacy: Carl Schmitt, Hans Kelsen, and Hermann Heller in Weimar* (Oxford: Clarendon Press, 1997), 69.

20 The period of the reform bills; democracy in the modern sense was not acknowledged in the British constitution until the reform of the House of Lords in 1911. A. V. Dicey, *Introduction to the Study of the Law of the Constitution* (Indianapolis: Liberty Classics, 1982).

21 Carl Schmitt, *Verfassungslehre,* 5.

22 Ibid., 31, 53–54: "Such a compromise can never be a genuine thing."

23 Ibid., 55.

24 The relation of "legal" and "actual" power was a persistent theme in the jurisprudence of the empire and the Republic, for which Georg Meyer's comment regarding the "normative power of the factual" is symbolic. The practical effect of Meyer's *Lehrbuch des deutschen Staatsrechts* (1878) in Weimar came through Gerhard Anschütz's revision. Meyer had written that "the competence to use state power does not come from its legal acquisition, but its actual possession." In his 1914 edition, Anschütz added: "Legitimacy is not an essential moment of state power." The ambiguity of their relation—the right to use power and the competence to do so—became the leitmotiv of the Republic, and its struggle for constitutional stability can be read in terms of that problem. For a discussion of the imperial sources of this problem, see E. R. Huber, *Deutsche Verfassungsgeschichte seit 1789,* vol. 6, *Die Weimarer Reichsverfassung* (Stuttgart: W. Kohlhammer, 1981), 5–23.

25 And therefore the subject of an "in principle unlimited power that was not constitutionally bounded" (Schmitt, *Verfassungslehre,* 55).

26 *Amtliche Sammlung der Entscheidungen des Reichsgerichts in Zivilsachen* (hereafter cited as RGZ) 100 (8 July 1920): 26; RGZ 104 (4 April 1922): 258; quoted in Schmitt, *Verfassungslehre,* 57.

27 "The German people, united in every branch, and determined to renew and strengthen its empire in freedom and in justice, to serve domestic and international peace and promote social progress, has given itself this constitution." Article 1, Weimarer Reichsverfassung, in *Die deutsche Verfassungungen des 19. und 20. Jahrhunderts,* ed. Horst Hildebrandt (Paderborn: Schöningh, 1979).

28 Otto Kirchheimer, "Wandlungen der politischen Opposition," in *Politik und Verfassung* (Frankfurt: Suhrkamp, 1981), 126.

29 Carl Schmitt, *Verfassungslehre,* 20ff.; Pasquale Pasquino, "Die Lehre vom 'pouvoir constituant,'" in *Complexio Oppositorum: Über Carl Schmitt,* ed. Helmut Quaritsch (Berlin: Duncker und Humblot, 1988), 380.

30 Schmitt, *Verfassungslehre,* 45.

31 Ibid. Schmitt notes further that the Magna Carta was but one of many late medieval agreements between princes or kings and a class.

32 Ibid., 47–48. The old Reich was also a Rechtsstaat in requiring permission from the princes for a declaration of emergency by the kaiser.

33 Ibid., 49.

34 The American example is disregarded in this context, possibly because of its English heritage; by contrast, the American Bill of Rights is the first modern declaration of these for Schmitt.

35 Quentin Skinner, *Liberty before Liberalism* (Cambridge: Cambridge University Press, 1998), 76.

36 Ernst-Wolfgang Böckenförde comments that from then on, constitutional law and theory must assume that "people, from their own will and through a sovereign decision, determine their own fate and order the world with their own hands" (Böckenförde, "Die verfassungsgebende Gewalt des Volkes—ein Grenzbegriff des Vervasungsrechts," 12, quoted in Pasquino, "Die Lehre vom 'pouvoir constituant,' " 373).

37 Carl Schmitt, *Verfassungslehre*, 50.

38 Michael Oakeshott, introduction to *Leviathan, or The Matter, Forme, and Power of a Commonwealth, Ecclesiastical and Civil*, by Thomas Hobbes (Oxford: Blackwell, 1960), xi.

39 G. W. F. Hegel, *Phänomenologie des Geistes*, vol. 4 (Frankfurt: Suhrkamp, 1970).

40 G. W. F. Hegel, *The Phenomenology of Mind*, ed. and trans. James Baillie (London: Allen and Unwin, 1971), 231–33.

41 Schmitt, "Der Begriff des Politischen" (1927), 4. The 1932 edition adds that conflicts of this sort cannot be regulated through a general norm agreed in advance or the decision of a neutral or nonpartisan judge (Schmitt, *Der Begriff des Politischen* [1932], 27).

42 Carl Schmitt, *Die geistesgeschichtliche Lage des heutigen Parlamentarismus* (Berlin: Duncker und Humblot, 1979), 71.

43 Carl Schmitt, *Politische Theologie: Vier Kapital zur Lehre von der Souveränität* (Berlin: Duncker und Humblot, 1985), 78.

44 Carl Schmitt, *Die geistesgeschichtliche Lage des heutigen Parlamentarismus*, 58.

45 Ibid., 87.

46 The artist Balthus, quoted in the *New York Times*, 20 February 2002, on morality and art.

47 Schmitt, "Der Begriff des Politischen" (1927), 5.

48 "All political concepts, images, and terms have a polemical meaning. They are focused on a specific conflict and are bound to a concrete situation; the result (which manifests itself in war or revolution) is a friend-enemy grouping" (Schmitt, *Der Begriff des Politischen* [1932], 30).

49 For the same reason that natural man cannot lay down the right of self-preservation. It is "the absence or epistemological impossibility of defining an objective criterion of what constitutes a threat to the individual's self preservation which transforms the natural right into the origin of the potential war of all against all." Pasquale Pasquino, "Hobbes, Natural Right, Absolutism, and Political Obligation," quoted in John McCormick, "Fear, Technology, and the State: Carl Schmitt, Leo Strauss, and the Revival of Hobbes in Weimar and National Socialist Germany," *Political Theory* 22, no. 4 (1994): 623.

50 Schmitt, *Der Begriff des Politischen* (1932), 29–31.

51 Schmitt, "Der Begriff des Politischen" (1927), 7; *Der Begriff des Politischen* (1932), 29.

52 G. W. F. Hegel, *Elements of the Philosophy of Right* (Cambridge: Cambridge University Press, 1991), 361.

53 Schmitt, "Der Begriff des Politischen" (1927), 5; *Der Begriff des Politischen* (1932), 29.

54 Schmitt, "Der Begriff des Politischen" (1927), 7.

55 Carl Schmitt, "Das Rheinlande als Objekt internationaler Politik" (14 April 1925), in *Positionen und Begriffe im Kampf mit Weimar–Genf–Versailles, 1923–1939* (Hamburg: Hanseatische Verlagsanstalt, 1940), 26–33.

56 "One hears so much about the 'self-determination' of peoples that one might believe that today no nation could any longer be the object of international politics because self-determination must mean that a people subject determines its own political and state existence—that is the opposite of being an object" (ibid., 27).

57 Carl Schmitt, "Um das Schicksal des Politischen," *Die Schildgenossen* 5 (1924–25): 313–22.

58 Schmitt, *Der Begriff des Politischen* (1932), 13.

59 Rheinische Friedrich Wilhelms-Universität Bonn, Philosophische Fakultät, Geschichtlich-Staatswissenschaftliche Abteilung, *Vorlesungen die hauptsächlich für Studierenden der Staatswissenschaften in Betracht kommen, 1925–26*, 49.

60 Carl Schmitt, "Der Begriff des Politischen" (1927), 6, 15. In *Theorie des Partisanen* Schmitt sees the capacity to command killing and being killed as having passed, significantly, to organizations that are not unlike the modern state bound to a territory. These *tellurische* organizations are characterized by their irregularity, mobility, partisanship intense to the point of fanaticism, and a characteristic use of terror that ignores the civilian/combatant distinction of the jus publicum Europaeum. Carl Schmitt, *Theorie des Partisanen: Zwischenbemerkung zum Begriff des Politischen* (Berlin: Duncker und Humblot, 1975).

61 Carl Schmitt, *Die Kernfrage des Völkerbundes* (Berlin: Dümmlers Verlagsbuchhandlung, 1926).

62 In fact, Western policy—in particular, U.S. policy in 1919—helped preserve German unity, but the condition of Wilson's offer of aid to the civilian populations (which had been besieged for most of the Great War and were, especially in the large cities, half starved) was that a communist government not come to power. Hagen Schulze, *Weimar: Deutschland, 1917–1933* (Berlin: Siedler, 1998), 21.

63 Schmitt, *Der Begriff des Politischen*, 70. *Politische Theologie* (1922) develops a method Schmitt calls "radical conceptualization" to uncover "the ultimate, radical structure" of an intellectual world. Such an approach assumes that a conceptual construction can be compared to the social structure of a given period, so that its analysis explains why certain ideas appear as "self-evident" in a given historical period. "Metaphysics is the most intense and clearest expression of an epoch" (Schmitt, *Politische Theologie*, 58–60).

64 It is remarkable that there is no mention of fascism in editions of *Der Begriff des Politischen* prior to 1933, despite the attention Schmitt gave it in *Die geistesgeschichtliche Lage des heutigen Parlamentarismus* (1923) as an ideology of equal rank to communism. Mussolini had been in power for nearly five years when Schmitt spoke, and his admiration for Il Duce extended in the book on parliamentarism to comparing him with Machiavelli: "As in the sixteenth century, again it is an Italian who articulates the principle of political reality" (89). The reference is to Mussolini's October 1922 speech in Naples.

65 Hugo Preuß, "Volksstaat oder Verkehrter Obrigkeitsstaat?" *Berliner Tageblatt*, 11 November 1918, reprinted in *Staat, Recht, und Freiheit: Aus 40 Jahren Deutsche Politik*, by Hugo Preuß (Tübingen: Mohr, 1926). Preuß's article appeared two days after Scheidemann had proclaimed the Republic from the balcony of the Reichstag

in Berlin. Max Weber saw the Russian Revolution as an attempt to superimpose conditions of modern political rationality on a primitive agrarian society. The "unique" constellation of factors that led in the West to capitalism and liberalism was absent in Russia, and the consequence of imposing their political institutions on that country could not, he argued, support freedom. David Beetham, *Max Weber and the Theory of Modern Politics* (Oxford: Blackwell, 1985), 46.

66 Schmitt, "Die Rheinlande als Objekt internationaler Politik," 22. Liberalism, a nineteenth-century doctrine, showed the same face internationally and domestically. In both spheres, liberal argument ignored the material in favor of the formal. Just as liberal equality is a legal form, not an actual equality, so too liberal international law disregards the unequal power positions of nations. The liberal definition of "economics" as an unpolitical sphere follows from this and allows liberal imperialism after World War I to present itself as essentially different from older military forms of domination because *as* economics "it serves peaceful expansion." Thus the imperialism of the United States is regarded as the most modern precisely because it is primarily economic, not military. Historically significant imperialism depends, he wrote, "not only on military and marine armaments, not just on economic and financial wealth, but on the ability to determine the content of political and legal concepts." Schmitt, "Volkerrechtliche Formen des modernen Imperialismus," reprinted in *Positionen und Begriffe im Kampf mit Weimar-Genf-Versailles, 1923–1939* (Hamburg: Hanseatisches Verlagsanstalt, 1940), 179.

67 Schmitt, "Die Rheinlande als Objekt internationaler Politik," 29–30. Herbert Marcuse later developed a similar critique of liberalism in which concepts such as "toleration" became their opposition. See Herbert Marcuse, Robert Paul Wolff, and Barrington Moore Jr., "Repressive Tolerance," in *A Critique of Pure Tolerance* (Boston: Beacon Press, 1965).

68 Schmitt quotes an American delegate to the Peace Conference as saying that it is not part of the concept of self-determination that a people controls the mineral wealth of its own territory. Carl Schmitt, "Die Rheinlande als Objekt internationaler Politik," 31.

69 "The League of Nations today exists principally as an organization of governments" (Schlücking and Wehberg, *Das Kommentar zur Satzung des Völkerbundes* [1924], 138); "The League of Nations is, in its essence, an association of peoples and not just of governments" (Wehberg, *Revue de droit internationale et de législation compareé* [1924], 560); both quoted in Schmitt, *Die Kernfrage des Volkerbundes*, 4.

70 Carl Schmitt, "Reichstagsauflösungen: Nochmalige Reichstagsauflösung—ein staatsrechtlicher Hinweis" (1924), reprinted in *Verfassungsrechtliche Aufsätze* (Berlin: Duncker und Humblot, 1973); Schmitt, *Unabhängigkeit der Richter, Gleichheit vor dem Gesetz und Gewährleistung des Privateigentums nach der Weimarer Verfassung—ein Rechtsgutachten zu den Gesetzentwürfen über die Vermögensauseinandersetzung mit den früher regierenden Fürstenhäusern* (Berlin: Walter de Gruyter, 1926); Schmitt, *Volksentscheid und Volksbegehren: Ein Beitrag zur Auslegung der Weimarer Verfassung und zur Lehre der Unmittelbaren Demokratie* (Berlin: Walter de Gruyter, 1927).

71 Winston S. Churchill, *The Unknown War: The Eastern Front* (New York: Schreibner, 1931).

72 I am indebted to Mr. David Leslie for details about the fighting around Moncelul.

73 The promises of reform made by the provisional government did not threaten the

power of finance, which blocked demands from the peasants and zemstvos: "the banks will only give credit to those who (1) continue the war for the time being and (2) whatever happens, keep the peasants in subjection, as their ideals are incompatible with the interests of the Russian state creditors." Max Weber, "Russia's Transition to Pseudo-Democracy," in *The Russian Revolutions,* trans. Gordon C. Wells and Peter Baehr (Ithaca, N.Y.: Cornell University Press, 1995), 250–51.

74 The Great War defined their identity "not as a zone of dates . . . it is more like a magnetic field at the center of which lies an experience or a series of experiences. It is a system of references that gives priority to some experiences and devalues others." Robert Wohl, *The Generation of 1914* (London: Weidenfeld and Nicholson, 1980), 210. On this war as the source of subsequent conflicts and political instability in Europe, including the rise of Hitler and World War II, see Niall Ferguson, *The Pity of War: Explaining World War I* (New York: Basic, 1999); and John Keegan, *The First World War* (New York: Knopf, 1999). Keegan's analysis of war monuments, public mourning, and the culture of grief in the Allied versus Germanic nations is especially telling and forms a first chapter of the story that Alexander Mitscherlich would tell in the 1950s as "the inability to mourn" (Mitscherlich, *Die Unfähigkeit zu Trauern* [1958]). The Germans cannot decently mourn their dead of the two wars, Keegan notes. The atrocities of World War II compromise the ability to mourn; the physical fact that most German war dead lay on foreign soil, and the rancor of the Allies, made even the construction of cemeteries difficult: "The French and Belgians found little room in their hearts or in the national soil for the creation of German war cemeteries. While the British were accorded a *sepulture perpétuelle* for their places of burial . . . the Germans were obliged to excavate mass graves in obscure locations to contain the remains of their casualties." Only in east Prussia, at the Tannenberg site, was there a monumental edifice, and it was destroyed during World War II. Only a single lion of the originally huge mausoleum remains, now located on the main square in Olstzyek (Allenstein) in Poland, several miles away from the original site, which is totally overgrown with weeds.

75 Its argument originated in works that appeared during the war and its immediate aftermath and in articles from the mid-1920s addressing Germany's international position under the Treaty of Versailles. These mark not only Schmitt's break with the legal formalism and normative assumptions of his writing before 1914 but the beginning of Schmitt's critique of liberal political ideas and institutions. The primary texts of this period are *Politische Romantik* (1919), *Die Diktatur* (1921) and *Politische Theologie* (1922), *Römischer Katholizismus und politische Form* (1923), and *Die geistesgeschichtliche Lage des heutigen Parlamentarismus* (1923). Among the articles on international relations are "Der Status Quo und der Friede," *Hochland,* December 1925; "Die Kernfrage des Völkerbundes," *Schmollers Jahrbuch* 48, no. 4 (1925); "Um das Schicksal des Politischen," *Die Schildgenossen* 5 (1924–25); and "Illyrien: Notizen von einer dalmatinischen Reise," *Hochland* 23, no. 1 (1925–26).

76 Preuß, "Volksstaat oder Verkehrter Obrigkeitsstaat?"

77 Schmitt, *Hugo Preuß: Sein Staatsbegriff und seine Stellung in der Deutschen Staatslehre* (Tübingen: Mohr, 1930), 17. He refers to Preuß, "Volksstaat oder Verkehrter Obrigkeitsstaat?"

78 Stone, M. E. *The Russian Revolution* (1917), 283.

79 Richard Abraham, *Alexander Kerensky: The First Love of the Russian Revolution* (New York: Columbia University Press, 1987), 209.

80 Schmitt, *Der Begriff des Politischen* (1932), 63.

81 Ibid.

82 Ibid. Schmitt is quoting from Georg Lukacs, *Geschichte und Klassenbewußtsein* (1923), and *Lenin* (1924). These comments do not appear in the 1927 version.

83 Ferguson, *The Pity of War,* 318–19.

84 "Such sloppy thinking," Ferguson remarks, "was common in London in 1914" (*The Pity of War,* 319).

85 Ibid., 336. There were a total of 9,450,000 deaths in the Great War, for which $208.5 billion was paid.

86 Those motivations weakened over the course of the war, as the cynicism of the following poem indicates:

I do not wish to hurt you
But (Bang!) I feel I must.
It is a Christian virtue
To lay you in the dust.
You—(Zip! That bullet got you)
You're really better dead.
I'm sorry that I shot you—
Here, let me hold your head. (Ferguson, *The Pity of War,* 356–57)

Such sentiments are captured cinematically in the shell hole scene of *All Quiet on the Western Front.* In *The Great War and Modern Memory* (Oxford: Oxford University Press, 1975), Paul Fussell argues that the experience of war on the Western front forever changed the literary imagination and emptied the tropes of romantic sacrifice.

87 Ferguson, *The Pity of War,* 358.

88 Ibid., 359. This makes explicit Freud's connection between Eros and Thanatos.

89 Ernst Jünger, *The Storm of Steel: From the Diary of a German Storm-Troop Officer on the Western Front,* trans. Basil Creighton (London, 1929), 22; quoted in Ferguson, *The Pity of War,* 359.

90 An image captured in Hermann Broch, *Die Schlafwandler, eine Romantrilogie* (Zurich: Rhein-Verlag, 1931).

91 Ernst Jünger, "Die totale Mobilmachung," in *Werke,* vol. 5 (Stuttgart: Klett, 1960–65), 131–32; italics mine.

92 Carl Schmitt, "Totaler Feind, totaler Krieg, totaler Staat," in *Positionen und Begriffe,* 335–39.

93 Schmitt's reference to the position of German cities on page 236 of "Totaler Feind, totaler Krieg, totaler Staat" compares their situation to the Prussians in the Seven Years' War—a clear indication that the age of "cabinet wars" had ended, in his view.

94 Ibid.

95 Ibid. Schmitt expanded this argument during the war in *Land und Meer: Eine weltgeschichtliche Betrachtung* (1944).

96 Schmitt, "Totaler Feind, totaler Krieg, totaler Staat," 237.

97 These are references to the incorporation of parliamentary and presidential institutions from those nations in the Weimar constitution by Preuß and others.

98 Carl Schmitt, *Der Nomos der Erde* (Berlin: Duncker und Humblot, 1974), 123.

99 Schmitt, *Die geistesgeschichtliche Lage des heutigen Parlamentarismus,* 77.

100 Carl Schmitt, conversation with author, 12 May 1982. See also Schmitt, *The Crisis of Parliamentary Democracy,* trans. Ellen Kennedy (Cambridge: MIT Press, 1985), 106 n. 16.

101 Noakes and Pridham, *Documents on Nazism, 1919–1945,* 664–66. The speech had little effect on civilian morale, as Security Service reports clearly indicate. The population continued, however, to insulate the führer from their overall dislike and criticism of the party (666–69). See also Ian Kershaw, *Der Hitler-Mythos: Volksmeinung und propaganda im Dritten Reich* (Stuttgart: Deutsche Verlags-Anstalt, 1980).

102 The editiorial note to Schmitt, "Um das Schicksal des Politischen," *Die Schildgenossen* 5 (1924–25): 313–22.

103 Schmitt, *Politische Theologie,* 12.

104 Ibid., 20; Schmitt, "Die Kernfrage des Völkerbundes," 22.

105 Schmitt, "Die Kernfrage des Völkerbundes," 15.

5 Constitutional Theory

1 Article 1, *Weimarer Reichsverfassung* (Weimar constitution) (1919).

2 Quoted in Hagen Schulze, *Weimar: Deutschland, 1917–1933* (Berlin: Siedler, 1998), 43. The "manageable" economy had already left the agricultural sector behind, as a spontaneous protest of 100,000 farmers in Schleswig-Holstein on January 28, 1928, demonstrated. "In speeches all across the province, peasants demanded higher tariffs, lower taxes, cheaper credit, and reduced welfare expenditures," Tom Childers writes, and as the protests spread, political resentments—"vitriolic denunciations of Versailles, reparations, the parliamentary system, 'Jewish international finance' and 'the Marxist welfare state' "—accompanied these economic demands. By taking advantage of rural fragmentation and resentment, the NSDAP laid the groundwork for its electoral success in 1930 (Childers, *The Nazi Voter,* 147, 149).

3 Childers, *The Nazi Voter,* 124–25.

4 Ibid., 126–27.

5 Taking 1928 as the base (100 percent) the figures were: 1929 (100); 1930 (87); 1931 (70); 1933 (66). See D. Petzina, W. Abelshauser, A. Faust, *Sozialgeschictliches Arbeitsbuch: Materialien zur Statistik des Deutschen Reiches, 1914–1945* (Munich: Deutscher Taschenbuch Verlag, 1978), 61; Wolfgang Michalka and Gottfried Niedhard, *Die ungeliebte Republik: Dokumente zur Innen- und Aussenpolitik Weimars, 1918–1933* (Munich: Deutscher Taschenbuch Verlag 1980), 403.

6 So too did the cost of living. If 1928 equals 100 percent, the figures for wages and cost of living were as follows: 1929 (101); 1930 (97); 1931 (93); 1932 (87); 1933 (91).

7 Childers, *The Nazi Voter,* 191.

8 Report of September 1930, *Documents on British Foreign Policy, 1919–1939,* 2d series, i. 512, no. 2; cited in F. L. Carsten, *The Reichswehr and Politics, 1918–1933* (Oxford: Clarendon Press, 1966), 310–11.

9 Peter Merkel, *Political Violence under the Swastika: 581 Early Nazis* (Princeton: Princeton University Press, 1975), 236. Merkel's study is based on Theodore Abel's *Why Hitler Came to Power* (1938) and uses contemporary interviews now housed at the Hoover Institute in Stanford. Merkel's analysis draws a correlation between a certain type of privatized freedom and political disaffection that led ultimately to radical opposition.

10 Schulze, *Weimar: Deutschland, 1917–1933*, 323; Heinrich August Winkler, *Weimar 1918–1933* (Munich: Beck, 1993), 334ff.

11 Herbert Michaelis and Ernst Schraepler, eds., *Ursachen und Folgen: Vom deutschen Zusammenbruch 1918 und 1945 bis zur staatlichen Neuordnung Deutschlands in der Gegenwart*, vol. 7, doc. 1580 (Berlin: H. Wendler, 1958), i.

12 The first version of *Der Begriff des Politischen* was presented in a lecture on May 10, 1927, as part of a series titled "Probleme der modernen Demokratie." The proofs of the *Verfassungslehre* were corrected in December 1927. Despite their coevality and central place in Carl Schmitt's corpus, the texts have seldom been read as addressing a single question. When they have, Schmitt's constitutional theory has been overshadowed either by the history of emergency powers in late Weimar and the descent into sovereign dictatorship under Hitler or more generally by Schmitt's reputation as a theorist of exceptional powers and politics as enmity. Ernst-Wolfgang Böckenförde is a notable exception; see "The Concept of the Political: A Key to Understanding Carl Schmitt's Constitutional Theory," in *Law as Politics: Carl Schmitt's Critique of Liberalism*, ed. David Dyzenhaus (Durham, N.C.: Duke University Press, 1998), 37–55.

13 This expression signifies the construction of sovereignty in the commonwealth for Hobbes as the recognition of a common identity that constitutes political association not as an abstraction but as an existence (Thomas Hobbes, *Leviathan*, chap. 17).

14 "In contrast to commentaries and glossaries, and unlike reduction into isolated studies, a systematic framework is intended here. Neither are all the questions of state law answered nor those of general state theory," but a "constitutional theory." Carl Schmitt, foreword to *Verfassungslehre* (Berlin: Duncker und Humblot, 1970), x–xi.

15 Ibid., 338.

16 Ibid., 126. Schmitt quotes from the opening statement of Kant's "Perpetual Peace" and "On the Relation of Theory to Practice in State Law."

17 Among them legality, administrative adjudication, prescribed state competencies, the independence of judges, and conformity to law (Schmitt, *Verfassungslehre*, 129ff.).

18 Ibid., 130–31.

19 See Schmitt's sketch of this argument in *Verfassungslehre*, 139–40. Only absolutism departs from this modern theory, he notes, with reference to Hobbes's "command theory" of law.

20 The classical sources are Locke and Montesquieu, but Schmitt notes Otto Meyer's link between such organizational features and the "absolute norm" *(unverbrüchliche Norm)*. This is "the real core of all rule-of-law thinking," Schmitt comments (*Verfassungslehre*, 140).

21 Kant, *Perpetual Peace*; Hegel, *Philosophy of Law*. Quoted in Schmitt, *Verfassungslehre*, 141.

22 Schmitt, *Verfassungslehre*, 138–39.

23 The text contains a "historical overview of the development of the parliamentary system" beginning with the later Middle Ages in England and with particular attention to developments in France and Belgium after Napoleon. Half of this section deals with German parliamentary theories and experiences after 1848 and provides an excellent survey of influences on the authors of the Weimar constitution and the National Assembly (Schmitt, *Verfassungslehre*, 320–38).

24 Schmitt, *Der Begriff des Politischen,* 28–29. On the various concepts of the political in Schmitt's work, see Vilmos Holchauser, *Konsensus und Konflikt: Die Begriffe des Politischen bei Carl Schmitt* (Berlin: Duncker und Humblot, 1990).

25 Schmitt, *Verfassungslehre,* 224.

26 Ibid., 225.

27 The United States and England are examples of "strong states" for Schmitt. See "Staatsethik und pluralistischer Staat," *Kantstudien* 35, no. 1 (1930): 28.

28 Schmitt, *Verfassungslehre,* 223.

29 Ibid., 224. The reference is to James Bryce, *Modern Democracies* (New York: Macmillan, 1921), and Richard Thoma, "Der Begriff der modernen Demokratie in seinem Verhältnis zum Staatsbegriff," in *Erinnerungsgabe für Max Weber,* vol. 2, ed. Melchior Palyi (Munich: Duncker und Humblot, 1923). The practical ambiguity of "the majority" in modern democracy is obvious in this discussion, and various "majorities" are possible: the majority of those voting in a given election; the majority of all active citizens without regard for their electoral participation; the majority of all those belonging to the state (i.e., of state nationals); the majority of the population of a country.

30 Schmitt, *Verfassungslehre,* 226.

31 Schmitt's list of politicians and authors who have so enlarged democracy includes L. T. Hobhouse, Jaurés, Kautsky, Bernstein, MacDonald, Herriot, Paul Boncour, Thomas, Branting, Vandervelde, and Masaryk (*Verfassungslehre,* 225–226).

32 Ibid., 227.

33 By extension, nonmembers of a state might receive equal treatment in the other spheres (moral, economic, aesthetic), but always with the reservation that the political distinction is decisive.

34 "All Germans are equal before the law" (Weimar constitution, Art. 109). Similar specifications are found in contemporary Swiss and Japanese constitutions. Even the French Declaration of Rights of Man and of the Citizen (1789) presumed, Schmitt asserts, "the French nation" despite its assumption of "natural human equality" (*Verfassungslehre,* 227). The constitution of the Federal Republic adopts the universal phrase "All men are equal before the law" (Art. 3, sec. 1).

35 Schmitt, *Verfassungslehre,* 228.

36 Schmitt, *Der Begriff des Politischen* (1932), 26–27.

37 Schmitt, *Verfassungslehre,* 234.

38 Schmitt's lecture was delivered on May 10, 1927, at the Deutsche Hochschule für Politik in Berlin, one of five public lectures in the series "Probleme der modernen Demokratie." The other topics reflect widely differing notions of what politics and the problems of democracy are. Ernst Michel presented politics as service to the community and the struggle for community based on a notion of the general good. Fritz Berber lectured on English democracy as a "rhythm of life" from which the spirit of liberalism developed, but cautioned that the English way of life could not simply be applied to German circumstances. Max Hildebert Boehm presented a typology of democracies emphasizing the difference between the romantic "centralized-state absolutist" form of the French and the "Germanic-corporatist" version of democracy. See Arnold Wolfers, foreword to *Probleme der Demokratie: Schriftenreihe der Deutschen Hochschule für Politik in Berlin und des Instituts für Auswärtige Politik in Hamburg,* vol. 5 (Berlin: Rothschild, 1928). Schmitt's conception of democracy in terms of homogeneity was explicitly rejected by Hermann Heller in

this lecture series. See Heller, "Politische Demokratie und soziale Homogenität," in *Hermann Heller: Gesammelte Schriften,* ed. Martin Drath et al. (Leiden: A. W. Sijthoff, 1971), 421–33.

39 "Parliamentarism . . . , government by discussion, belongs to the intellectual world of liberalism. It does not belong to democracy" (Schmitt, *Die geistesgeschichtlich Lage des heutigen Parlamentarismus,* 13).

40 Ibid., 26. This is also the basis of Locke's theory of consent, Schmitt notes (23–24).

41 Schmitt, "Der Begriff des Politischen" (1927), 5.

42 Heller, "Politische Demokratie und soziale Homogenität," in *Gesammelte Schriften,* vol. 2, 425.

43 This part of the text is prefaced by a discussion of earlier political theories of democracy found in the work of Plato and Aristotle, Thomas Aquinas, Montesquieu, and Rousseau (Schmitt, *Verfassungslehre,* 228–30).

44 Ibid., 231.

45 Ibid.

46 Schmitt notes the following: (1) immigration laws, especially those in effect in the United States and Great Britain; (2) annexations, including the establishment of colonies, protectorates, mandates, and intervention; (3) tariffs, laws limiting foreign populations, capital export and import limits; (4) newer versions of citizenship laws, including expatriation regulations, denaturalization; and (5) in the newly created Czechoslovakia, exclusion of non-Czech and non-Slovak populations [largely German] from constitutional deliberations (ibid.). In this text, as in *Parlamentarismus,* Schmitt remarks on the practice of British citizenship law excluding immigration from the colonies as a means to prevent those populations from acquiring metropolitan citizenship (Schmitt, *Verfassungslehre,* 232; *Parlamentarismus,* 14–15).

47 Equality is an existential concept for Schmitt. "Every equality relates to a species, to which the compared are subordinate. . . . Equality is the relation of things, which are subordinate to one and the same species." Where there is nothing superordinate, "equality" ceases to have any meaning. Edmund Husserl, *Logische Untersuchungen,* vol. 2, 112; quoted in Schmitt, *Verfassungslehre,* 235–36. Only he governs who has the trust of the people. He has no authority from a special existence. When the best and most gifted are chosen by the people, so much the better; the kind of choice and selection of the most virtuous, however, should never lead in a democracy to the creation of a special class that endangers the qualitative and substantial equality of all, that is, the total assumption of every democracy.

48 Schmitt, *Verfassungslehre,* 235.

49 Ibid., 24–25; "the constitution of a state, that is, the political unity of a people" (3).

50 Ibid., 251.

51 Article 73, sections 2–3.

52 Schmitt, *Verfassungslehre,* 241.

53 In the Weimar constitution, assembly appears in part 2, "The Rights and Duties of Germans," as a guaranteed "civil right" defined through organization law *(Vereinsrecht)*—the particular and fractional, not the unitary (Art. 124) (Schmitt, *Verfassungslehre,* 244). Schmitt comments that liberal rule-of-law constitutions always ignore the sovereign, whether a monarch or the people.

54 Ibid., 245.

55 The secret ballot was specified in Articles 125, 22, and 17 and in statutes requiring that the individual not be "observed" casting a vote. See also Schmitt's description of

voting machines and other devices (design of ballots, etc.) in *Verfassungslehre,* 245–46.

56 Schmitt, *Verfassungslehre,* 246.

57 Ibid.

58 Ibid., 247.

59 Ibid.

60 In contrast to the United States, where, Schmitt notes, such rights were private civil rights (*Verfassungslehre,* 248–49).

61 Among the sources cited by Schmitt are F. Tönnies, *Kritik der öffentlichen Meinung* (1922); James Bryce, *American Commonwealth* (1901); A. V. Dicey, *Law and Public Opinion in England* (1905); and Lawrence Lowell, *Public Opinion and Popular Government* (1913) (*Verfassungslehre,* 249).

62 Ernst Jünger's *Der Arbeiter* (1932; Stuttgart: Klett-Cotta, 1982) was an attempt (with silent reference to Schmitt's concept of the political and the people) to recover this figure as a "Gestalt" against the treason of the Bürger (40).

63 Schmitt, *Verfassungslehre,* 250.

64 Parliamentarism is the opposite of dictatorship because discussion is "human, peaceful and progressive" (Schmitt, *Verfassungslehre,* 315–16; see also *Parlamentarismus,* 43, 57, 61, 62). Schmitt quotes Marx's *Eighteenth Brumaire of Louis Bonaparte,* "parliamentary regimes live from discussion" (*Verfassungslehre,* 316).

65 Schmitt notes the resulting absurdities of legal definitions: "bread is what the holder of a bread card is entitled to receive on the basis of his bread card" (*Verfassungslehre,* 143).

66 Ibid., 144.

67 Carl Schmitt, "Die Lage der europäischen Rechtswissenchaft," in *Verfassungsrechtliche Aufsätze aus den Jahren 1924–1954: Materiailen zu einer Verfassungslehre* (Berlin: Duncker und Humblot, 1970), 404ff.

68 Schmitt took up the Hugo Preuß Chair at the Handelshochschule in spring 1928.

69 Lutz-Arwed Bentin, *Johannes Popitz und Carl Schmitt: Zur wissenschaftlichen Theorie des totalen Staates in Deutschland* (Munich: C. H. Beck, 1972), 144.

70 Wilhelm Röpke, "Staatsinterventionismus," *Handwörterbuch der Staatswissenschaften,* ed. L. Eisler, A. Weber, and F. Wieser (Jena: F. Fischer, 1923–29), 861–82.

71 Hans Ritschl, *Gemeinwirtschaft und kapitalistische Marktwirschaft* (Tübingen: J. C. B. Mohr, 1931). The text echoes Tönnies's *Gemeinschaft und Gesellschaft* (1887), and for many the statement "The same money runs in society, the same blood in community," appeared obvious.

72 Bentin, *Johannes Popitz und Carl Schmitt,* 146–47.

73 John Maynard Keynes, *The End of Laissez-Faire* (London, 1923).

74 Those questions could be subjected to a referendum only by the president. Carl Schmitt, *Volksentscheid und Volksbegehren: Ein Beitrag zur Auslegung der Weimarer Verfassung und zur Lehre von der unmittlebaren Demokratie* (Berlin: Walter de Gruyter, 1927).

75 Schmitt, *Verfassungslehre,* 238–52.

76 Schmitt, *Volksentscheid und Volksbegehren,* 22.

77 Robert Dahl, *Dilemmas of Liberal Democracies* (New Haven: Yale University Press, 1982). See also Paul Hirst, *Law, Socialism, and Democracy* (London: Allen and Unwin, 1986).

78 The current fashion for privatizing state functions and elevating "civil society"

obscures the reality of the modern state. Proponents of civil society theory want to identify it with democracy as such, but the focus on private individuals pursuing private pleasure—"bowling alone"—makes the political theory of democracy impossible. See, for example, John Keane, *Democracy and Civil Society* (London: Verso, 1988).

79 David Dyzenhaus, "Putting the State Back in Credit," in *The Challenge of Carl Schmitt,* ed. Chantal Mouffe (London: Verso, 1999), 75–91.

80 Schmitt, "Staatsethik und pluralistischer Staat," 28–43.

81 Ibid., 36. Schmitt remarks critically that here as in other social theories, "the political" is conceived as something with a "content" alongside other "social associations" such as churches, the economy, culture, et cetera.

82 Ibid., 39. Dyzenhaus notes the similarity of this view to that advanced by Isaiah Berlin at the end of his essay "Two Concepts of Liberty" (in Berlin, *Four Essays on Liberty* [Oxford: Oxford University Press, 1969]).

83 Schmitt quotes Weber, *Politik als Beruf,* 2d ed. (1926); see Max Weber, "The Profession and Vocation of Politics," in *Weber: Political Writings* (Cambridge: Cambridge University Press, 1994), 311.

84 Schmitt, "Irrationalist Theories of the Direct Use of Force," in *Parlamentarismus.*

85 Schmitt, "Der Begriff des Politischen" (1927), 3. The term *Große* in Schmitt's original is ambiguous and can mean "power," "authority," or the more neutral "entity."

86 Schmitt, *Verfassungslehre,* 314–15; previous quote, 318.

87 Jürgen Habermas, "Verfassungspatriotismus," in *Normalität einer Berliner Republik* (Frankfurt: Suhrkamp, 1995).

88 Carl Schmitt, *Der Hüter der Verfassung* (Tübingen: J. C. B. Mohr, 1931), 71.

89 Schmitt, foreword to *Der Hüter der Verfassung.*

90 Schmitt, "Staatsethik und pluralistischer Staat," 31.

91 Schmitt, *Der Hüter der Verfassung,* 83.

92 Ibid., 83–84.

93 Ibid., 84. See also Carl Schmitt, *Hugo Preuß: Sein Staatsbegriff und seine Stellung in der Deutschen Staatslehre* (Tübingen: J. C. B. Mohr, 1930); and "Weiterentwicklung des totalen Staats in Deutschland" (1933), in *Verfassungsrechtliche Aufsätze,* 365. The article was written in late 1932, during Schleicher's chancellorship and published before January 30, 1933.

94 Schmitt, *Der Hüter der Verfassung,* 84ff.

95 In the *Verfassungslehre,* Schmitt distinguishes between "real" and "dilatory" compromises (31ff).

96 Proponents of a unitary central state at the National Assembly were to be found mostly on the Left, where it was believed that social revolutionary change could be achieved most efficiently through the state. Liberal democrats favored a decentralized state. Had the first constitutional form been decided, it would have been necessary to dissolve Prussia (and possibly the other states as well), or at the very least, it would have required placing Prussia under the authority of the central government. That such changes in the structure of the Reich were not made in 1919 followed from several factors including continued attachment to the Länder as sites of personal and collective identity, separatist tendencies above all in the Rhineland and Bavaria ("away from Berlin" movements), and internal changes within and conflicts among the political parties represented in the Assembly. The conflict of federal and unitary state forms was not new; the relationship between Bodinian sovereignty (the

unitary state) and federalism bedeviled the German empire, as it had the young United States, and was resolved in the nineteenth century only through a formula: not *Bundesstaat* but *Staatenbund.* The organizational question was old, dating back to the seventeenth-century circumstances of the Holy Roman Empire of the German nation, and it reached a new high in the period immediately before 1848. The classical statement, Georg Waitz, "Das Wesen des Bundesstaates," in *Allgemeine (Kieler) Monatsschrift für Wissenschaft und Literatur* (1853), 494–530, was written under the influence of Tocqueville's *Democracy in America* and the arguments of John Calhoun. See Stolleis, *Geschichte des öffentlichen Rechts in Deutschland,* 365ff.; and Rupert Emerson, *State and Sovereignty in Modern Germany* (New Haven: Yale University Press, 1928), 92–129.

97 E. R. Huber, *Deutsche Verfassungsgeschichte seit 1789: Die Weimarer Reichsverfassung,* vol. 6 (Stuttgart: Kohlhammer, 1981), 65.

98 Ibid., 92.

99 Fritz Hartung, *Deutsche Verfassungsgeschichte vom 15. Jahrhundert bis zur Gegenwart* (Stuttgart: K. F. Köhler, 1950), 330–31.

100 See, for example, Johannes Popitz, *Die künftige Finanzausgleich zwischen Reich, Ländern und Gemeinden* (Berlin, 1930), and "Die Probleme der Finanzpolitik des Reichs," in *Strukturwandelungen der Volkswirtschaft,* ed. Bernard Harms (1928), 373–97.

101 Popitz, *Die künfige Finanzausgleich,* 6; cited in Bentin, *Johannes Popitz und Carl Schmitt,* 14. Only a few pages of *Der Hüter der Verfassung* deal with "polyarchy," and they are drawn from Popitz's work. See Schmitt, *Der Hüter der Verfassung,* 91–94.

102 Johannes Popitz, "Schlußwort zur Aufsatzreihe 'Gesetzgeberische Zukunftsaufgaben,'" *Deutsche Juristen Zeitung,* no. 6 (1931): 11–17.

103 Bentin, *Johannes Popitz und Carl Schmitt.*

104 Carl Schmitt was the leading advocate of this view, but it was taken up by his student Otto Kirchheimer, who made Schmitt's formulaic description of Weimar as a "dilettantish formal compromise" the basis of a radical critique.

105 Jennifer Nedelsky, *Private Property and the Limits of American Constitutionalism: The Madisonian Framework and Its Legacy* (Chicago: University of Chicago Press, 1990).

106 Ibid., 208.

107 "The inequality of property had to be reflected in political inequality: the protection of property required disproportionate power for the few with property since they needed to defend themselves against the many without" (ibid., 209).

108 The exception is, of course, the Civil War (1861–65), which was fought over federalism (states' rights versus federal rights), but also over the constitutional status of a specific kind of property, the "peculiar institution" of slavery.

109 After the murder of Rathenau on June 24, 1922, the mark fell sharply. When the Reichsbank stopped supporting it on April 4, 1923, one goldmark was worth ten thousand paper marks, and by the second week in November 1923, Germany's paper currency was virtually worthless. Before the Rentenmark was introduced, it took more than one billion paper marks to buy less than ten goldmarks.

110 Wilhelm Cuno (independent) and Gustav Stresemann (German Peoples Party).

111 Harold James, *The German Slump: Politics and Economics, 1924–1936* (Oxford: Oxford University Press, 1986), 29. See also Luther's memoirs, *Politiker ohne Par-*

teie: Erinnerungen (Stuttgart: Deutsche Verlagsanstalt, 1960), on the "chaos" that would have ensued without the Enabling Law of February 14, 1924, and its constitutionality (238ff).

112 The Rentenmark reforms were introduced on October 16, 1923.

113 *Das Kabinette Marx I (30 Nov. 1923–2 Juni 1924)*, ed. Günter Abramowski, Akten der Reichskanzlei, Weimarer Republik (Boppard: Boldt, 1973), 128.

114 The phrase is Carl Schmitt's in *Die Diktatur*, 25–42.

115 Walter Jellinek, "Das Märchen von der Überprüfung verfassungswidriger Reichsgesetze durch das Reichsgericht," *Juristische Wochenschrift* (1925): 454ff.; Gustav Radbruch, "Richterliches Prüfungsrecht?" *Die Justiz* (1925): 12ff.; and for a review of this debate, Friedrich Karl Kübler, "Der deutsche Richter und das demokratische Gesetz," *Archiv für die civilistische Praxis* (1963): 104ff.

116 Huber, *Deutsche Verfasungsgeschichte seit 1789*, 565.

117 *Juristische Wochenschrift* 15, no. 1 (1924).

118 In March 1909, Herr S. borrowed 50,000 Reichsmarks from Herr G. As security, Herr S. offered a piece of land, agreeing to pay back the entire debt in five years at an interest rate of 5 percent. By 1914 only RM 5,000 of the original debt had been repaid, and Herr G. foreclosed the mortgage. At auction, the land brought all but RM 2,110.87 of the total owing. During the Great Inflation of 1922 to 1923, Herr S. repaid the remaining sum through a third party—in money very much reduced in value from that in which the debt had originally been incurred. When in 1925 a federal law revalued preinflation debts, Herr G. sued to recover more of the value of the money he had loaned in 1909 to Herr S. The lower courts decided in his favor, and when the case reached Germany's highest court of appeal, the Reichsgerichtshof, it confirmed their decision.

119 *RGZ* 111 (1925): 320.

120 Carl J. Friedrich, "The Issue of Judicial Review in Germany," *Political Science Quarterly* 43 (128): 188–200, is a useful summary of the debate which sees it as basically a conflict between legislature and judiciary.

121 Staatsgerichtshof für das Deutsche Reich (StGH), 15 October 1927.

122 Heinrich Triepel, "Wesen und Entwicklung der Staatsgerichtsbarkeit," in *Veröffentlichung der Vereinigung der Deutschen Staatsrechtslehrer*, vol. 5 (Berlin: Walter de Gruyter, 1929), 8. Meetings of the Vereinigung der Deutschen Staatsrechtslehrer focused on a single theme with two or more paper presenters, in this case Triepel and Kelsen. Both their remarks carried the same title, 'Wesen und Entwicklung der Staatsgerichtsbarkeit."

123 Triepel objected to the term "Staatsgerichtsbarkeit," introduced by Rudolf Smend in *Verfassung und Verfassungsrecht* (1928), as confusing. A "state court" does not review the constitutionality of laws in Germany; this is the function of all courts (Triepel, "Wesen und Entwicklung der Staatsgerichtsbarkeit," 3).

124 Kelsen, "Wesen und Entwicklung der Staatsgerichtsbarkeit," 83.

125 Schmitt, *Der Hüter der Verfassung*, 78–81.

126 Ibid., 100–103. In the deeper crisis of 1932, Schmitt would add the military to these "Stüzen der Gesellschaft."

127 Ibid., 115.

6 Constitutional Failure

1 Dieter Grimm, "Verfassungserfüllung—Verfassungsbewahrung—Verfassungsauflösung: Positionen der Staatsrechtslehre in der Staatskrise der Weimarer Republik," in *Die Deutsche Staatskrise, 1930–1933: Handlungsspielräume und Alternativen*, ed. H. A. Winkler (Munich: Oldernbourg, 1992), 184.

2 I draw on the categories of constitutional failure defined in Mark Brandon, *Free in the World: American Slavery and Constitutional Failure* (Princeton: Princeton University Press, 1998), 18ff.

3 H. A. Winkler, *Weimar 1918–1933: Die Geschichte der ersten deutschen Republik* (Munich: C. H. Beck, 1993), 332.

4 Winkler calls the events of late 1922 "an avoided catastrophe." The Bavarians did not want to separate that Land from the Reich, he notes, so much as they wanted to prepare for a "march on Berlin" on the model of fascist Italy (Winkler, *Weimar 1918–1933*, 223).

5 Schmitt, *Der Hüter der Verfassung*, 107.

6 Ibid., 114ff. (neutral power) and 96ff. (economic constitution). It was especially important to remove the central bank and railways from the polycratic/party system, Schmitt thought. Both were dependent on the Reichstag for funding and so carried the interests of the "pluralistic party state" into their spheres of relative autonomy from executive direction. Discussion of the historical literature on public finances in late Weimar would take me too far from immediate concerns. Any judgment of the Brüning years must, however, consider the evidence now available on government spending and the public quota of the national economy. See the contributions by Knut Borchardt, "Wirtschaftspolitische Beratung in der Krise: Die Rolle der Wirtschaft," and Carl-Ludwig Holtfrerich, "Vernachlässigte Perspektiven der wirtschaftlichen Probleme der Weimarer Republik," in Winkler, *Die deutsche Staatskrise 1930–1933*, 109–54.

7 Schmitt notes the resulting absurdities of legal definitions: "bread is what the holder of a bread card is entitled to receive on the basis of his bread card" (*Verfassungslehre*, 143).

8 Ibid., 144.

9 "The people as a collectivity can never democratically govern itself, but the rulers change constantly." Robert Michels, *First Lectures in Political Sociology*, ed. Alfred de Grazia (New York: Harper and Row, 1965 [translation from the Italian edition of 1927]), 63.

10 Joseph A. Schumpeter, *Capitalism, Socialism, and Democracy* (London: Allen and Unwin, 1981), 273–74.

11 Max Weber, "Parliament and Government in Germany under a New Political Order," in *Political Writings*, 130–271. Originally published in the *Frankfurter Zeitung*, the article was subtitled "Toward a Political Critique of Officialdom and the Party System." Authors of Federal Germany's Basic Law, conscious of these critical faults in the Weimar constitution, corrected both by introducing the "5 percent hurdle" denying seats in parliament to parties winning less than 5 percent of the total votes cast, and by requiring votes of no confidence to be "positive," with a government in place before one falls.

12 Schulze, *Weimar: Deutschland, 1917–1933*, 72.

13 Fritz Hartung, *Deutsche Verfassungsgeschichte* (Stuttgart: Koehler, 1950), 337–38.

14 Richard Thoma, "Die rechtliche Ordnung des parlamentarischen Regierungssystems," in *Handbuch des deutschen Staatsrechts,* vol. 1, ed. Gerhard Anschütz and Richard Thoma (Tübingen: Mohr-Siebeck, 1930), 503.

15 Hugo Preuß, *Staat Recht und Freiheit* (1926), quoted in Thoma, "Die rechtliche Ordnung," 510.

16 Hartung, *Deutsche Verfassungsgeschichte,* 338.

17 Wilhelm Hennis, "Richtlinienkompetenz und Regierungspolitik," in *Regieren im modernen Staat* (Tübingen: Mohr, 2000), 106–42.

18 Thoma, "Die rechtliche Ordnung," 507.

19 These were personal freedom (Art. 114), privacy of dwelling (Art. 115), privacy of the post, telegraph, and telephone (Art. 117), freedom of expression and press (Art. 118), freedom of assembly (Art. 123), freedom of association (Art. 124), and private property (Art. 153).

20 Hans Boldt, "Article 48 of the Weimar Constitution: Its Historical and Political Implications," in *German Democracy and the Triumph of Hitler,* ed. Anthony Nicholls and Erich Matthias (London: Unwin, 1971), 90.

21 Ibid.

22 Ibid., 90–91.

23 Schmitt, "Die Diktatur des Reichspräsidenten nach Artikel 48 der Weimarer Verfassung," in *Die Diktatur,* 218–19.

24 Carl Schmitt, *Die Diktatur: Von den Anfängen des modernen Souveränitätsgedankens bis zum proletarischen Klassenkampf* (1928; Berlin: Duncker und Humblot, 1978).

25 Ibid., 1–3.

26 Ibid., 35.

27 Clinton Rossiter, *Constitutional Dictatorship: Crisis Government in the Modern Democracies* (New York: Harcourt Brace, 1948), 69.

28 Ibid.

29 Schmitt, *Verfassungslehre,* 91–99.

30 Schmitt, *Der Hüter der Verfassung,* 135–37.

31 Ibid., 115–16.

32 Ibid., 111ff.

33 Schmitt, *Verfassungsrechtliche Aufsätze,* 358.

34 Schmitt, *Der Begriff des Politischen* (1927), 27.

35 Richard Thoma, in *Recht und Staat im neuen Deutschland,* ed. Bernard Harms (Berlin: Hobbing, 1929), 120.

36 Schmitt, "Reichstagauflösungen," in *Verfassungsrechtliche Aufsätze,* 26, 25.

37 Winkler, *Weimar 1918–1933,* 374.

38 Ibid., 472.

39 That it would not be a parliamentary system on the original model is obvious, and the reforms advanced in late summer 1932 by Gayl bear a certain resemblance to provisions designed to avoid the negative politics of Weimar's proportional representation. The substantive context of Germany after 1945 was, however, dramatically changed; radicalism had been thoroughly discredited, and West German integration into the American sphere took place on the condition of a liberal-democratic, federalist constitution.

40 See the comments of Eberhard Kolb in Winkler, *Die deutsche Staatskrise, 1930–1932,* which found little resonance among other conference participants (49).

41 Lutz Berthold, *Carl Schmitt und der Staatsnotstandsplan am Ende der Weimarer Republik* (Berlin: Duncker und Humblot, 1998), 12; Schmitt, *Legalität und Legitimität*, in *Verfassungsrechtliche Aufsätze*, 263–350.

42 Schmitt, "Legalität und gleiche Chance politischer Machtgewinnung," *Deutsches Volkstum* 15 (1932): 557–64.

43 Schmitt, *Legalität und Legitimität*, 263ff.

44 Ibid., 274ff.

45 Ibid., 284. In his foreword to the English translation of this text, John McCormick demonstrates the significance of Schmitt's mobilization of the Kantian "right to resist" in this context. See Carl Schmitt, *Legality and Legitimacy*, trans. Jeffrey Seitzer (Durham, N.C.: Duke University Press, 2004).

46 Schmitt, *Legalität und Legitimität*, 288.

47 Ibid., 344–45.

48 Berthold, *Carl Schmitt und der Staatsnotstandsplan*, 15.

49 Ibid., 17.

50 August 30, 1932.

51 E. R. Huber, "Carl Schmitt in der Reichskrise der Weimarer Endzeit," in *Complexio Oppositorum: Über Carl Schmitt*, ed. H. Quaritsch (Berlin: Duncker und Humblot, 1988), 33–70.

52 Ibid., 40.

53 Hans Mommsen, "Entscheidung für den Präsidialstaat: Komplott der Machteliten oder Selbstpreisgabe einer Demokratie?" in Winkler, *Die deutsche Staatskrise, 1930–1932*, 1–18.

54 In an article of the same name, Kirchheimer too explored the emergence of the civil service as "a new legitimate power" in spring 1932, but he was far more critical of it than Schmitt. Kirchheimer acknowledged that government by emergency decree was no longer a temporary measure but had assumed a "permanent character," and it is against the background of "the illegality of groups struggling against it" that this government is "legal." Kirchheimer, "Legality and Legitimacy," in *Social Democracy and the Rule of Law: Otto Kirchheimer and Franz Neumann*, ed. and trans. Keith Tribe (London: Allen and Unwin, 1987), 130–48. After Schmitt's *Legalität und Legitimität* was published, Kirchheimer (with Nathan Leites) reviewed it critically in the *Archiv für Sozialwissenschaft und Sozialpolitik* 68 (1933): 457–87; translated in Tribe, *Social Democracy and the Rule of Law*, 149–78. On the relation of Franz Neumann's work to Schmitt's, see Tribe's nuanced "Franz Neumann in der Emigration: 1933–1942," in *Die Frankfurter Schule und die Folgen*, ed. Axel Honneth and Albrecht Wellmer (Berlin: de Gruyter, 1986), 259–74.

55 Huber, "Carl Schmitt in der Reichskrise," 46.

56 Berthold, *Carl Schmitt und der Staatsnotstandsplan*, 26.

57 *Preußen contra Reich* (1932) is the subject of David Dyzenhaus's *Legality and Legitimacy.*

58 See Schmitt's comments in *Verfasungsrechtliche Aufsätze* (350) to that effect, a denial he repeated in conversations with me during 1982.

59 Berthold, *Carl Schmitt und der Staatsnotstandsplan*, 38.

60 Ibid., 550, on the relation between those arguments and Schmitt's political theory.

61 There was agreement in the cabinet on this plan, although some discussion about whether to announce a new date for elections (ibid., 25).

62 Kaas to Schleicher, 26 January 1933, in Rudolf Morsey et al., eds., *Das Ende der*

Parteien 1933: Darstellung und Dokumente (Königstein/Tr.: Droste, 1979), 428–29. Schmitt's presumption, probably correct, was that Kaas had direct contact with Hindenburg as well.

63 As Ernst Fraenkel demonstrates, provisions of the civil and criminal law continued to be applied, but prejudicially toward the Jews and political enemies of the Reich. See Fraenkel, *The Dual State: A Contribution to the Theory of Dictatorship*, trans. E. A. Shils et al. (New York: Oxford University Press, 1941).

64 The Presidential Decree for the Protection of People and State (28 February 1933).

65 Second Law for the Coordination of the Länder and the Reich (7 April 1933).

66 Law for the Reconstruction of Parties (14 July 1933). Further laws and order consolidated the totalitarian state, and one made Hitler head of state and of government (Law on the Head of State of the German Reich, 1 August 1934).

67 Winkler, *Weimar 1918–1933*, 11.

68 Lutz Berthold's correct characterization of an early German study of Schmitt by Jürgen Fijalkowski, *Die Wendung zum Führerstaat: Ideologische Komponenten in der politischen Philosophie Carl Schmitts* (1958). Later studies including Christian Graf von Krockow, *Die Entscheidung: Eine Untersuchung über Ernst Jünger, Carl Schmitt, und Martin Heidegger* (1958), Kurt Sontheimer, *Antidemokratisches Denken in der Weimarer Republik: Die politische Ideen des deutschen Nationalismus zwischen 1918 und 1933* (1962), and Hasso Hofmann, *Legitimität gegen Legalität: Der Weg der politischen Philosophie Carl Schmitts* (1964), while critical, were more nuanced (Berthold, *Carl Schmitt und der Staatsnotsplan*, 11).

69 Ingeborg Maus, "Zur Zäsur von 1933 in der Theorie Carl Schmitts," in *Rechtstheorie und politische Theorie im Industriekapitalismus* (Munich: Fink, 1986), 93–110. Gary Ulmen has recently tried to argue against Maus that 1933 marks an absolute break in his work. See Ulmen, "Between the Weimar Republic and the Third Reich: Continuity in Carl Schmitt's Thought," *Telos* (2000): 18–31.

70 F. A. Hayek, *Law, Legislation, and Liberty* (Chicago: University of Chicago Press, 1979). On the model constitution (i.e., liberalism and the free market), see vol. 3, *The Political Order of a Free People*, 105ff. Hayek makes extensive use of Schmitt's critique of the "weak" total state. See also Scheuerman, *Carl Schmitt: The End of Law*, for an excellent analysis of their relationship; and Renato Cristi, *Carl Schmitt and Authoritarian Liberalism: Strong State, Free Economy* (Cardiff: University of Wales Press, 1998).

71 Ulmen, "Between the Weimar Republic and the Third Reich," 18–31.

72 This is especially true of William Scheurman in *Carl Schmitt: The End of Law.* (1999).

73 Yossi Shain and Juan Linz, "The Role of Interim Governments," *Journal of Democracy* (1991): 73–87.

74 Schmitt, *Verfassungslehre*, 23–24.

75 Based on the concept of a "constitution-giving power" which is ever-present and distinct from all forms of constitutional legislation.

76 Schmitt, *Verfassungslehre*, 98–99; Huber, "Carl Schmitt in der Reichskrise."

77 Schmitt, *Verfassungslehre*, 24. Schmitt remarks on the error of prewar jurisprudence, continued in contemporary positivism, to regard such proclamations as are found in Article 1 and its preamble as "mere declarations." See the long note criticizing Anschütz's argument that because such elements cannot be adjudicated, they are irrelevant.

78 Among them are oaths to the constitution and the nonjustifiable character of the core decisions.

79 Katzenstein, Proceedings of the National Assembly, 186, quoted in Schmitt, *Verfassungslehre,* 30.

80 Among the "dilatory" compromises were provisions dealing with church-state relations (Articles 137, 138) and schools (Article 149) (Schmitt, *Verfassungslehre,* 32–35.

81 Ibid., 99–102.

82 Ibid., 109–10.

83 *Verfassungslehre,* 27; "Freiheitsrechte und institutionelle Garantien der Reichsverfassung" (1931), in *Verfassungsrechtliche Aufsätze aus den Jahren 1924–1954: Materialien zu einer Verfassungslehre* (Berlin: Duncker und Humblot, 1973), 140ff., and "Grundrechte und Grundpflichten (1932), in *VRA,* 181ff.

84 Schmitt, "Staatsethik und pluralistischer Staat" (1930).

85 H. L. A. Hart, *The Concept of Law* (Oxford: Oxford University Press, 1986).

86 Schmitt, *Verfassungslehre,* 43.

87 Ibid., 76–77.

88 Schmitt, *Ex captiviate Salus: Erfahrungen der Zeit, 1945–47* (Cologne: Greven, 1950), 12. In reference to the Greek myth of the doomed Titan, and to his friend Konrad Weiß; see Weiß, *Der christliche Empimethius* (Edwin Runge, 1933).

89 Ernst Nolte, *The Three Faces of Fascism: Action française, Italian Fascism, National Socialism* (New York: Signet Classics, 1969), 537; Hermann Raushning, *Die Revolution des Nihilismus* (Zurich: Europa, 1938).

90 This is implicit in references to the Holocaust. In that perspective, the death of millions and of everyone in the Nazi genocide can only be understood theologically, as "a burnt offering." Yehuda Bauer, *The Holocaust in Historical Perspective* (Seattle: University of Washington Press, 1978). A powerful addition to our understanding of these events within the larger horizon of modernity and the modern state is Giorgio Agamben's *Homo Sacer: Sovereign Power and Bare Life* (Stanford: Stanford University Press, 1998). Agamben's argument begins with Schmitt's definition of the sovereign as a decision about the exception, enlarging and extending in a comprehensive political theory of the material and theological terms of man's present existence.

91 Ernst Cassirer, *The Myth of the State* (New Haven: Yale University Press, 1946).

92 Michael Burleigh, introduction to *The Third Reich: A New History* (New York: Hill and Wang, 2000). Burleigh's argument has a long history, beginning with Talmon's "totalitarian democracy" critique of Rousseau.

93 Schmitt, *Römischer Katholizismus und Politische Form* (Stuttgart: Klett-Cotta, 1984), 31–32.

94 Patrick Riley, *The General Will before Rousseau: The Transformation of the Divine into the Civic* (Princeton: Princeton University Press, 1986). Riley builds on Judith Shklar's remark that while the general will is associated with Rousseau, "he did not invent it, but he made its history."

95 Ibid., 4–5. The Pauline text is 1 Tim. 2:4.

96 Pierre Bayle had written to Leibniz: "The God of the Christians wills that all men be saved; he has the power necessary to save them all; he lacks neither power nor good will, and nonetheless almost all men are damned" (quoted in Riley, *The General Will before Rousseau,* 5).

97 Schmitt, *Verfassungslehre,* 75. Schmitt applies these concepts to the League of Na-

tions and the International Tribunal in the Hague, concluding that the League has neither auctoritas nor potestas, while the tribunal has the "authority of a court" (75–76).

98 Jerry Muller, *The Other God That Failed: Hans Freyer and the Deradicalization of German Conservatism* (Princeton: Princeton University Press, 1987).

99 Martin Brozat, *The Hitler State: The Foundation and Development of the Internal Structure of the Third Reich* (New York: Longman, 1981).

100 "Your great enemy is truly the Spaniard," said Oliver Cromwell in a speech against the Spanish and the Papacy (1656). Schmitt, *Der Begriff des Politischen* 67; *Verfassungslehre,* 230.

101 Schmitt, *Der Leviathan,* 82.

102 Hobbes, *Leviathan,* ed. Richard Tuck (New York: Cambridge University Press, 1991), chap. 41, p. 145.

103 Schmitt, *Der Leviathan,* 84.

104 Title page of the 1651 edition; current editions, including Richard Tuck's, omit the subtitle, although they reproduce the original frontispiece. Secularized readings of Hobbes are common.

105 Schmitt, *Der Begriff des Politischen,* 122.

106 Ibid., 59.

107 Hannah Arendt, "The Public and the Private Real," in *The Portable Hannah Arendt* (Penguin: 2000), 184.

108 Christian Meier, *Die Entstehung des Politischen bei den Griechen* (Frankfurt: Suhrkamp, 1980), 15. This work and Meier's biography of Caesar are the most effective antidotes to the German tendency to romanize the Greeks—unless one prefers Nietzsche's robust rejection of Plato in *Götterdämmerung.*

109 Meier, *Die Lehre Carl Schmitts* (Stuttgart: Metzger, 1994), 260.

110 "Da sprach Gott der Herr zu der Schlange: Weil du das getan hast, seist du verflucht, verstossen aus allem Vieh und allen Tieren auf dem Felde. Auf dem Bauche sollst du kriechen und Erde fressen dein Leben" (Gen. 14). "Und ich will Feindschaft setzen zwischen dir und dem Weibe und zwischen deinem Nachkommen und ihrem Nachkommen; der soll dir den Kopf zertreten, und du wirst ihn in die Ferse stechen" (Gen. 15).

111 Meier, *Carl Schmitt and Leo Strauss,* 68.

112 Jacob Taubes, "Staat einer Einleitung: Leviathan als sterblicher Gott," in *Der Fürst dieser Welt: Carl Schmitt und die Folgen* (Schöningh: Fink, 1983), 9–15. See the now definitive work by Manfred Dahlheimer, *Carl Schmitt und der Deutsche Katholizismus, 1888–1936.*

113 Schmitt, *Theodor Däublers Nordlicht* (1916), "Die Sichtbarkeit der Kirche" (1917), *Römischer Katholizismus und politische Form* (1923).

114 Schmitt, *Der Begriff des Politischen,* 121–22. On the Catholic reception of Schmitt, and the incompatibility of his "primacy of politics" with Catholic natural-law teaching, see Dahlheimer, *Carl Schmitt und der Deutsche Katholizismus,* 330–34.

115 Jacob Taubes, *Ad Carl Schmitt: Gegenstrebige Fügung* (Merve, 1987), 7.

116 Meier, *Die Lehre Carl Schmitts,* 260.

117 Schmitt, *Der Nomos der Erde,* 29.

118 Meier, *Carl Schmitt and Leo Strauss,* 55. His second book continues and concludes the argument of *Carl Schmitt and Leo Strauss,* with the question that is always asked of Schmitt: "How, looking back from the vantage of 1945, could he see his

decision in 1933 as compatible with his political theology?" The philosophers Spinoza, Mendelssohn, and Stahl appear as the central influence on the modern process of secularization. They represent "the restless spirit of the Jews" that brought about a new stage in the two-thousand-year struggle between Christianity and Judaism. With this, Meier comes full circle in his reading of Schmitt to the explanation: "Schmitt's anti-Semitism is deeply rooted in his belief in Revelation" (Meier, *Die Lehre Carl Schmitts*, 234).

Afterword

1 Schmitt, *Politische Theologie*, 49.

2 Ibid., 26.

3 "Every specific parliamentary arrangement and norm take their meaning from discussion and publicity" (*Die geistesgeschichtliche Lage des heutigen Parlamentarismus*, 7).

4 Schmitt, *Politische Romantik*, 121. Schmitt quotes Novalis, an exemplary romantic, here.

5 Leo Strauss, "Notes on *The Concept of the Political*," in *The Concept of the Political*, by Carl Schmitt, trans. George Schwab (Chicago: University of Chicago Press, 1996), 92.

6 Michael Burleigh, *The Third Reich: A New History* (New York: Hill and Wang, 2000), 7–9.

7 Schmitt, *Ex captiviate Salus* (Cologne: Greven, 1950), 9.

Bibliographic Note

Carl Schmitt was a prolific author whose work provoked an immense literature during his lifetime, and whose death in 1985 has increased that literature's size, especially in the English-speaking world. Therefore this book contains no comprehensive bibliography of the usual sort. However, the first Festschriften for Carl Schmitt each contain extremely useful bibliographies by Piet Thommassen. These should be the starting point for the study of Schmitt's work: Hans Barion, Ernst Forsthoff, and Werner Weber, eds., *Festschrift für Carl Schmitt zum 70. Geburtstag dargebracht von Freunden und Schülern* (Berlin: Duncker und Humblot, 1959); and Hans Barion, Ernst-Wolfgang Böckenförde, Ernst Forshoff, and Werner Weber, eds., *Epirrhosis: Festgabe für Carl Schmitt* (Berlin: Duncker und Humblot, 1968).

In addition to those (primarily German) bibliographies, recent American publications on Schmitt and Weimar constitutional theory also contain useful bibliographies: David Dyzenhaus, *Legality and Legitimacy: Carl Schmitt, Hans Kelsen, and Hermann Heller in Weimar* (Oxford: Clarendon Press, 1997). Dyzenhaus, ed., *Law as Politics: Carl Schmitt's Critique of Liberalism* (Durham, N.C.: Duke University Press, 1998), does not contain a summary bibliography, but the contributions allow one to trace the major debates and their literature in North American and English debates. Chantal Mouffe, *The Challenge of Carl Schmitt* (London: Verso, 1999), similarly omits a summary bibliography but does usefully list Schmitt's works in English translation and also contains a new translation of Schmitt's "Ethic of State and Pluralistic State." George Schwab, *The Challenge of the Exception: An Introduction to the Political Ideas of Carl Schmitt between 1921 and 1936* (New York: Greenwood Press, 1989), was the first study in English; it originally found no American publisher and appeared in 1970 with Duncker und Humblot. While now somewhat dated, Schwab's work remains an important introduction to Schmitt's arguments in these years. Joseph Bendersky, *Carl Schmitt: Theorist for the Reich* (Princeton: Princeton University Press, 1983), remains an excellent introduction to the man, his times, and his work. The appearance of Bendersky's study at Princeton coincided with three new translations of Schmitt at the MIT Press—*The Crisis of Parlia-*

mentary Democracy, Political Theology, and *Political Romanticism*—giving readers without German access to a significant body of Schmitt's work.

I have attempted to give full bibliographical references in the notes both to printed materials and to archival documents. Schmitt's Nachlaß is now housed in the Stadtarchiv at Düsseldorf, Germany, and has been admirably cataloged by Dirk van Laak and Ingeborg Villinger in *Nachlass Carl Schmitt: Verzeichneis des Bestandes im Nordrhein-Westfälischn Hauptstaatsarchive* (Siegburg: Respublica, 1993). Schmitt was a lifelong diarist who kept his daily thoughts and reflections in a stenography now read by only a very few. The first volume, edited by Eberhard Freiherr von Medem, is *Glossariarium: Aufzeichnungen der Jahre 1947–1951* (Berlin: Duncker und Humblot, 1991). Others are presently in preparation.

Index

Ellen Kennedy is a professor of political science at the University of Pennsylvania. She is the author of *The Bundesbank: Germany's Central Bank in the International Monetary System* (1991); *Freedom and the Open Society: Henri Bergson's Contribution to Political Philosophy* (1987); and coeditor, with Susan Mendus, of *Women in Western Political Philosophy: Kant to Nietzsche* (1987). She is the translator of *Crisis of Parliamentary Democracy*, by Carl Schmitt (1985).

Library of Congress Cataloging-in-Publication Data

Kennedy, Ellen
Constitutional failure : Carl Schmitt in Weimar / Ellen Kennedy.
p. cm.
Includes bibliographical references and index.

ISBN 0-8223-3230-2 (cloth : alk. paper)
ISBN 0-8223-3243-4 (pbk. : alk. paper)

1. Constitutional history—Germany. 2. Germany—Politics and government—1918–1933. 3. Schmitt, Carl, 1888—Views on constitutional law. I. Title.

KK4710.K46 2004 342.4302'9—dc22 2004007045